For John & Sarah

Nov 2001

STOLEN GLORY

The McKinley Assassination

Alamar Books
P.O. Box 2876, La Jolla, California 92038

Web Sites: alamarbooks.com
mckinleyassassination.com

E mail alamarbooks@aol.com

Toll Free: 877-861-9252

ISBN 0-9661772-1-5

Printed in the United States of America

STOLEN GLORY
The McKinley Assassination

Jack C. Fisher M.D.

[signature]

Published in cooperation with
Buffalo and Erie County Historical Society

Alamar Books • La Jolla

2001

For

Jack Anthony

Who first stimulated my
interest in history

Contents

PLENTY OF ROOM FOR EVERYBODY.

BUFFALO EVENING NEWS.

TEN PAGES
EIGHTY COLUMNS.

VOL. XLII—NO. 126.   BUFFALO, N. Y., FRIDAY, SEPTEMBER 6, 1901.   PRICE ONE CEN

EXTRA! EXTRA! EXTRA! EXTRA!

PRESIDENT M'KINLEY SHOT

Two Bullets Sent Into His Body By a Stranger at the Pan-American.

He Sank Down and Was at Once Taken to the Exposition Hospital.

Pan-American Grounds --4:15 P. M.--Bulletin--President McKinley has been shot at the Temple of Music.

He was taken to the hospital on the Exposition grounds.

It is feared the President is fatally shot.

One bullet took effect in his right breast and another in his abdomen.

The name of his assailant not yet known.

The villain shot the President as he was shaking hands with people at the public reception in the Temple of Music.

Officers Foster and Ireland of the U. S. Secret Service were stationed at the time on the lookout. Mr. Cortelyou was on the left of the President, while Mr. Milburn was on the right. They saw a man with a black mustache approach the President from the left. He had a handkerchief on his left hand. They supposed the man's hand was injured, but kept an eye on him.

He walked up to shake the President's hand when suddenly he fired two shots in rapid succession from a revolver concealed beneath the handkerchief. Detectives Foster and Ireland sprang upon him, disarmed and arrested him. He was taken at once to No. 13 Police station.

The assassin's voice a student's cap.

One bullet lodged against breast bone. This has been taken out. The other perforated the walls of the abdomen and was not extracted by a surgeon. President McKinley is conscious and resting easily.

EXCITING RACE BETWEEN TWO FAST TRAINS.

Speedy Special Chasing Lake Shore Flyer With Important Mail for England.

WOULDN'T TAKE M'KINLEY'S DOLLAR.

Programme Boy Made Himself Happy by Giving President a Present.

ADJUDGED IN CONTEMPT AND FINED $6000.

Heavy Punishment Meted Out to John F. Moffett by Justice Lambert.

THE SHERIFF O' LONDON TOWN.

An Exalted Official of the English Metropolis and M. P. Visits the Pan.

HIS ACQUAINTANCE WAS A SHARPER.

William Jeffries of Louisville, Separated From His Wallet and $40.

STEEL MEN'S LAST OFFER IS REJECTED.

BIG SHAKE-UP OF POLICE OFFICERS

Capt. Michael Regan Transferred to No. 1 Station and Capt. John Taylor to No. 3.

CAPT. FRANK KILLEEN SENT TO NO. 13 AT BLACK ROC

Capt. Burfeind Transferred to No. 4—Inspectors Martin and Donovan Change Places—Two Precinct Detectives Shifted.

Today at the Exposition.

5 O'CLOCK BULLETINS.

Friday, September 6, 1901

PROLOGUE

William McKinley, twenty-fifth president of the United States, stood in a reception line at Buffalo's Pan-American Exposition on Friday afternoon, September 6, 1901. To his left, Exposition President John Milburn beamed with anticipation and pride. Milburn already knew that Buffalo's grandest public event would sustain a severe financial loss,[1] but he wasn't going to let that spoil his moment in the spotlight. Standing to McKinley's right was his personal secretary, George Courtelyou, who glanced warily toward the advancing line of well-wishers.

Courtelyou's responsibilities included reading all letters of aggressive intent mailed to the White House and then forwarding those letters to John Wilkie, director of the Secret Service.[2] Despite President McKinley's remarkable popularity, the frequency and emotional intensity of the disparaging letters addressed to the president had increased following the recent American aggression in the Philippine Islands. Thus, Courtelyou was more apprehensive than usual over the president's habitual need for contact with an admiring public. Although at the peak of his national acclaim, McKinley continued to seek affirmation at every opportunity.

Three Secret Service agents protected the president that day.[3] Exposition police, Buffalo police detectives, and a unit of the U.S. Coastal Artillery stationed nearby assisted them. Courtelyou had been assured that the crowds would be adequately controlled, and they were. However, no one spotted a self-proclaimed anarchist standing in line with a .32 caliber revolver concealed in his handkerchief-wrapped hand.

At 4:07 P.M., McKinley turned to greet this man. Two shots were fired before the gunman, Leon Czolgosz (shole-gawz), could be wrestled to the floor. The president stood firm, barely wavering, until someone brought a chair forward for him. He did finally sit down, but not before urging that his assailant be spared any further mistreatment. Secretary Courtelyou asked the president if he felt any pain. McKinley responded by nodding, then slipped his hand inside his jacket. His fingertips were blood coated when he withdrew his hand. The sight of fresh blood removed all doubt. The president had been seriously injured.

McKinley was quickly transferred to a nearby emergency medical facility, where the nurses and medical students on duty provided for his immediate needs. Meanwhile, a call for help went out to several of Buffalo's surgeons. The first to arrive was Dr. Herman Mynter, followed soon after by Dr. Matthew Mann, and then Dr. John Parmenter. Notably absent was Dr. Roswell Park, a nationally recognized surgeon, who was at that moment performing surgery on a patient in Niagara Falls, twenty-five miles away. Therefore, Mann, a distinguished gynecologist and dean of the University of Buffalo's Department of Medicine, was asked to take charge. He sought counsel from his colleagues and received unanimous support for the decision to operate immediately.

One of the bullets had bounced harmlessly off McKinley's breastbone; it fell to the floor as the president's clothing was being removed. The other passed through the stomach and imbedded itself deep within the abdomen. It was never found. Mann located two holes in the stomach wall and repaired both. Just as he was closing the initial incision and preparing to bring the operation to a close, Dr. Park arrived. Having missed the surgery, he contented himself with arranging for McKinley's aftercare.

All of the president's attending physicians (including Dr. Park) pledged that they would not speak individually to the press but would instead issue joint daily statements regarding McKinley's condition. Those reports were initially optimistic; for several days all were convinced that their patient would recover fully. However, by the sixth day following surgery, the president's rapid pulse began to weaken. Despite the use of every therapeutic measure known at the time, William McKinley, at the age of 58, died early on the morning of Saturday, September 14, 1901.

The entire nation was stunned. A president beloved by the vast majority was gone. Had he lived, McKinley's popular leadership might have led to an unprecedented third term in office, especially if the economy continued its steady improvement. Instead, Theodore Roosevelt, at the age of 49,[4] became the youngest president in United States history.

McKinley's surgical team had been granted heroic stature during the few days following surgery, but everything changed the moment their patient died. Now, it seemed everyone, laymen and professionals alike, found fault with the surgery. The press was especially ruthless. How could such a dire outcome follow so closely on the heels of so much optimism about the chances for recovery?

Surgeons in Boston, New York, and Philadelphia expressed regret that McKinley had required surgery in a "backwater community."[5] Even Buffalo's medical establishment took sides, one camp supporting Dr. Mann and the other convinced that waiting for Dr. Park would have assured a better outcome, not only for McKinley but also for Buffalo's reputation. Attorneys advised Mann, Park, and the others that their reputations were being slandered, and that they ought to take legal action against their accusers. They never did.[6]

Roswell Park waited until 1914 to publish his own *"Reminiscences of McKinley Week."* He had long avoided expressing any criticism or even appearing to break ranks with his colleagues. When his son, historian Julian Park, gave the original, unedited draft of the recollection to the Buffalo Historical Society in 1945, it became clear that Dr. Park had harbored strong convictions about surgical errors he thought had been made on that tragic day in 1901.[7]

* * * *

My interest in the McKinley assassination commenced one afternoon in 1961 when, as a medical student in Buffalo, I was browsing in a secondhand medical bookstore.[8] I purchased a slightly worn copy of Roswell Park's *Selected Papers: Surgical and Scientific*[9] and discovered in it Park's recollection of the McKinley tragedy. I read the story with great fascination but very limited comprehension of the president's medical fate. Later, while training as a resident in general surgery, I gained enough experience with traumatic injuries to the abdominal organs to understand why the president's condition had deteriorated so rapidly, despite the best efforts of his physicians.

Many years later, I visited the Buffalo and Erie County Historical Society, where I enjoyed an exhibit featuring the Pan-

Roswell Park

American Exposition and its most notorious incident. On display was the original, unedited draft of Park's version of the McKinley tragedy. I obtained a copy for study and took note of several lines and paragraphs the author had marked for deletion. Nearly all were comments critical of the management of the president's surgery.

Since those tragic events in Buffalo, a century has passed, but the circumstances surrounding McKinley's death remain enveloped in myth. The popular press at the time-and much of the historiography that has followed-mistakenly identified Leon Czolgosz as an immigrant, in part because of his name, but also because violence at the hands of foreign anarchists was widely feared. The president's surgeons were declared incompetent, and Matthew Mann especially so. People from all walks of life wondered why a gynecologist was selected to perform an operation involving bullet injuries to the stomach. The prevalent conclusion is that a serious blunder was made. Many also assumed (both then and now) that had the other doctors awaited Roswell Park's arrival, the president's life would have been spared. Those who enjoy dissecting the surgery's many details have offered their opinions about where the procedure ought to have been conducted, when it should have been done, and whether or not the abdominal cavity should have been "drained." Nearly every historical interpretation of the McKinley era concludes that "bungled surgery" cost the nation its twenty-fifth president.

Today, a re-examination of the medical evidence in light of a more thorough understanding of surgical physiology suggests a different explanation. A better grasp of the type and extent of damage the assassin's bullet inflicted on McKinley makes possible a more convincing interpretation of the causes of his death and a more balanced appraisal of the efficacy of his surgeons' efforts.

The impetus for re-examining the events surrounding McKinley's assassination goes well beyond the simple desire to set the medical record straight, however. Glory was stolen on that tragic day by a desperate and deluded man, not only from the city of Buffalo, its surgeons, and its grandest public event, but also from McKinley and the American people. Had the polling methods available today existed in 1901, McKinley surely would have received very high voter approval ratings. America's economy was steadily expanding, reversing the period of misfortune precipitated by the Panic of 1893,[10] and the public generally attributed that upturn to McKinley's stewardship. Moreover, the United States was launching itself as an active participant on the world stage. Because of his decision to go to war against Spain, friend and foe alike would remember McKinley as the first imperial president. Immediately after he died, the reins of power were automatically transferred to his vice president. Although this succession occurred exactly as provided by the United States Constitution, many were deeply displeased by the idea of Theodore Roosevelt holding the nation's highest office. "I told McKinley it was a mistake to nominate that damned cowboy!" fumed Mark Hanna, longtime friend and advisor to the murdered president.[11] Others questioned where the hot-blooded Roosevelt, hero of a valiant charge up Cuba's San Juan Hill, would take the nation in its quest for global recognition. The new president made clear that his appetite for action would become the defining characteristic of the new administration. "We are not, and cannot be, and never will be one of those nations that progress from century to century doing little and suffering little, standing aside from the great world currents," he proclaimed. "We must either succeed greatly or fail greatly."[12]

As the chapters that follow will explain, part of the responsibility for President McKinley's death lies far from Buffalo. Despite having lost two presidents to assassins in less than twenty years, the U.S. Congress still had not officially assigned to any agency the role of protecting the president. McKinley's death resulted in a redefinition of the Secret Service's powers, but only after Congress debated the issue for several more years. The government eventually accepted the premise that maintaining security for its leadership was of paramount importance to the nation. Future presidents would need to make their own personal adaptations to the security barriers placed between them and their public.

Of course, no matter how large a budget is allocated for protecting our leaders, no matter how many agents are put on the job, no public figure is ever completely safe from attack. And those like McKinley, who have a deep desire for direct contact with the electorate, are especially vulnerable. Still, even a reclusive president cannot be assured longevity; history shows that determined assassins will triumph. McKinley's assassination, like all others except Lincoln's, was the act of a lone gunman, not the result of coordinated efforts among co-conspirators.[13] As a nation, we find it almost impossible to believe that any individual acting alone can succeed in killing a national leader. Thus, in coming to terms with McKinley's assassination, it is especially important to understand what prompted Leon Czolgosz's action. A self-defined anarchist, Czolgosz truly believed that it was up to him to rid America's "good working people" of their gravest "enemy." How did he reach that tragic conclusion? The story begins with the anarchists who mistrusted every form of ruling authority, even a democracy governed by elected leaders.

❖

Emma Goldman

Alexander Berkman

1

ANARCHISTS

"A single deed is better propaganda than a thousand pamphlets! Words are lost in the air like the sound of church bells."

Peter Kropotkin, 1877[1]

Hidden in the ranks of those who were captivated by the vision of a stateless society, one without government or the restraint of written laws, there stood a few who were willing to punctuate the idea of anarchy with a murderous deed. They were the terrorists of their day, desperate men mostly, responsible for bringing a tragic end to the lives of French President Carnot in 1894, Spanish Premier Canovas in 1897, Austrian Empress Elizabeth in 1898, Italian King Humbert in 1900, U.S. President McKinley in 1901, and another Spanish Premier, Canalejas, in 1912.[2]

Not one of these slain rulers was considered a tyrant; instead, each was beloved by the majority. The willing assassin, however, rarely extended goodwill to any member of the ruling class, beloved or reviled. The signature belief of these zealots was that ownership of property was the root cause of all social evil. Eliminate an individual's possession of either land or the means of industrial production and no one would ever again be forced to live off the toil of another. Presumably, replacing organized government with voluntary cooperation among all people was considered sufficient for maintaining a stable society. Leaders of the anarchist movement were unconcerned by the absence of any historical precedent for this utopian condition.

The term "an-archy," literally meaning "without a ruler," was first used in Paris during the mid-nineteenth century. Anarchists believed that social reform through a gradual process of persuasion or popular vote was futile; the ruling class would never voluntarily relinquish either its power or its property. Two early prophets of the movement were Pierre Proudhon, a

Frenchman, and Michael Bakunin, a Russian exile living in Paris. "Whoever lays his hand on me to govern me is a usurper and a tyrant," Proudhon wrote in 1848, "I declare him to be an enemy. Government of man by man is slavery; its laws cobwebs for the rich and chains of steel for the poor." At public forums, Proudhon would often ask, "What is property?" The countless revolutionaries who followed in his path would quote or paraphrase his reply, "Property is theft!" Less commonly cited was Proudhon's belief that mankind could be persuaded by reason to adopt a society without structure. Bakunin's views were considerably more popular: words would never be enough; violence was necessary; widespread revolt would be required to achieve meaningful change in the social order.[3]

Bakunin's chief rival among the believers in violent change was another expatriate, Karl Marx, twice evicted from his native Germany.[4] Both men championed the violent overthrow of existing governments, but they differed on who might carry out such a revolt. Marx believed it would come from the laborers toiling in already industrialized nations. Bakunin thought the uprising would emerge from backward nations like Italy, Spain, or Russia, where workers had less to lose by abandoning their jobs.

This distinction was a subtle one, particularly within the social context of pitting a massive labor force against "mankind's tormentors," as Bakunin liked to characterize monarchs, statesmen, soldiers, officials, financiers, moneylenders, lawyers, and priests. For most workers, however, the rich were a more distant threat than the landlord, the boss, the factory owner, or the police. The task for revolutionaries of every breed, anarchists included, was to awaken the laboring class to the need for change. The spark that would eventually ignite the anticipated uprising, they believed, would surely be recognized when it came. The 1871 Paris Commune seemed to fit the bill, but to Bakunin's dismay, it died quickly and without leading to widespread insurrection. "We reckoned without the masses who did not want to be roused to passion for their own freedom," he wrote, with despair. He died in 1876, "a Columbus without America," according to one admirer.[5]

Bakunin and Marx also disagreed concerning the relative

merits of government. As a socialist, Marx accepted the idea of a controlling central authority, but he insisted that this agency be one dominated by common men. As an anarchist, Bakunin rejected every form of government organization. Although an extreme position, anarchism attracted its share of enthusiasts, both theorists and activists. The former were men of greater intellectual bearing, focused primarily on ideology and polemic discourse, but generally opposed to violent deeds. They included artists and writers like Camille Pissaro, Georges Seurat, Oscar Wilde, and even Henry David Thoreau. The latter were poorly educated and usually impoverished men who were driven either to act against their oppressors or to convince others to act on behalf of their cause. This inherent polarity rendered a unified organization of anarchists hopeless.

Unlike the socialists and communists, who claimed Karl Marx as their leader, the anarchists had no heroes. They made do, instead, with very colorful characters. Prince Peter Kropotkin, for example, was a Russian aristocrat by birth who managed to transform himself into a revolutionist by conviction. Educated as a geographer, he served briefly as a cossack in Siberia, and then later was secretary of the geographical society in St. Petersburg, Russia. When his radical political beliefs became known, he was promptly arrested and imprisoned. One of the very few ever to escape Peter the Great's imposing fortress on the banks of St. Petersburg's Neva River, Kropotkin fled first to Switzerland and then to France where, for awhile, he edited *La Revolte*. When he eventually reached England, he published both a series of pamphlets fomenting social rebellion, and his classic *Memoirs of a Revolutionist*.[6] Although Kropotkin never openly advocated assassination, he nevertheless left little doubt about his ultimate objective. Social transformation, he believed, would be achieved, " ...first by speech and written word, then by dagger, gun, and dynamite." He sought "...men of courage willing not only to speak but also to act, pure characters who prefer prison, exile, and death to a life that contradicts their principles."

Kropotkin reminded every crowd with the potential for sedition that "A single deed is better propaganda than a thousand pamphlets...words are lost in the air like the sound of church

bells." London intellectuals, recognizing Kropotkin's scholar-
ship, invited him to join the Royal Geographic Society; he
declined, citing the group's royal patronage. Even as a guest at a
Society dinner, he refused to stand and join his colleagues in a
toast to the king.

An equally colorful contemporary of Kropotkin was Enrico
Malatesta, an Italian firebrand who carried a symbolic torch for
anarchism wherever he traveled in Europe. Malatesta, who had
aristocratic origins, was a medical student at the University of
Naples until he was dismissed for leading a student riot. Thereafter,
his personal reading turned to the writings of Bakunin and Marx.
For the rest of his life, Malatesta seemed to be either freshly released
from prison or just returning to a cell. Referring to his friend's
episodic appearances, Kropotkin once described Enrico as "...just as
we saw him last, always ready to renew the struggle, with the same
love of man, with the same absence of hatred for adversaries or jail-
ers." In 1899, shortly after escaping from a prison in Tunisia, he
arrived in Paterson, New Jersey.[7]

The anarchist movement eventually had to confront the central
question of how to account fairly for the distribution of material
goods and personal services. Proudhon's and Bakunin's solution-
payment in proportion to what each man produced for society-
implied the existence of an organized authority, an anathema to any
practicing anarchist. Kropotkin and Malatesta conceived of a different solution, one that assumed any citizen would be willing to work
for the good of everyone else, that all work would be agreeable, and
that everyone would give to and take from the storehouse only what
he or she needed, never more. Their notion, which they called
"mutual aid," was intended to replace Darwin's theory of survival,
which most anarchists dismissed as a capitalist corruption.[8]
Kropotkin's interpretation of the function of government, like his
theory of mutual aid, was fanciful, at best. He cited "free" street-
lights and water and "free" parks, museums and libraries as proof
that public authority was not required, missing altogether the point
that these forms of social welfare were widely considered the happy
result of effective government.

In 1881, the populist movement in Russia pleaded for com-
munal use of land by all peasants. An extremist segment of this

group, known as the Narodniki, believed that only by eliminating the highest levels of government leadership could a people's revolutionary spirit be aroused. Accordingly, they struck a blow for their cause by tossing a fatal bomb into the carriage of Tsar Alexander II, one of the few Russian monarchs ever to display genuine interest in the plight of ordinary citizens. Perpetrators of the crime hoped their act would be the equivalent of Parisians storming the Bastille in 1789. In fact, the Russian people suffered an even more savage repression during the decades that followed. And, ironically, Alexander II, victim of violent death at the hands of his people, is remembered as the "Tsar liberator of the serfs".[9]

All this savagery and public violence was viewed as Europe's predicament, not America's. Why should a revolutionary spirit emerge in America, where no monarchy existed, where personal freedom and economic opportunity awaited all? Why were anarchists congregating in large numbers in cities like Paterson, New Jersey? One reason was that the United States had been experiencing the same social pressures typical of rapid industrialization everywhere. Immigrants were arriving from Europe at an unprecedented rate. Most arrived motivated to work, to support a family, and eventually to own land. Some, however, continued to live as they had in Europe, surrounded by filth, hunger, disease, prostitution, and violent crime. A few brought with them a firmly established hatred of all authority. They could still hear the echoes of anarchist rhetoric that emanated from Europe's ghettos, and they were listening to the calls for violent action that would come from America's expanding factories and tenements.

One newcomer was far more literate than most of his compatriots. Johan Most had been a bookbinder in Germany until police were alerted to his authorship of propagandist literature. Exiled first to England and then in 1882 to America, Most supported himself in two ways: he worked shifts in a New Jersey explosives factory and he edited *Freiheit*, New York City's most successful anarchist weekly. Combining knowledge gained from his two occupations, he wrote and published a book with the unsuitabtle title, *Science of Revolutionary Warfare: A Manual of Instructions in the Use and Preparation of Nitroglycerine, Dynamite, Gun-Cotton, Fulminating Mercury, Bombs, Fuses, Poisons, Etc.*[10] It was an instant bestseller among men with notions of destroying the ruling class, and it caught the eye of police investigating an 1886 explosion in Chicago's Haymarket Square.

The antecedent of the violence in Haymarket Square was a demonstration among laborers that had attracted police in great numbers, setting off brawls that left one striker dead and several others wounded. August Spies, editor of Chicago's anarchist daily, *Die Arbeiter-Zeitung*, issued a call to action, headlining the next day's paper, "A Pound of Dynamite is Worth a Bushel of Bullets!" Indeed, dynamite had become the poor man's preferred weapon; only the wealthy man, Spies pointed out, could afford a Winchester rifle. Handbills, produced and distributed throughout the city by Johan Most, urged, "Revenge! Revenge! Workingmen to Arms!" Exaggerating the death toll, he added, "Your masters sent out bloodhounds - the police killed six of your brothers!"

In response, strikers next gathered in the Old Haymarket on the evening of May 4, 1886. Just as a phalanx of police advanced on the angry mob, someone tossed a pipe bomb filled with dynamite into the front ranks, killing seven officers and wounding seventy. Spies was promptly arrested along with seven of his anarchist colleagues. Not one of them, of course, admitted to flinging the bomb into the police brigade. In the end, authorities concluded that the man who precipitated the crime had eluded them and had successfully fled the country.[11]

The public's disdain for anarchists was vividly demonstrated by the court's frustrated effort to empanel an impartial jury. Seven hundred fifty-seven prospective jurors were excused for cause; another two hundred were rejected on peremptory challenge. Presiding Judge Joseph Gary eventually accepted anyone who thought he could reach a decision based on fairness. When the jury returned its guilty verdict, Judge Gary sentenced all eight to be hanged, despite the absence of an identified murderer. One of the sentenced men managed to blow himself up the night before his scheduled execution with a capsule of fulminate of mercury smuggled into his jail cell by a compatriot. Four of the remaining men were hanged and three were imprisoned.[12]

The American public's reaction to the Haymarket incident was contrary to the primary objective of revolutionists everywhere.

Anarchism, not the anarchists, was on trial. With the full approval of the American public, and the press, anarchism was duly convicted. Instead of rallying to the revolutionist cause, most citizens viewed the movement with alarm, believing that anarchism was one of the most dangerous theories yet encountered by a civilized society. Its followers appeared to be more committed to violence than to creating a more effective social order. The newspaper cartoonist's typical image of the anarchist displayed a swarthy, unkempt, sinister-looking man with a dagger braced between his teeth, a smoking revolver grasped in one hand and a bomb held in the other. Illinois Governor John Peter Altgeld's decision (several years later) to pardon the three surviving anarchists served to destroy his political career.[13]

In 1892, the American public had yet another opportunity to display its abhorrence of anarchic behavior. Russian-born anarchist Alexander Berkman sought revenge for violence inflicted by Pinkerton agents hired to protect Andrew Carnegie's steel mill in Homestead, Pennsylvania during a prolonged strike. Learning that Carnegie, his intended victim, was in Scotland did not deter Berkman. After draping his body with explosives, he forced himself into the office of Henry Clay Frick, Carnegie's business partner. When Berkman discovered that he could not activate his bombs' fuses, he drew his revolver, fired once, then a second and a third time. All three bullets missed their target. The assailant next lunged with a dagger and stabbed Frick seven times. Miraculously, the victim survived. Berkman was subsequently tried, convicted, and sentenced to a prison term of sixteen years.[14]

This incident left the nation reeling. Remarkably, Johan Most, no stranger to inspiring terror, denounced Berkman's attempted murder on the pages of *Freiheit*. Most explained that the likelihood of a revolt in America was now slim, there being precious little class consciousness among its people. When he expressed this reversal of position at a public forum, a woman in the audience sprang onto the stage, brandishing a horsewhip. She began to lash at Most's face and body, with bloody and deforming results.

The whip-wielding woman was Emma Goldman. She had come to America from Russia at the age of twenty-one. Her first job was sewing for ten hours each day, for the meager payment of $2.50 per week. Appalled by the conditions that she and her co-workers suffered, as well as by the exploitative wages they received, Goldman longed to punish all the responsible authorities, and she sought others who shared this desire. She adopted Alexander Berkman as her mentor for a revolutionist education. Thus, she was not prepared for any compromise in ideologic zeal, especially from Johan Most, with whom she had been romantically involved in the past. The scandal of two anarchists and former lovers slugging it out at a public forum attracted considerable attention from the press.[15]

Newspaper accounts of anarchist activities had by this time captured the interest of Leon Czolgosz,[16] a twenty-year-old factory worker living in Cleveland, Ohio. Unimpressed by the land of freedom and opportunity to which his Polish immigrant father had fled, he sought a different ideology. While toiling in a wire factory, he joined co-workers demonstrating for higher wages. Thereafter branded as a striker, he was forced to use an alias (Fred Nieman) in order to find work. His timing was poor. Within a few weeks, Czolgosz, along with twenty percent of the American labor force, was out of work, the result of a financial collapse that history would call The Panic of 1893.

A first-generation American,[17] Leon Czolgosz was born in 1873, and raised, together with his five brothers and two sisters, in Detroit and several other midwestern communities. After his mother died (giving birth to an eighth child), his father moved repeatedly from one job and community to another. Leon's oldest brother, Waldeck, and his oldest sister, Cecili, looked after him during these formative years. By the time he was five, Leon had taught himself to read; his family eventually labeled him as the intellectual in their midst.

Czolgosz's father later recalled Leon as the quietest of his children, one never inclined to maintain friendships with other children. He was very often angry, but never able to explain why. When his father remarried, Leon developed an intense hatred for his stepmother. His formal schooling amounted to less than five years. Yet Leon, according to his siblings, always appeared to be thinking more than most children his age. Gradually realizing that none of his prayers were being answered, young Czolgosz repudiated all of the teachings of his family's faith, Roman Catholicism. What, he asked, was the validity of any religion or any god, if incessant prayer led only to unhappiness and misery? He turned his attention instead to the daily newspapers and read about the socialists and, especially, about the exciting anarchists.

In 1898, Czolgosz grew weary of looking for work and announced to his family that he was ill. His father had purchased a farm in Bedford, Ohio, just outside of Cleveland. He rejected older brother Waldeck's urging that he seek care from doctors, or at least go to a hospital. There was no place in any hospital for someone as poor as he, he declared. No adequate explanation for Leon's "ill health" was ever found. However, because he was able to obtain a doctor's certificate documenting illness, his labor union, the Benevolent Knights of the Golden Eagle, paid him sixteen weeks of sickness benefits.

Whenever Czolgosz wasn't sleeping or reading, he repaired machinery on the farm. Family members considered him their best hunter; he always preferred the challenge of shooting rabbits with a revolver instead of a shotgun. Czolgosz also occupied his time by visiting the local saloon. It wasn't beer (he rarely drank anything other than a soda), or companionship he sought; it was newspapers that drew him. Sometimes he stayed all day, rereading every issue from front to back.

Early in August, 1900, headlines announced the assassination of Italy's King Humbert. On July 29, 1900, as Humbert was distributing awards to athletes near his summer residence outside Milan, a man suddenly stepped up and shot him four times. Italy's king fell to the ground and quietly expired. The assassin, Gaetano Bresci, was a thirty-year-old silk weaver from Paterson, New Jersey, whose journey to Italy had been financed by conspiring anarchists.[18]

Czolgosz was thoroughly captivated by the story. For the first time, he realized that someone like himself, a common laborer, might some day strike a similar blow for social justice. He clipped the article and carefully folded it into his wallet. Periodically, he removed the clipping to reread it, savoring the details.[19]

The time eventually came when Czolgosz wanted to leave the farm and live in a city, perhaps Cleveland, although sometimes he spoke of going to Kansas, or even to California for his health.

Believing that his work at the family farm justified a share of its value, Leon asked to exchange his interest for a payment that might support his life elsewhere. His repeated demands went unanswered until the summer of 1901, when his father finally agreed.

Meanwhile, frequent trips to Cleveland provided Czolgosz with an opportunity to attend lectures and speak to others sharing his interest in anarchy. At first, he visited the city for one day, then lengthened his stays to two or sometimes three days at a time. When his family asked what occasioned these trips, he said only that he attended meetings, offering few details. One of those anarchist gatherings was a lecture given by Emma Goldman, by then the most famous and outspoken of radical women orators. She traveled constantly to meet with fellow anarchists, bringing a plea for social revolt to workers in every city she visited. For her audiences, she would often recall the inspiring words of her mentors, Alexander Berkman mainly, but Johan Most as well. Her many collaborators were scattered in all of the great industrial cities, from New York and Philadelphia to Chicago and St. Louis.

On May 5, 1901, Goldman was scheduled to speak to the Franklin Liberal Club in Cleveland. Czolgosz had seen the notice in a newspaper, recognized her name, and arranged to be there. Arriving early, he took a seat in the last row and watched the room fill with men, most of whom were recent immigrants. For this particular event, there were several women present as well. Unwilling to engage others in conversation, Czolgosz devoted his full attention to Goldman's words. Hearing the noted anarchist leader in person for the first time, he listened raptly as she painted her image of a world where "...men are no longer under the galling yoke of government, ecclesiasticism, and prejudice." She distinguished her ideological position from that of the socialists: "We do not favor the idea of converting men and women into mere producing machines under the eye of a paternal government. We go to the opposite extreme and demand the fullest and most complete liberty for each and every person to work out his own salvation..."

Czolgosz was enthralled by Goldman; she was more dynamic than any radical he had ever read about or listened to. Afterward, he summoned the courage to approach her, introduced himself as Fred Nieman, and asked for literature.

Remarkably, she would later recall this brief encounter, including the name he gave her.[20]

In June, Czolgosz returned to Cleveland and introduced himself, again as Fred Nieman, to Emil Schilling, a local anarchist leader. Czolgosz expressed disappointment that members appeared to spend most of their time quarreling. When, he asked, would someone be willing to act for social justice? Schilling, who clearly was not excited about violent acts, responded by loaning him *Chicago Martyrs*, a book about the Haymarket Square incident. Returning a few days later and irritating Schilling when he interrupted his dinner, Czolgosz declared that he didn't have time to read Schilling's book or any other books, for that matter. The time had come, he believed, for someone to do something. He wanted to know about any secret societies that might be plotting something-anything-including, for example, a deed like Breschi's attack in Italy. Stunned by the young man's brashness, Schilling turned him away, declaring that the anarchists he knew in Cleveland didn't engage in that sort of violent action.

Early in July, Czolgosz sought out Emma Goldman in Chicago. She introduced 'Nieman' to several of her anarchist friends, including Abe Isaak, editor of the newsletter *Free Society*. Isaak offered Nieman lodging and help finding a job locally, but he balked at a request for funds. Nieman lacked authenticity in Isaak's view; his knowledge of the movement seemed woefully limited. Thinking him a spy, Isaak so warned readers of *Free Society*. Few took immediate notice of Isaak's published impressions of Nieman, but police later would.

Before leaving Chicago to return to Cleveland, Czolgosz read newspaper reports that President McKinley would be visiting Buffalo's Pan-American Exposition in September. Early in August, he had a final brief encounter with Schilling in Cleveland. As the two parted, Schilling inquired where he might travel next. Czolgosz replied, "Maybe to Buffalo".[21]

❖

McKinley's favorite presidential photograph.

2

McKINLEY

*"As a result of our free institutions, the great body of men
who control public affairs come from the ranks of
the plain people of these United States."*

William McKinley, 1900[1]

All American presidents are vulnerable. Some, though, are more acutely conscious of potential danger than others. Unlike President Grover Cleveland before him, William McKinley resisted all efforts to limit his contact with the American public. His first executive order following inauguration in 1897 authorized removal of the guard booth that Cleveland had installed in front of the executive mansion.[2] McKinley considered himself personally secure from attack, despite awareness that two previous American Presidents, Lincoln and Garfield, had fallen victim to assassins' bullets.[3]

Prior to Lincoln's mortal injury in 1865, only Andrew Jackson among U.S. presidents had faced the threat of an intended assassin. Yet no formal security measures were established following that incident because few people were surprised that someone might wish to end Jackson's life. "Old Hickory" had already survived twenty-six duels and collected numerous enemies along the way. In 1835, the president faced a man in the Capitol rotunda whose first and second revolvers both misfired, earning for Jackson, once again, his reputation for being as indestructible as the tree for which he was nicknamed.[4] The assailant, Richard Lawrence, was never found guilty of a murderous act. Such was the prevailing cultural attitude that men at all levels of society could draw revolvers to solve their problems.

Presidential security was first considered a priority during the Civil War years. Because the capital district was located well within the war zone, protecting the commander in chief became the War Department's responsibility, backed by the Metropolitan

Police. When Lincoln would impetuously decide to stroll through the streets of Washington, he would be chased after by a cavalry detail. Nevertheless, significant security gaps remained, as the president's encounter with assassin John Wilkes Booth at Ford's Theater clearly demonstrated. The man who had been assigned to guard Lincoln that evening was later found sipping his drink in a tavern next to the theater.

James A. Garfield, twentieth President of the United States, met his assassin, Charles Guiteau, in the capital's Baltimore and Ohio Railroad terminal. Guiteau, a self-styled lawyer/politician with neither the education nor the experience to justify either title, was disgruntled over his failure to secure a government position. He took revenge by following Garfield into the station and shooting him in the back. Later, Guiteau boasted that he had successfully stalked Garfield in numerous public places, always escaping detection until his final desperate act.

Grover Cleveland genuinely feared personal attack. His wife, aware of threats against her husband, was even more apprehensive about his safety, particularly when they vacationed at Gray Gables, their Massachusetts summer home on Buzzard's Bay. She directed the Secret Service to send "operatives," as they were known in that day, to Massachusetts even before her husband could voice his needs. Subsequently, the press called attention to this use of government personnel as unauthorized. Congress had long opposed the formation of federal policing authorities, their only exceptions being the U.S. Marshals Service formed in 1789 to help maintain order, and a "Secret Service" established to deal with rampant counterfeiting after the Civil War. Ultimately, the Secretary of the Treasury did authorize agents to protect President Cleveland, and this habit continued without congressional approval throughout McKinley's term of office, although in a more restrained and less visible manner.

McKinley's comfort with himself and his surroundings had been a lifelong feature of his personality. Beginning in childhood, he spoke with clarity and confidence. In school, he enjoyed reciting and often volunteered his willingness to do so. Later, he was recognized for his public speaking, and he would further develop his rhetorical skills while competing in debating society events.[5]

Major William McKinley

Nancy Allison Mckinley

Senator Mark Hanna

President McKinley

Born in Niles, Ohio on January 29, 1843, the future president was the seventh of nine siblings. His father, William McKinley, was the prosperous owner of several pig iron foundries. His mother, Nancy Allison McKinley, a devout Christian, hoped that young William would apply his oratory skills to his childhood faith and become a Methodist minister. When the schools in Niles proved inadequate for developing William's obvious potential, the family moved closer to Union Seminary in Poland, Ohio (near Youngstown). There, the young boy excelled for eight years before a sudden bankruptcy of the family iron enterprise cut his education short. All the McKinley children went to work; William was a clerk in the Poland post office.

He hoped to become a schoolteacher, but the shots fired at Fort Sumter were heard at least as far as Poland, Ohio. Negotiating an agreement with his weeping mother, the eighteen-year-old William promised to come back to her alive and healthy if she would approve his decision to enlist. On June 11th, 1861, he (and a cousin) joined the Union Army's Twenty-third Ohio Volunteer Infantry Regiment. They were sent to the Shenandoah Valley to fight under General Sheridan.

Young McKinley proved a daring and courageous soldier. In September 1862, during the heat of battle at Antietam, he drove a mule cart loaded with hot food into the center of combat. McKinley's valor caught the eye of his immediate commanding officer, a Cincinnati lawyer named Rutherford B. Hayes, who promoted him to the rank of commissary sergeant, in charge of an entire brigade's nourishment and supply. Not content with an enlisted man's rank, McKinley soon achieved an officer's commission and served Hayes in an administrative capacity throughout their remaining days in America's bloodiest war.

In letters to home, Hayes described his young Ohio protege as "...a handsome, bright, gallant boy, and one of the bravest and finest officers in the Union Army...someday, he will be President." McKinley learned on March 13, 1865 that he had been promoted to the rank of Brevet Major. His certificate, signed by A. Lincoln just one month before the president's tragic assassination, became a cherished possession. For the rest of his life, McKinley preferred "Major" to all other titles, including "Mr. President."

In 1865, with the war over, both Hayes and McKinley returned to Ohio. Hayes ran successfully for governor, and a dozen years later, he became nineteenth President of the United States. McKinley returned to Poland in remarkably fine condition, much to his mother's great delight. His war experiences had given him greater discipline and poise and a clear awareness of his personal strengths as a leader. Influenced by his model, Colonel Hayes, McKinley decided to study law. When he announced his plans to the colonel, Hayes, now a congressional representative, reflected a moment and said, "With your business capacity and experience, I would have preferred for you a career in railroading or some commercial business...As a lawyer, a man sacrifices independence to ambition which is a sorry bargain at best."

McKinley ignored his mentor's skepticism. He enrolled at the Albany Law School and completed the necessary requirements in one year. While a student there, his Methodist upbringing continued to guide his behavior; he abstained from alcohol, tobacco, dancing, and card playing, a regimen he had maintained during the war years, as well. Writing to a younger nephew, he offered his credo, "Look after your diet and living, take no intoxicants, indulge in no immoral practices."

Despite his exemplary conduct, McKinley was ill at ease in Albany's sophisticated social circle. The company of young women made him bashful and his rural background left him unacquainted with the rituals and novelties of his hosts.[6] Therefore, it was easy for him to return to his native state after passing the necessary examinations at the law school. He set up his practice in Canton, a city of 10,000, where an older sister had already established herself. Other members of the family, including his mother, soon joined them there. McKinley's practice flourished, and he became active in the local veteran's organizations, the Masonic Lodge, the Knights of Pythias, and the YMCA.

He also offered his support to the local Republican Party committee, taking strong positions on issues such as women's suffrage (which he favored). In time, his skillful political oration earned him a reputation throughout Stark County. His mother, delighted with most of her son's achievements, was dubious of his interest in politics (and even more chagrined by his newly established love of cigars).

Mrs. McKinley also had reservations about her son's evolving romantic attachment to Ida Saxton, eldest daughter of Canton's principal banker. She had attended fashionable academies in Cleveland and Philadelphia, and then enjoyed a grand tour of Europe. The townspeople considered Ida spoiled, demanding, and used to getting whatever she wanted.[7] What she wanted after meeting William McKinley at a church social was his hand in marriage. They married in 1871 and honeymooned in New York City. Their first daughter, Katie, was born one year later, and a second daughter, Ida, came in 1873. The second baby was frail from the outset, and she died before her fifth month.

This tragedy devastated both parents, but it was especially hard on Ida. Immediately following delivery, she had developed two serious conditions—severe phlebitis in both legs and a seizure disorder. Once carefree, physically active, and fun-loving, Ida became a lifelong invalid, ever prone to brief lapses of consciousness and limited in the use of her chronically painful and swollen legs.[8] Although his wife's handicaps never appeared to weaken McKinley, they did change him. He grew both more serious and more compassionate toward all people who suffered. He also devoted even more time and attention to Ida. Instead of taking walks together, the couple enjoyed long rides in their carriage, more often in the evening when bright sunlight would be less likely to trigger her attacks. In public places, he sat close by her and deftly placed a handkerchief over her grimacing face during the seizures. Fortunately these episodes were brief. Often, following recovery, Ida would continue a conversation that had been interrupted by a seizure, not seeming to be aware of the intervening episode.

The only remaining brightness in the McKinleys' lives was snuffed when little Katie died in 1876. The only pleasing diversion McKinley could find was politics. In the midst of a most depressing year, Rutherford Hayes, by then Republican candidate for president, asked him for help. McKinley stumped for his mentor throughout Ohio, and so thoroughly enjoyed campaigning that he decided to give up his law practice in favor of a run for the United States Congress. Remarkably, McKinley won his election in 1876 more easily than did Hayes, whose victory was determined in 1877 by Congress, following one of the closest votes in the nation's history.[9]

With both men living in Washington, their friendship deepened and widened to include their families. Ida's health improved enough to permit her to attend receptions and dinners, and she once happily took on the task of caring for the Hayes children in the executive mansion while the president and his wife traveled.

When the Republicans regained the executive office in 1889, replacing Grover Cleveland with Benjamin Harrison[10], they also re-established leadership of both Houses of Congress for the first time in sixteen years. McKinley was held in sufficiently high regard to be proposed for Speaker of the House of Representatives. His chief competition was the formidable Thomas Reed of Maine, who read widely, kept his diary in French, and spoke with an erudition and historical perspective that McKinley could never match. Reed's election as Speaker came as a relief to McKinley, who later reflected that his own success might have destined him to a lengthy but mediocre career in Congress.

Congressman McKinley chose to focus on the nation's trade policy. As chairman of the House Ways and Means Committee, he was primary author of a protective tariff act. In 1890, what became known as the McKinley Tariff Act passed after intense debate. For McKinley, Congress took the place of a college education. Although he respected men of culture and erudition, often seeking their company throughout his political career, he learned to assert the advantage of practical skills over theoretical knowledge, never forgetting the disadvantage of his own abbreviated schooling. "I would rather have my political economy founded upon the everyday experience of the puddler or potter than the learning of the professor," he liked to say. To his stenographer, he once observed that he learned more from people than from books. "Of course, people do write the books," he added with amusement.

In 1892, at the age of forty-nine, McKinley accepted nomination as governor of Ohio and won that office handily. Friends and colleagues were already saying that the former congressman was destined to be president someday. Both Hayes and Garfield had shown that Ohio politics was an effective launching platform for the nation's leadership. Others wondered how Ida could possibly perform as an effective first lady. Might she be the lodestone that prevented McKinley from attaining the presidency? Now childless, Ida was growing increasingly depressed. She required maids and nurses in attendance more frequently as her husband's mounting responsibilities drew him away from her side. Even at his busiest, however, McKinley spent many hours each day comforting his wife. This intense devotion, as it gradually became more widely known, served only to increase the public's respect and admiration for the man.

Ida's many needs, combined with her expensive tastes, were an added burden on the family's already strained finances. As a congressman, McKinley had been forced to borrow on his real estate holdings in Canton in order to defray the costs of caring for Ida, living and socializing in Washington, and funding his office expenses and campaigns. As Ohio's new governor, he at last found the financial security that had eluded him throughout his early political career. His gubernatorial salary was $8,000, significantly more than the $5,000 congressional stipend. The state of Ohio provided very comfortable living quarters, and McKinley's social obligations were not as personally burdensome as they had been in Washington. He might have become a very wealthy man had he accepted the corporate directorships and paid lecture assignments he was offered, but he did not. He preferred a clear conscience.

McKinley found the challenges of Ohio politics far less daunting than the obligations of his position in the House of Representatives. His greatest source of joy during the years he spent between national responsibilities was the fact that Ida felt so much better. She participated in the social duties of gubernatorial leadership with a predictability that led her closest friends to imagine the possibility of full recovery. Unfortunately, that would never happen, not in Columbus, and not when she returned to Washington.

As he was leaving Congress in 1891, McKinley had told reporters that he was looking forward to private life someday, probably in Canton, the place he called home. Left out of these conversations was any mention of his friendship with Mark Hanna, a coal and iron millionaire and major contributor to the Ohio Republican Party. Hanna, who respected and admired McKinley, firmly believed in putting his money behind the right man. And, as was becoming increasingly clear to many in the Republican party, William McKinley was the right man. In addition to being talented and accomplished, McKinley had the serendipitous advantage of not being associated with Washington when the Panic of 1893 struck.

Shortly after Grover Cleveland's second term began in 1893, the national economy plummeted. Foreign creditors' demands and the enormous debt held by the overextended railroads precipitated a collapse of the stock market, and widespread bank and business failures. President Cleveland and his administration appeared helpless to ease the calamity, which included four million workers—Leon Czolgosz among them—suddenly without jobs. Nor did the new Democratic administration seem able to bank the flames of revolutionary activism spreading throughout the nation. Democrats were in disgrace, despite the fact that they had little to do with causing the economic disaster that confronted them. The president's failure to display sufficient sympathy for the victims of the economic depression only made matters worse.[11]

The Republicans bided their time, eagerly awaiting the next presidential election. In 1896, McKinley easily won his party's nomination for president on the first ballot. His opponent was not Cleveland, but William Jennings Bryan, hero of the populist movement and fierce opponent of a currency traditionally based only on gold. Bryan had become the surprise nominee of the Democratic Party after giving one of the most stirring speeches in U.S. political history. The Populists nominated Bryan, as well, leading to a fusion of the two parties that eventually proved fatal to the causes of each.

One issue overshadowed all others during the 1896 campaign: whether or not free coinage of silver would be allowed, thereby diluting the value of all existing currency and stimulating a sharp price inflation. The Republicans, led by McKinley, believed that future prosperity depended on a firm monetary policy, which they argued meant preserving the gold standard and not allowing monetary dilution. The "Silverites," led by Bryan, advocated coining silver at a 16:1 ratio with gold. Western silver mining interests foresaw a ready government market for their product; farmers looked forward to an increase in prices paid for their products, plus the convenience of paying off their debts with cheaper money. During the summer and fall of 1896, Bryan campaigned across the country. He captivated audiences with his brilliant oratory, warning his opponent, "...you shall not press down upon the brow of labor this crown of thorns; you shall not crucify mankind upon a cross of gold!"

McKinley, meanwhile, conceived a daring strategy. He stumped from his front porch in Canton, Ohio. The Republican National Committee cooperated, as did the railroads; the former organized numerous delegations that the latter allowed to travel to Canton at reduced rates. There, the delegates would meet McKinley in person and listen to his campaign message. Each morning, the candidate would appear on his porch, flanked by his mother and (whenever her health permitted) his wife. He would deliver his address and talk with delegates. Then, after taking a midday break, he would repeat the scenario in the afternoon. Thus, a carefully crafted image of a serious, honorable man, forever devoted to his invalid wife, was carried home by steelworkers from Pittsburgh, railroad men from the western states, farmers' organizations, hardware men, and representatives of nearly every other trade group in the nation. By September, trains were arriving in Canton from dawn to dusk, bringing as many as 30,000 people each day. McKinley gave as many as sixteen speeches daily, except for Sundays, which the family reserved for worship.

McKinley's appeal was greatest in the industrialized cities of the Northeast, where workers of every social and economic class, every ethnic background, wanted the factories to resume full production. He benefited, as well, from the support of bankers who believed that their future stability depended on a strong currency. And big business backed him as a man who could be depended upon to maintain the protective barriers that kept foreign competitors' lower-priced products out of local markets.

As the election approached, the southern states were solidly behind Bryan, as were nearly all of the far west states. But it was the "sound money interests" that carried the election. Bryan lost.[12] When the call to Canton came to announce that another Ohioan had earned the nation's presidency-and with a popular vote greater than for any candidate since Ulysses S. Grant-McKinley's mother's first reaction was to pray, "Oh God, keep him humble."[13]

While the campaign had proceeded through the late summer and fall of 1896, events not anticipated by anyone involved in the election were taking place thousands of miles away in Canada's Yukon Territory. Sixty-eight miners worked their claims alongside a tributary of the Klondike River, renamed Bonanza Creek by an American and two Indian sidekicks who discovered gold in its rich bed.[14] The resulting infusion of $175 million in gold bullion into the North American economies over a few years contributed significantly to renewed economic stability. By the time McKinley became the Republican candidate for re-election in 1900, the nation had experienced twelve consecutive quarters of economic expansion. Then, as now, presidents were rewarded for a rising economy whether or not their decisions were responsible for it.

On March 1, 1897, McKinley, his wife, and his mother arrived in Washington. The president-elect's first meeting with Grover Cleveland was warm, candid, and mutually respectful. The topic that dominated that first conversation was one largely ignored during the campaign: Spain's persistent meddling in the political affairs of Cuba. United States policy was consistent with the provisions of the Monroe Doctrine, which called for protecting Western Hemisphere nations from European domination. A peaceful resolution, perhaps even involving Spain's sale of Cuba to the U.S., had seemed likely. Now, on the eve of the inauguration, Cleveland was convinced that war was inevitable, thanks to zealous calls from Congress for aggressive intervention.

In the short term, the possibility of an international war was trumped by the gala events associated with the transition to the new administration. Inauguration Day was bright, clear, and windy; a multitude of flags snapped above the crowds lining Pennsylvania Avenue. Detachments of regular army troops escorted Cleveland and McKinley to the Capitol, followed by a procession of diplomats and other officials. At the designated moment, Chief Justice Melville Fuller administered to McKinley the oath by which he became the twenty-fifth President of the United States. The presidential party viewed the grand parade that followed from a platform in front of the executive mansion, specially constructed for Mrs. McKinley's comfort.[15]

The new president's capacity for hard work and his administrative efficiency were quickly evident. He arose early to read the newspapers and attend to his wife's needs. Following breakfast, he remained at his desk until 1:30 P.M., receiving visits from senators, congressmen, cabinet members, and foreign ambassadors. Some days, he set aside an hour to receive members of the general public, as well. The new president was unusually adept at developing empathy and rapport with both legislators and the public. Following a meeting with his political adversaries, McKinley was approached by Democratic Senator Cullom, who remarked, "Mr. President, I could not get mad at you if I tried!" After lunch and a visit with Mrs. McKinley, he returned to his desk until late afternoon. Weather permitting, he would then take his wife for a carriage ride. Although Ida was pleased to serve as the president's first lady, she was not particularly anxious to assume the role of hostess. Instead, she busied herself knitting small items for eventual donation to charitable organizations. (Before she left Washington, Ida had knit 3,500 pairs of slippers.) The president's mother, on the other hand, who entered the Washington political scene at 87, had sufficient energy and enthusiasm to delight the public and serve as a source of amusement for the press.

Occasionally, the president walked the streets of Washington with colleagues or rode on horseback alongside the Potomac River. He always appeared at dinner in a full dress suit. After the meal and conversation with family or friends, McKinley would return to his desk for two or three hours. He saved his hardest work, writing his replies to correspondence or to Congressional bills submitted to him for comment, for this period. The staff could not recall a president who routinely put in as long a workday as McKinley.

Accustomed to monitoring domestic legislation, the president was confident about his judgments in such matters. On

President McKinley's War Cabinet, 1848.

President and Mrs. McKinley, Executive Mansion.

international questions, he accepted the counsel of his advisors and declared an unwillingness to interfere in the affairs of foreign governments. His conviction that "...we must avoid the temptation of territorial aggression. War should never be entered upon until every agency of peace has failed..." was severely tested early in the second year of his presidency. On the night of February 16, 1898, a courier from the Navy Department arrived at night with news that the battleship Maine had exploded in Cuban waters during the previous evening, taking 268 men with her to the bottom of Havana's harbor. It was considered a calamity unmatched since the 1881 assassination of then-president James Garfield. McKinley was immediately pressured to declare war on Spain. He resisted steadfastly for several weeks. Criticism came from all sides—from the Congress, from the press, even from the president's own Assistant Secretary of the Navy, Theodore Roosevelt, who declared McKinley to be "...as spineless as a creampuff" for postponing a declaration of war. Following an unsuccessful board of inquiry to determine exactly what happened to the Maine and why, and several failed attempts to compromise with Spanish President Canovas, McKinley reluctantly submitted a proposal for articles of war to a Congress he knew would jump at the opportunity to support armed conflict. And so it was: Congress declared war on April 25, 1898. Within a few days, troops were on their way to Cuba, among them Theodore Roosevelt, whose personal ambition to take part in combat had been apparent to his colleagues for several months.

Even before the advent of war, McKinley's personal secretary, George Courtelyou, had been concerned about the president's safety. The number of angry letters received at the executive mansion, including some with threats against McKinley's life, had increased. Courtelyou knew that the executive mansion was not secure, especially at night, when a lone watchman patrolled the nearby grounds. There was no guard at all for the second floor living quarters. John Wilkie, director of the Secret Service, responded to Courtelyou's apprehension by assigning two Secret Service operatives to the mansion full time, plus a night watchman for the bedroom corridor. Windows and doors that had long been left unlatched day and night were secured. Courtelyou understood that it was useless to speak of these matters with McKinley, who continued to greet dozens of visitors each day and to take walks on the nearby streets of Washington without concern.

The war lasted only three months. Between April and August, United States armed forces occupied Cuba and Puerto Rico, while naval forces in the Pacific, under the command of Commodore George Dewey, destroyed a squadron of Spanish warships in Manila Bay. Even the most vehement critics of American imperialism were awed by this display of might. For President McKinley, there was clear evidence of restored prestige throughout the world. Emissaries from London spoke of his popularity there. Republican newspapers compared him with Lincoln, while even the Democratic press acknowledged an obligation to stand behind the president in time of war. The conflict with Spain was formally brought to a close in February 1899, when the Treaty of Paris was signed. Regrettably, in the Philippine Islands, hostile actions persisted. Misunderstandings with revolutionary leader Emilio Aguinaldo led to prolonged guerilla-style clashes between American and Philippine forces over a period of several months, with bloodshed, casualties, and loss of life of a scope and style that would be repeated in Vietnam, later in the twentieth century.[16]

When Secretary of State John Hay recommended that 5,000 American troops be forwarded from Manila to China, where dozens of diplomats were trapped in the midst of the Boxer Rebellion, McKinley agreed. It was a decision the president took considerable pride in. America, he believed, was showing itself to be a moral leader among nations. McKinley's decision also represented a precedent: It was the first time a sitting president had sent troops to foreign soil without first consulting Congress. In 1899, as another presidential election campaign drew near, McKinley's popularity was virtually unquestioned. When his party nominated him for a second term, however, the ticket included as his running mate a man McKinley did not particularly like. The choice for vice president was a hero now renowned for his bravery under fire in Cuba, the recently elected governor of New York State, Theodore Roosevelt.

Out of deference to Mrs. McKinley's physical limitations,

and because the strategy had worked in 1896, McKinley again chose to conduct his campaign from Canton, Ohio. Meanwhile, Roosevelt boarded trains and campaigned for the Republican ticket in nearly every state of the union. McKinley and Roosevelt won easily, despite having to compete again with William Jennings Bryan and his colorful oratory. This time the issue wasn't monetary reform. Bryan's campaign was based on the perils of imperialism, in his words, "...the most dangerous trend in America". American voters preferred the Republican Party's vision of "Prosperity at home; prestige abroad!" When the votes were counted, McKinley had received the largest popular majority of any presidential candidate in the nation's history.

Soon after his second inauguration (held on March 4, 1901), McKinley scheduled an extensive journey throughout the western states. Mrs. McKinley had conserved her energy during the recent campaign. She believed she was strong enough to accompany her husband on a six-week tour that would culminate in Buffalo, New York, where the president would preside over the opening of the Pan-American Exposition. The westbound party included forty-three officials, friends, staff, servants, and journalists. Among them was the president's personal physician, Dr. Presley Rixey, a bushy-mustached naval surgeon from Virginia. McKinley's special train departed Washington on April 29, 1901 and took the southern route, through Texas, bound for Los Angeles. Arrival was anticipated in time for that city's annual fiesta.

Rixey knew that the president's health was rarely in question, and that he would likely devote most of his attention to Mrs. McKinley. After studying her medical history, he decreased the dosage of bromides that were used to help keep her calm. As a result, Ida was far more alert, and even appeared to enjoy herself throughout the long ride across the country. However, as the train crossed the southwestern desert, she developed signs and symptoms of a felon: an abscess-like infection of the fingertip. The pain and swelling became so severe that Rixey was forced to lance the infection before they reached Los Angeles. Following arrival, her finger was lanced again, but not soon enough to prevent a life-threatening fever. Mrs. McKinley missed the fiesta parade and most other social events but later seemed improved enough to continue the trip. As the party reached San Francisco, her fever returned, along with a renewal of the seizures. When her heart weakened, Ida was given injections of salt solution, a new form of therapy that provided her with sudden improvement in health.

Although the president managed to launch the new battleship Ohio while in San Francisco, he remained distracted from other public responsibilities throughout his wife's convalescence. A continuation of his planned tour was out of the question, as was his scheduled opening of the Pan-American Exposition in Buffalo. Vice President Roosevelt would be sent in his place. Only when his wife was strong enough to depart did McKinley summon everyone still traveling with him and direct that the train return to Washington promptly. After returning to the capital, Ida McKinley was diagnosed as having bacterial endocarditis, an infection of the lining of the heart. She continued to rally slowly and asked her husband if she might spend a quiet summer in Canton. Naturally, he agreed.

Secretary Courtelyou therefore commenced planning for the nation's governance to be conducted from the library of McKinley's Ohio home. The president and his party left the capital on July 5th with the intention of remaining in Canton for three months. A side trip to Buffalo was still on McKinley's agenda, but Courtelyou hoped to talk him out of it. The president's security was one kind of challenge in Canton, but quite another at a crowded exposition in Buffalo.

❖

TEN PAGES EIGHTY COLUMNS.

BUFFALO EVENING NEWS.

LAST ED

VOL. XLII—NO. 23.   BUFFALO, N. Y., MONDAY, MAY 20, 1901.   PRICE ONE C

THE EXPOSITION DEDICATED

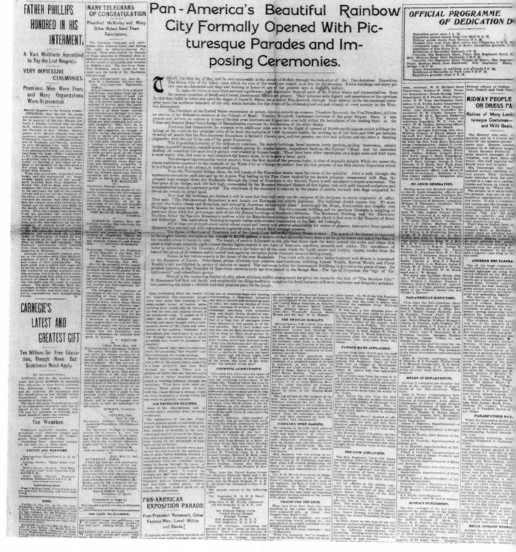

FATHER PHILLIPS HONORED IN HIS INTERMENT.

A Vast Multitude Assembled to Pay the Last Respects.

VERY IMPRESSIVE CEREMONIES.

Prominent Men Were There and Many Organizations Were Represented.

CARNEGIE'S LATEST AND GREATEST GIFT

Ten Millions for Free Education, Though None But Scotchmen Need Apply.

MANY TELEGRAMS OF CONGRATULATION

President McKinley and Many Other Rulers Send Their Felicitations.

Pan-America's Beautiful Rainbow City Formally Opened With Picturesque Parades and Imposing Ceremonies.

PAN-AMERICAN EXPOSITION PARADE

Vice-President Roosevelt, Other Famous Men, Local Militia and Bands.

OFFICIAL PROGRAMME OF DEDICATION D

MIDWAY PEOPLE ON DRESS PA

Natives of Many Lands in Picturesque Costumes and Wild Beasts.

ST. LOUIS DELEGATES.

PAN-AMERICAN DIRECTORS.

HEADS OF DEPARTMENTS.

Monday, May 21, 1901

3

EXPOSITION

"Expositions are the timekeepers of progress."

William McKinley, Sept. 5, 1901[1]

Planners of Buffalo's Pan-American Exposition optimistically designated May 1st as the date of the grand opening, hoping to exploit a full season of visitors. They also eagerly anticipated President and Mrs. McKinley's presence at the ribbon-cutting ceremonies. Most of all, Buffalo's leaders wanted to place their city in the world's spotlight; they envisioned the exposition earning a place on history's list of memorable events. Their objectives were achieved, but not in a manner that any of them would have wished or could have imagined.

Expositions have a long history.[2] They began centuries ago as weekly community-based events; in time, they grew into annual displays of an entire nation's unique products. The first international world's fair, housed in an enormous steel and glass enclosure (dubbed "The Crystal Palace"), was held in London in 1851. Loathe to be outdone by the English, the French organized the "Exposition Universelle" on Paris's Champs Elysees in 1855. Unlike the London fair, which paid for itself, the exposition in Paris sustained an enormous financial loss, establishing a woeful precedent.

In the U.S., expositions typically were organized to commemorate great historical events, beginning with the 1876 Centennial Exposition in Philadelphia. In 1893, Chicago launched its Columbian Exposition to mark the four hundredth anniversary of Columbus' discovery of America. Despite the misfortune of opening shortly after the stock market crash that touched off the Panic of 1893, that exposition drew 27 million visitors and turned a respectable profit. Buffalo's event was conceived as an equally grand affair from the beginning. Inspired by his visit to the 1895 Cotton States Exposition in Atlanta, Georgia, Buffalo newspaperman Richard Hill met with business executives and politicians in Buffalo and Niagara Falls in 1897, urging that a site for a huge event–one that would attract participation from the entire Western Hemisphere–be identified approximately halfway between their respective communities.

The first choice was Cayuga Island on the Niagara River, close to the American shore and four miles above the falls. Early word of the planned exposition was conveyed to President McKinley, who not only offered enthusiastic support but also viewed the proposed island site during a visit to Buffalo in August 1897. War with Spain, however, brought the enterprise to an abrupt halt.[3]

The military conflict did no more than postpone the Pan-American Exposition, however, thanks to a nucleus of enthusiasts that included Buffalo's mayor, Conrad Diehl. Summer 1901 was designated as the target for a fair that would celebrate economic progress and political union among all nations in the Western Hemisphere. Fund-raising efforts in the community produced gratifying results: Nearly three hundred of Buffalo's wealthiest citizens quickly purchased stock worth $500,000; an additional 12,000 individuals purchased shares worth a total of $1,325,000. Mayor Diehl was thrilled by this outpouring of community support. To raise the remaining funds required to underwrite the huge event, he turned to the state and federal governments. The United States Congress, well aware of President McKinley's support, appropriated $500,000 for government exhibits. Another $500,000 was to be raised from the state assembly for construction of a New York State building at the Exposition.[4] Because most of the initial backing had come from Buffalo's business leaders, their commercial interests took precedence, and the Cayuga Island site was abandoned in favor of a location in Buffalo.[5]

Ease of visitor access is a critical requirement for any exposition. Buffalo benefited from being a major railroad hub with a track network denser than any other city in the nation. Its rail belt line carried thousands of workers each day from the inner city to factories along the northern perimeter and river shoreline and its electric streetcar system was modern, clean, and efficient. The city's overall layout (designed by Joseph Ellicott) featured broad boulevards radiating from a central area, mirroring French architect Pierre L'Enfant's design for the District of Columbia.

Initially, many Exposition backers supported a lakefront site, following Chicago's lead. When it became clear that the amount of landfill needed to create enough usable land would entail prohibitively high costs, attention shifted to a tract of land north of the city center. Owned by Dexter Rumsey, patriarch of one of Buffalo's wealthiest families, the tract lay between Delaware and Elmwood Avenues, two of Buffalo's radial boulevards, and extended for one mile north of Park Lake. Measuring 350 acres, the site was half the area of Chicago's Columbian Exposition but still large enough to be considered adequate. Also, the location offered the potential for providing visitors with a grand spectacle when viewed from the south, across Park Lake. Furthermore, since the railway belt line crossed the plot's northern border, it would be comparatively easy to add a new terminal that would provide direct access to the Exposition.

Rumsey agreed to a short-term (two-year) lease of the land, and the charter for "The Pan," as the Exposition was soon nicknamed, was signed early in 1899. John G. Milburn, a prominent Buffalo attorney, was elected exposition president. William I. Buchanan, former United States ambassador to the Argentine Republic, was recruited to serve as director-general. Roswell Park, Buffalo's most respected surgeon, was appointed as the exposition's medical director. He was assisted by Vertner Kenerson whose specialty was public health.

The city that would soon host this world-class exposition had come a long way from its humble beginnings. One hundred years before, Buffalo, originally named Buffalo Creek, had been a modest settlement of simple houses perched on an embankment overlooking the southern shore of Lake Erie, at the head of the Niagara River. The village was burned to the ground during British attacks in 1813 and 1814 and then later rebuilt and incorporated as the City of Buffalo. After completion of the Erie Canal in 1825, Buffalo's rapid growth was assured, and it became the "Queen City of the Great Lakes."

Immigrants and finished goods traveled north on the Hudson River, then west through a system of locks on the Erie Canal to Buffalo, then on to the western territories. Traveling the route in reverse came raw materials—grain, livestock, and iron ore-to feed the people and factories of the northeast. The Erie Canal flourished until the railroads came. Buffalo evolved easily into a rail center, served by as many as fifteen railroads at one time. By 1900, the city's rail traffic was second only to Chicago's.[6]

The Erie Canal had stimulated Buffalo's growth; the railroads made the city rich. The key to Buffalo's new wealth lay in the role it played in the transfer of goods from lake steamers into railcars departing for Atlantic coastal cities. Tonnage that had required seven days to be removed from a boat's cargo hold in 1840 could, in 1890, be transferred in seven minutes. Charges as high as 25 cents for each ton of goods trans-shipped, when multiplied by the total weight passing through Buffalo, resulted in the accumulation of enormous local wealth. Great family dynasties grew from these commercial endeavors: the Albrights (coal and iron), Larkins (soap), Rumseys (tanning), Scatcherds (lumber), Urbans (flour), and many more.

Buffalo's steady industrialization was not without a dark side, however. Across town from the broad boulevards and parkways where the city's newly rich erected large, elegant homes, lay the overcrowded neighborhoods of Buffalo's rapidly expanding immigrant population. The narrow streets were filled with a blend of decent people, prostitutes, thieves, and beggars, along with the combined odors of boiled cabbage, stale beer, and rancid garbage. Alleys were crowded with children playing and drunks sleeping off their intoxication. In overcrowded tenement buildings as many as ten people lived in a single room, all eating, sleeping, arguing, defecating, and eventually dying within the same space. These were the same living conditions that approximated the ghettos of Europe, where socialist and anarchist movements had first taken root.

The central rail terminal on Exchange Street served as Buffalo's Ellis Island, receiving thousands of immigrants-Greeks, Germans, Irish, Italians, Poles, Russians, and Scandinavians-each week. Many were farmers who would continue westward to claim the tillable land promised to them by the Homestead Act; those inclined toward factory work might remain in Buffalo. Those who were skilled with machines, and who owned their own tools, were absorbed quickly into specialized manufacturing activities such as tool and die making. These workers would prosper like no others. Then as now, success in America depended on the development of technical skills, not on a birthright.

Like most industrialized cities of the northeast, Buffalo experienced its share of labor unrest. Despite a growing economy, unemployment remained at 20 percent, primarily because no limits were placed on the number of immigrants permitted to enter the nation or the city. The Pan-American Exposition's executive committee, chaired by John Scatcherd, grappled with labor issues very early in the planning process. A suggestion to organize all laborers at the work site according to union principles quickly met with vigorous opposition, especially from the building contractors. Compromises ensued. Men living in Buffalo for at least one year were given hiring preference, but the development zone was declared an open shop, so men who didn't belong to a union could still be hired. Most important for union interests, the designated workday would be eight hours; time-and-a-half wages would be paid for overtime. Some problems remained. Contractors who made individual agreements to extend the defined workday or went outside of Buffalo to find cheaper labor provoked on-site protests from unionists.

Ground was broken on September 26, 1899. The magnitude of construction required within the limited time available exceeded anything Buffalo had ever experienced. The first task was grading the site for its planned canals, reflecting pools, and fountains. Trees, plants, and perennial flowers were planted in the spring of 1900 to allow time for growth before the opening in May 1901. Construction of the rail terminal was begun promptly, as this was the portal through which several hundred thousand tons of construction materials would pass. Of the more than one hundred structures to be erected, including a stadium and a grand tower, only the New York State building was designed for permanence. The remaining structures were built using techniques that had worked well in Chicago: first, a wood framework was erected and then that was wrapped with wire mesh and covered with plaster of Paris mixed with hemp fiber. This approach allowed each building's surface to be sculpted to achieve the detail required for the designer's selected architectural theme, which in most cases was Spanish Renaissance. In place of the all-white surfaces that had earned Chicago's Columbian Exposition the moniker "White City," Buffalo's "Pan" would be a "Rainbow City," filled with buildings resplendent in colors.

Exposition planners hoped to draw visitors both day and night. They authorized the installation of a multitude of electric lights, many times more than for any prior "electrified" exposition. The power for this man-made spectacle would come from western New York's natural spectacle, Niagara Falls. Although hydroelectric power was not new, alternating current was. Buffalo was one of America's testing grounds for this new technology developed by Nickola Tesla and further refined by George Westinghouse. Their opponent in the "battle of currents" was Tesla's former employer, Thomas Edison. Edison favored direct current and steadfastly maintained that the high voltage delivered by alternating current was dangerous for individual users. He was eventually proven wrong. The new current could travel greater distances, and individual homes could be protected by using transformers to step down the high-powered current. Many of the great homes and mansions along Buffalo's grand avenues were already supplied with alternating current. These beautifully lit homes were not only brighter at night, they were healthier, as well. Gaslight consumed much of a household's available oxygen.

To fully illuminate the Exposition would require 5,000 electric horsepower (about 4,500 kilowatts) each day, an amount equal to nearly half the requirements of the city's entire population (350,000 in 1901).[7] Most of the additional power demand would occur at dusk, when the Exposition's daytime image gave way to a true spectacle of illumination. Instead of using arc lights, which he considered unreliable, lighting designer John Ruskin chose the newer incandescent lamps. The latter glowed with a softer radiance and offered greater flexibility in alignment. When completed, the installation drew on light from more than 200,000 individual fixtures.

The enormous amount of power required to sustain this nighttime extravaganza created another unprecedented diversion. Americans inaugurated a new form of civic protest.

The Exposition's Pan-American Hospital.

Hospital Staff (Roswell Park rear right).

"Preservationists" argued that water flowing over a natural wonder should not be wasted for the benefit of a temporary spectacle that fed the egos of the wealthy. Gaslight was of already proven effectiveness; electric lighting, they believed, was yet another frivolity of the rich. The emotions displayed in the ensuing debate were just as intense as those surrounding environmental issues today.

Planning for the Exposition's medical and public health needs was the combined responsibility of Doctors Park and Kenerson. Their work commenced during the summer of 1900. A stenographer and two nurses were employed to assure that an emergency medical facility would be satisfactorily appointed, equipped, and supplied for the fair's anticipated crowds. Once the event opened, nurses would be drawn from local hospitals as well as medical institutions throughout the nation. Buffalo's physicians would make themselves available on a rotational basis. And student-volunteers from the city's medical school and local nursing schools would supplement the facility's staff during peak attendance. A fleet of newly purchased electric-powered ambulances would be available to transport injured or ill visitors from any location on the Exposition site to the medical facility. Dr. Kenerson took charge of overseeing the sanitary arrangements, including water supply, food inspection, restaurant hygiene, and proper removal of all waste. Dr. Park concentrated on the medical facility, ensuring that it would be suitable for treating victims of accidents and other injuries. An operating room was equipped for minor surgical and fracture setting needs. Park also insisted that the latest telephone equipment be installed to allow immediate consultation with specialists, should the need arise.[8]

The Exposition's expenses mounted. Revenue from stock subscriptions was higher than expected and local banks happily issued mortgage bonds, but these resources were not sufficient. The original $4 million budget prepared by Mr. Buchanan was revised upward twice. As opening day approached, anticipated costs stood at $7 million. Gate revenues were expected to make up the difference. Buffalo's weather, always unpredictable, dealt the planners a major blow. As every local citizen knew, winters sometimes refused to end. What climatologists decades later

The Dexter Rumsey farm - Future site of the Exposition.

Uncompleted construction blanked with snow - March, 1901.

RAIL TERMINAL

Artist rendering of completed Exposition site.

Grand opening, May 20, 1901, Vice President Roosevelt presiding.

would call the "lake effect," an arctic-like microclimate caused by an ice-covered Lake Erie nearby, could bring heavy snowfalls, prolonged cold, and mixtures of rain and sleet throughout the spring months. This is exactly what happened in 1901. On March 1st, two months shy of the planned opening date, "The Pan" still lay under a heavy blanket of snow. Virtually no exhibit hall was yet finished.

Ground excavations, major framing of buildings, and most of the wire wrapping had been completed before the winter of 1900-1901 had begun. The final application of plaster and the fashioning of design themes remained to be done. Neither could be achieved in the presence of winter temperatures and heavy moisture. Because so many buildings were unfinished, early visitors would not have access to many of the event's planned attractions. This led some members of the executive committee to call for postponing the grand opening. They argued that all visitors should enjoy a comprehensive experience and depart singing their praises of the event. In the end, the committee forged ahead with plans to cut the ribbon and open the event on the first of May. That decision was a serious error. Those who came during the first month were extremely disappointed. Editorials in the Buffalo and Cleveland newspapers criticizing exposition management, and recommending that everyone postpone visiting until the end of June, further dampened the public's interest. A communication from secretary Courtelyou informing the executive committee that Mrs. McKinley's illness would prevent the president from attending the official opening (instead, Vice-President Roosevelt would come) didn't help matters.[9]

Revenue data reflected the early visitors' lackluster attitude. Only 179,000 admissions were paid during May, compared with one million for the Chicago event during the same month in 1893. The fact that the nation had been in a state of financial panic in 1893 but was experiencing an economic boom in 1901 made the situation even more ironic.

On the official grand opening day, May 20, 1901, local dignitaries joined the vice president and his party and brought them out Delaware Avenue, over the broad, tree-lined Chapin and Lincoln Parkways, then across Park Lake to the Triumphal

Bridge. Leaving their carriages, Roosevelt and his party continued by foot to the Esplanade, a grand plaza designed to accommodate 100,000 spectators. It was a beautiful sunny day; the winter's snow and ice had by then melted, and the wildflowers bordering the lake were in full bloom. All eyes were drawn to the Court of the Fountains and to the imposing Tower of Light in the background. At the northwest corner of the plaza stood the Temple of Music and at the northeast corner, the Temple of Ethnology. Everyone did their best to look past the scaffolding that still enveloped many of the unfinised buildings. Fortunately, the sun's daily heat was quickly drying the newly sculpted plaster on the surfaces of the fair's structures.

Walking further into the Court of the Fountains, the party of officials came to the Machinery and Transportation Halls on the left and the Liberal Arts Hall on the right. Beyond a transverse mall stood the Electrical and Agricultural Buildings. At the northeast corner, there was a stadium that would host a myriad of sporting events throughout the summer months. Other staged spectacles (some below currently acceptable standards, such as the daily re-enactment of an Indian uprising, each performance consuming 15,000 rounds of blank ammunition) were already under way. Shows often depicted tragic events such as the Johnstown flood or Jerusalem at the time of the Crucifixion. Finally, there was the Midway,[10] a popular assortment of rides, catch-penny games, and fabricated villages featuring ethnic life in every corner of the world (e.g., the Streets of Cairo, an African Village, Old Nurenberg). The Midway's "death-defying" rides were the biggest draw of all. In Chicago, the newly invented Ferris Wheel had attracted the greatest interest. In Buffalo, thousands clamored for rides on the Aerio-Cycle, a sealed car spinning as high as 275 feet in the air.

While Vice-President Roosevelt delivered his address (pledging, among other things, that the U.S. would not support "...policies for the aggrandizement of any nation here on this continent at the expense of any one else in the hemisphere" [11]) that afternoon in Buffalo, Leon Czolgosz was sitting quietly in a dim corner of his neighborhood saloon reading about the Exposition in the Cleveland Plain Dealer. Nothing he read surprised him. He was in full agreement with his socialist and anarchist mentors that world fairs and national expositions represented another way to exploit the working poor, an opportunity for the barons of industry to consume the public treasuries in order to glorify their fame and wealth. He believed that immigrant labor would sign up to work for any wage, then eventually lose their jobs when the capitalists wearied of selling their wares and returned to their mansions. What role did the nation's elected leader play in these alleged social debacles? According to the anarchists, a president's guilt was absolute, his complicity shameless, whether he represented the Democratic or the Republican Party.

Members of the Exposition's executive committee felt nearly as gloomy as Czolgosz, though for entirely different reasons. During the weeks that followed Roosevelt's visit, revenue continued to lag behind expectations. During July 1893, Chicago's Columbian Exposition had attracted nearly three million paid guests; for the same period, Buffalo recorded less than 800,000. Overnight lodging certainly wasn't the problem. There were more than 200 hotels, plus 600 boarding houses; rooms cost as lit-

Temple of Music.

Tower of Light.

tle as $2 per night and apartments, $30-40 per week. Add the 3,000 private homes with space available to take in guests and Buffalo was capable of absorbing 250,000 visitors each day. Attendance never came close to that capacity.[12]

Director-General Buchanan turned to the railroads for help, asking that special reduced fares be offered to stimulate travel to the Exposition. Railroads with east-west routes that didn't pass through Buffalo protested loudly that the railroad industry shouldn't have to subsidize Buffalo's event. Eventually, a desperate plea to reduce the roundtrip fare from Boston, New York, and Philadelphia from $9.00 to $6.00 was honored - in October, when it was too late to make any difference.

Exposition leaders were left with the hope of attracting McKinley to Buffalo early enough for him to draw attention to the exhibits and produce a swell of attendance during the final months, assuming the autumn weather held. The summer months in Canton had been idyllic for both McKinleys; secretary Courtelyou skillfully attended to most of the required matters of state. Mrs. McKinley had recovered sufficiently to be ready to accompany her husband to Buffalo before they returned to

Cleveland, where the president wished to visit the annual encampment of the Grand Army of the Republic. Courtelyou's final plea to cancel the Buffalo visit was unsuccessful, so he proceeded with trip planning. Following a visit from a delegation from Buffalo, September 5th was designated as President's Day at the Pan-American Exposition.

The president decided that he would deliver a major address in Buffalo, one in which he would promote reciprocal trade agreements with Western Hemisphere nations. He was looking forward to the Exposition. The well-publicized electrical display, plus fireworks and an excursion to Niagara Falls promised to make the trip thoroughly enjoyable for Mrs. McKinley, as well. One planned event, an afternoon reception following the excursion to Niagara Falls, worried Courtelyou. He tried to dissuade the president from mingling with crowds, the ranks of which could not be screened or controlled. He pointed out that in the brief time set aside for the reception, few people would be able to greet the president. Every time Courtelyou raised the subject, the result was the same: McKinley insisted the reception remain on the schedule.[13]

Czolgosz, traveling as Fred Nieman, first came to Buffalo in mid-July, not long after he had visited Emma Goldman in Chicago and learned of the president's planned trip. Departing his train in the suburb of West Seneca, he rented a room from a Mrs. Kazmarek. She thought him a secretive young man, keeping to himself and preferring to hire a boy to fetch food rather than visit a nearby cafe. Czolgosz took day trips into Buffalo and studied the Exposition site, often from outside its gates. He remained in the area for nearly six weeks, and when he departed, he was unable to pay his entire board. Czolgosz left behind an old pistol as collateral on the debt of $1.75 he still owed the Kazmareks and promised to return for his property when he could pay his tab in full.[14] He boarded a Lake Erie steamer bound for Cleveland on August 29th.

Czolgosz's stay in Cleveland was brief; he likely returned in order to collect the remainder of the money that represented his share of the family farm. When he returned to Buffalo on August 31st, he was better financed and took a more expensive room, staying at Novak's Saloon and Hotel on Buffalo's east side. There, he was observed taking a large roll of bills from his pocket. Once again, he registered under an assumed name, this time as "John Doe"! Immediately suspicious, the proprietor asked why he wasn't using his real name. In response, Czolgosz reverted to the already tested "Fred Nieman." When asked what his business would be in Buffalo, he explained that he would be selling souvenirs at the Exposition.[15]

On September 3rd, Czolgosz entered the Walbridge Hardware Store at 316 Main Street and asked to see an Iver Johnson .32 caliber revolver. As he knew from the carefully folded news clipping he carried in his wallet, this was very same type of weapon that Gaetano Bresci had used to shoot Italy's King Humbert I. The gun's compact dimensions permitted easy concealment in the palm of the hand, earning it, in time, the nickname "Saturday night special." Czolgosz paid a premium price, $4.50, for the Iver-Johnson product, considered at the time to be a particularly well-made gun. He also purchased Smith and Wesson .32 caliber cartridges. Soon after leaving the store, Czolgosz loaded his new weapon.

On the following morning, at the McKinley home in Canton, trunks were packed, as were the office files selected for reference should any national crisis arise. The McKinleys and their entourage (which included maids, messengers, and stenographers, as well as secretary Courtelyou and Dr. Rixey) departed at 10 A.M. for the ten-day journey. There were also three representatives of the Secret Service present, assigned by Director Wilkie to protect the president on this journey. The men were custodian George Foster, the president's permanent bodyguard, plus special operatives Samuel Ireland and Albert Gallagher, both recruited from regional offices.

In Dunkirk, on the outskirts of Buffalo, the train paused to allow John Milburn, William Buchanan, and other members of the Exposition's executive committee to board. At 5:55 P.M., McKinley's special train approached Buffalo's Terrace Station, where an inexperienced lieutenant had positioned his cannons too close to the tracks. When the signal came to fire the designated salute, the resulting blast blew out several of the train's windows. Next, every factory whistle within hearing range of the cannon fire added its own greeting. The train continued around the belt line, and at 6:20 P.M., came to a halt at the Exposition's terminal station, where a long line of prominent Buffalo citizens waited to welcome the presidential party. When Mrs. McKinley stepped off the train, she appeared still shaken from the cannon blast that had come unexpectedly near her car.

Standing nearby, in a crowd restrained by police and military personnel, was Czolgosz, who had consulted the newspapers to learn the president's exact route for the entire three-day visit. Pushing a little too hard to reach the front row, he annoyed an officer, who advanced toward him but then abruptly turned his attention back to the presidential party still alighting from the train. Police apprehension of Czolgosz at that moment would have altered the course of history.

Milburn and President and Mrs. McKinley boarded a carriage and rode through the Exposition. McKinley could see the Midway on his right as he passed the 409-foot, cream-colored Tower of Light and the beautiful Court of the Fountains. Filling the broad expanse of the Esplanade were many thousands of well-wishers. In a second carriage, Courtelyou kept attentive watch on his right for the Temple of Music, site of the reception to be held two days later, and on his left for the speaker's platform, already in place, where the president would deliver his speech the next day. The carriages continued over the Triumphal Bridge and down Lincoln Parkway to the Milburn residence at 1168 Delaware Avenue, where President and Mrs. McKinley would be staying. They spent a quiet evening preparing for the next day's many events.

September 5, 1901 might be considered Buffalo's finest day. Crowds began to gather early along Delaware Avenue and Lincoln Parkway, the president's route. The Exposition turnstiles never stopped that day, admitting more than 116,000 people, a new attendance record. Many thousands packed into the Esplanade in time for McKinley's arrival at 10:15 A.M. Overflow crowds extended past the Court of the Fountains toward the Tower of Light. A succession of military bands entered the Lincoln Parkway gate and crossed the Triumphal Bridge.

Nearby, the speaker's stand was wrapped in purple bunting; only guests with special invitations were admitted to the area. Nearly every chair was filled when the president's cavalcade first came into view. An escort of plumed horsemen preceded the open carriage in which McKinley stood, waving to the crowds. Mrs. McKinley, dressed in gray, with her face shaded in black lace, sat by his side. Everywhere in America, the frailty of the president's wife and her aversion to loud noise were well known. In deference to her needs, the assembly of excited people standing shoulder to shoulder in the Esplanade managed to quiet, allowing a remarkable hush to descend.[16]

When the carriage came to a halt beside the platform, the president stood and waved, then bent down to lift Mrs. McKinley up from her seat. Together they stepped down and, with his arm wrapped tightly about her waist, he helped her climb up the steps to their designated chairs in the center of the front row. When all were seated, John Milburn stepped forward to say, simply, "Ladies and gentlemen, the President of the United States." He then sat down. Startled by the brevity of this introduction, Mckinley quickly stood and received an immediate cheer from the crowd. Then another hush came as McKinley motioned for silence. Everyone prepared to listen to their president.

McKinley's custom, developed as a schoolboy, was to hold cards in his hand for reference as he spoke extemporaneously. For this occasion, however, he had prepared his speech in advance. Drawing the pages from his vest pocket, he began to read with care and deliberation: "Expositions are the timekeepers of progress." Great distances, he reminded his listeners, had been shortened by the telegraph, by transoceanic cables, by swifter steamships, and by ever faster trains. McKinley articulated two themes as he made his argument for easier commercial reciprocity between nations: first, the potential for unity in a modern world, and second, the opportunity for prosperity throughout the Western Hemisphere. "We must not repose in fancied security that we can forever sell everything and buy little or nothing...Isolation is no longer possible or desirable...God and man have linked the nations together. The period of exclusiveness is past."

Astute listeners would have noted the irony of these words

coming from a former Congressman who had championed an America-first protectionist policy for most of his legislative career, and who was largely responsible for passing the highest tariffs in the nation's history. Most members of the audience, though, were thoroughly pleased to hear a president they respected highly. They recognized the sincerity of McKinley's words and did not doubt that they reflected his thinking at the time. Contemptuous listeners like Leon Czolgosz, who was among the president's audience that day, took particular note of the president's habitual reference to prosperity. Czolgosz could not understand why McKinley, like every president before him, was blind to all poverty.

At the close of his speech, the president assisted Mrs. McKinley to a carriage waiting to take her to a luncheon in her honor given by Mrs. William Hamlin, chair of the exposition's board of women managers. This independently minded organization had declined a Women's Exhibit Hall, believing that its scope would be limited to "...embroidery, pickles, and pastry." Instead, they saw to it that the most important work of women throughout the Pan-American nations was represented within each of the major exhibits. Board members were looking forward to their audience with the president's wife, but she disappointed them. Pleading weakness, she begged her way out of the luncheon and returned to the Milburn home.

The president remained at the Exposition to enjoy himself. He began by giving an impromptu greeting to several individuals who had gathered by the speaker's stand. Secret Service agents Foster, Ireland, and Gallagher responded promptly to these unexpected moves; they were familiar with the president's gregarious nature. McKinley's next stop was the stadium, where numerous military units stood on parade waiting for his review. He went on to a luncheon in his honor at the New York State building. There, the two hundred assembled guests were treated to a meal prepared and served by kitchen staff and waiters on loan from Buffalo's grandest hotel, The Iroquois. Later, when McKinley returned to the Exposition to visit the U.S. government exhibit, he shared a joke with one of the guests, Dr. Herman Mynter, a retired surgeon of the Royal Danish Navy, now settled and practicing in Buffalo. Mynter told the president that he ought to be pleased to shake the hand of a man who wasn't asking for anything. McKinley laughed and said that it rarely happened to a politician. The president drew out his time at the Exposition, making unscheduled visits to several exhibit halls, enjoying the antics of the crowd, especially the popcorn boys, and stopping to sip coffee at the Puerto Rico exhibit.

That evening, McKinley and his wife returned to view the Exposition's special illumination. They boarded one of the small boats awaiting them at Park Lake and then reclined in comfortable chairs to watch a water-nymph ballet in the waters around them. The incandescent lamps on the Tower of Light and surrounding buildings steadily brightened to full intensity, and their reflection danced over the lake's surface. The evening's entertainment also included aerial fireworks, blazing ground displays of Niagara Falls spilling fire, and even a pyrotechnic presidential portrait, accompanied by the words, "Welcome to McKinley."

The entire day had been filled with grand events! By the time the president's carriage made its way back down Delaware Avenue to the Milburn home, everyone was as exhausted as they were elated. The McKinley's second floor bedroom lights were soon extinguished. Outside the house, a Buffalo police detail began its night vigil.

Czolgosz had not remained long at the Esplanade that morning; neither was he interested in nighttime displays for the amusement of the privileged. Returning to Novak's Saloon, he bought a glass of whiskey but drank little of it before retiring to his room. Czolgosz had for the first time observed a sitting American president and listened to his carefully chosen words. Now he was convinced that McKinley was just like every member of the ruling class, a champion of the wealthy and of the political principles that his fellow anarchists disdained. Czolgosz knew where his duty lay.

Foster, Ireland, and Gallagher returned to their hotel for some rest; Friday would be another busy day.

McKinley reviewing the troops at Exposition.

A parade along the Exposition mall.

4

GUNSHOTS!

"I have no enemies. Why should I fear?"

William McKinley, 1901[1]

On Friday, September 6th, the sun rose blood red.[2] The president was up early enough to see it. Newspapers listing McKinley's itinerary in Buffalo had omitted any mention of the president's affinity for early morning walks. Except for scattered police already on duty near the Milburn residence, the streets at sunrise were nearly deserted, allowing McKinley the pleasure of strolling unattended. His traveling party, which would include his wife, was scheduled to gather after breakfast for the excursion to Niagara Falls. Ida McKinley didn't mind rising early when a pleasant ride was in store; this was the part of the journey to Buffalo that appealed to her most. She planned to enjoy the natural beauty of the falls while the president inspected the recent expansion of Niagara's power station.[3]

Leon Czolgosz also awoke early. He dressed carefully in the dark suit he had purchased while visiting Emma Goldman in Chicago; he wore a string tie with his flannel shirt and folded a large handkerchief into his vest pocket. The Iver Johnson revolver lay concealed in his right front pants pocket. Skipping breakfast, he bought a cigar and left Novak's Hotel. Czolgosz arrived at the Exposition at 8.30 A.M., just in time to witness the president's carriage pass quickly through the grounds on its way to the terminal station, where the party would board a special train bound for Niagara Falls. Czolgosz planned to follow the president to the falls and murder him there, if he could position himself closely enough to shoot accurately.[4]

Friday was to be McKinley's "restful day," according to secretary Courtelyou's careful planning. Despite clear skies and the prospect of another warm day, the president, with the afternoon reception in mind, had dressed formally in a studded shirt, black satin cravat, vest, pinstriped pants, and heavy frock coat. He began to perspire as soon as his train left the Exposition at 9:00 A.M. An hour later, the train arrived in the town of Lewiston and the entire party, including diplomats and other distinguished guests, boarded electric cars from which they could observe the giant whirlpool, a natural wonder of the Niagara gorge below the falls, and then make their way along the brink of the gorge to the town of Niagara Falls. There, President and Mrs. McKinley transferred to a carriage and rode halfway across the international suspension bridge to a spot where they could best view the Canadian falls without departing American territory.[5]

Because of the ill effects of midday heat she experienced on the bridge, Mrs. McKinley asked to be excused from the rest of the tour. The president accompanied her to the nearby International Hotel where a parlor suite had been reserved for them. After assuring himself that she was comfortable, he resumed the planned tour. The next stop was Goat Island, a stony promontory at the crest of the American falls. The president was escorted by mounted cavalry and accompanied by Foster, Ireland, and Gallagher, his three Secret Service operatives. Despite his formal attire, McKinley seized the opportunity to climb to the very highest rock formations above the falls. Returning to the hotel, he and his party enjoyed a hearty lunch in the ballroom and then retired to the porch to smoke cigars. After checking on Mrs. McKinley's condition, the president departed for a visit to the nearby power station.

Plant construction had begun in 1890 and the first usable power was generated by diverting a portion of the Niagara River's flow over the falls in 1895. Few people could yet foresee the broad applications of cheap electric power for every citizen. The preservationists, who firmly believed that the natural beauty of the falls must not be disturbed, had gathered that day in hopes of drawing the president's attention to the validity of their position. Local police kept the protesters at a safe distance from the president's party. Secret Service operatives, wary of the demonstrators, continued to shadow McKinley for the duration of his visit to Niagara Falls.

Czolgosz quickly discerned that acute concern for the preservationists' activities would preclude any chance of his getting
within accurate shooting range of McKinley. Therefore, he
boarded a train that was returning to the Exposition, arriving
shortly after noon. He proceeded directly to the Temple of
Music, where a file of people hoping to greet the president was
already forming. Joining that line, Czolgosz waited silently,
barely noticeable in the noisy, perspiring crowd dense with
working men.

After touring the power facilities, the president and his
party re-boarded their parlor cars and departed for the
Exposition at 2:45 P.M. Mrs. McKinley had been transported
from the hotel directly to the train. Buffalo's late summer heat
and humidity had by this time taken its toll on the president,
and he expressed concern for his appearance at the 4:00 P.M.
reception. Before leaving Niagara Falls, Courtelyou sent word
to the Milburn home directing that a partial change of clothing
be available when McKinley reached the Exposition. When
they arrived, it was 3:30 P.M. Mrs. McKinley, with Dr. Rixey as
her escort, prepared to return to the Milburn residence for a
nap. Once settled in a carriage, she looked back, smiled, and
waved to her husband, who, after redressing, had paused to
watch her departure.[6] The president then turned away to join
Milburn and Courtelyou. As the men walked toward the
Temple of Music, they stopped for refreshment, and the president admired a display of Mexican handicrafts. A carriage took
the group the remaining distance to the reception site.

There had been no disagreement over Grand Marshal
Louis Babcock's selection of the Temple of Music as the site for
the reception. The building, positioned at the northwest corner
of the Esplanade, epitomized the Exposition motif. It was a
bulky structure of white stucco, garishly appointed, and topped
with a gilded dome. Spectators assembling nearby could view
the president arriving and departing the building, and the
number of people permitted entry could be controlled easily.
Earlier that morning, under Babcock's careful supervision,
laborers had moved chairs to establish an aisle twelve to fifteen
feet wide, extending from the east entrance to a midpoint, then

turning at a right angle toward the south doorway. At the center, where McKinley would stand, a large American flag draped inside a wooden framework served as a backdrop. Bunting, several potted palms, and two bay trees completed the decor. An organ console stood nearby.

After Grand Marshal Babcock and his colleague, attorney James Quackenbush,[7] were satisfied with the hall's appearance, they retired to a nearby restaurant for sandwiches and a pilsener beer. Quackenbush horrified Babcock with a flippant remark about Vice-President Roosevelt's luck if the president were to be shot that day. As he returned to the Temple of Music, Babcock found himself thinking about increasing the hall's security. At his disposal were Exposition police who were already handling the crowds outside and controlling the line of guests still forming. Inside, a detachment of the 73rd Coastal Artillery from nearby Fort Porter had arrived in full dress uniform, as requested. Babock asked this group to take positions on either side of the aisle and to watch for anyone suspicious among the people advancing to greet McKinley. Several Buffalo police detectives also stood waiting to receive their assignments.[8]

When the president and his party reached the Temple of Music, Babcock and Quackenbush were at the door to greet them. McKinley entered the building and without prompting walked directly to the precise location planned for him to stand. Now, many more eyes scanned the room, assessing its security arrangements. Secretary Courtelyou was pleased with Babcock's positioning of the military guards. Foster arranged the detectives in a loose ring around McKinley. The president, meanwhile, remained typically oblivious to security. He remarked to a few reporters (and anyone else who was listening) that the coolness of the hall was certainly a blessing on that hot afternoon. In fact, the Temple of Music was as cool as any place around; Babcock had wisely left all the doors and windows closed while the reception hall was being readied. Now, with the afternoon sun behind the building, the interior was not likely to overheat.

Ordinarily, Foster would have taken a position at the presi-

John Milburn, President McKinley (tipping hat) and George Courtelyou.

Site of the attack inside the Temple of Music.

dent's left where he could best observe everyone who approached. This time, however, he was informed by Courtelyou that Mr. Milburn would stand on the left in order to introduce recognizable guests to the president. Foster didn't care for this plan but he kept his opinion to himself. Instead, he positioned Ireland directly across the aisle from the president. Gallagher was assigned to a point ten feet to the left of Ireland where he could keep the line moving away from McKinley. Foster chose to stand to the right of Ireland and directly across from Milburn so that he could study the people approaching the president. Secret Service operatives familiar with McKinley knew that he liked to greet "50-a-minute," as he put it. Their job on that particular day, in addition to watching for suspicious characters, was to keep the public approaching and departing as quickly as possible.

Courtelyou stepped to the president's right side, took a watch from his pocket and looked toward Babcock at the east entrance. Meanwhile, the organist, W. J. Gomph, sat patiently waiting for his cue. At the stroke of 4:00, McKinley said, "Let them come." His pleasure at that moment was obvious to everyone present. The previous afternoon's event had been for the gentility. This reception was for the common people, those most responsible for the president's enormous popularity. As Courtelyou gave the signal, Gomph began to play a Bach sonata, and the waiting line surged forward.

Dr. Clinton Colegrove of Holland, New York was the first man to reach the president. McKinley grasped with his right hand while pulling the people past him quickly, sometimes adding a late push with his left hand. It was his way of greeting as many as possible within the time allotted. Still, with such a large crowd, the pace was uneven; at times the line slowed, and then it would move forward quickly again. A message came back down the line to Babcock: keep the line moving even faster!

Despite the relative coolness inside the Temple of Music, many people entered fanning themselves or wiping their brows with handkerchiefs. Thus, the crowd was dotted with dozens of hands holding something white. A man had already passed the president with a bandaged right hand. The president reached for the man's left hand, shook it, and offered his greeting. Czolgosz realized he would be under closer scrutiny once he entered the building. He took out his handkerchief and wrapped it over his right hand just as he withdrew the revolver from his pocket. He had practiced the maneuver several times and no one spotted his weapon. As he advanced, he grew increasingly nervous; but, even if he had wanted to retreat, he would have had little opportunity. The crowd pushing from behind propelled him forward to meet his fate.

Again the word was passed back to Babcock: Quicken the pace. Having people coming forward in clusters followed by gaps made surveillance all the harder for Ireland and Foster. As a group came between them and the president, they could not always see the hands extended to McKinley until the greeting was complete. Babcock walked closer, trying to gauge the effect of his efforts to speed up the line. He attracted Courtelyou's eye, saw the pocket watch in his hand, and knew that it was nearly time to close the doors. Courtelyou was determined that this event would not last a second longer than the agreed-upon ten minutes. A little girl passed by; McKinley leaned down, spoke to her, and shook her hand. Ireland's eye was drawn to the next man, dark complexioned and mustached, perhaps European. The man looked suspicious to him, especially when he lingered before the president a little too long. Ireland put a hand on his shoulder to move him along more quickly. Foster did the same.

Czolgosz was next in line! He had successfully passed by fourteen guards without drawing notice to his weapon. Foster and Ireland, distracted by the man who had seemed suspicious, had less time to study the person who truly embodied their greatest fear. McKinley, seeing the bandage in Czolgosz's right hand, prepared to shake his left. Deflecting the president's reach, Czolgosz brought his left hand over to steady his right wrist, thrust both hands forward to within inches of McKinley, and began firing.[9]

The time was 4:07 P.M., Friday, September 6, 1901.

Babcock, as he walked briskly toward the entrance to close the doors, heard a loud report pierce the air, followed quickly by another. Turning on his heel, he saw the president's startled expression, and then a struggling mass of people attempting to subdue a man standing in front of McKinley. Over their heads, he saw a rising wisp of smoke. Soon, the unmistakable smell of exploded gunpowder would permeate the hall.

Ireland had the best view of Czolgosz as the assailant brought his bandage-wrapped hand to within inches of the president's body. Hearing the shots, Ireland lunged for the man's right arm. James Parker, who was the next person in line, instantly understood what was happening and grasped the assailant's throat.[10] As Czolgosz went down, his right arm was still extended toward McKinley but no more shots were fired. Gallagher reached Czolgosz just as the revolver fell from his hand. Grabbing for it through the now-flaming handkerchief, Gallagher felt the burn just as an artilleryman, who mistook him for the villain, wrestled him to the floor. Foster, along with several others, threw himself on the assailant. Czolgosz was eventually freed, and as he stood, he directed his glance toward McKinley to determine his condition. Seeing this, Foster abandoned his attempt to restrain his anger and swung the full weight of his fist into Czolgosz's nose. Bright red blood began to flow instantly. A Buffalo police detective interceded to prevent further attacks on the gunman.

McKinley barely wavered as he stood watching the action unfold before him. Both Milburn and Courtelyou were urging the president to step away from the scene, but McKinley was more intent upon the blows being delivered to Czolgosz. "Go easy on him, boys!" were his first words. Someone brought a chair forward and convinced the president to sit down. When secretary Courtelyou asked if he felt any pain, McKinley nodded, pointing to his breastbone. Then, after reaching under his shirt, he noted blood on his fingertips when he withdrew his hand. Not wanting to believe what he saw, McKinley reached under his shirt a second time. More blood confirmed that he had been wounded. He looked up and said, "Mrs. McKinley—Be careful, Courtelyou, how you tell her. Oh, be careful."

Leaving the president momentarily, Courtelyou approached Gallagher to see about retrieving the weapon. The agent pointed to the soldier who had jumped him and who still refused to

Four artist's renderings of the shooting, none of them accurate according to eye witness acconts.

give up the gun. Courtelyou appealed to the man's commanding officer and the revolver was soon relinquished to the police
for examination.

Chaos prevailed in the Temple of Music. The men responsible for dealing with Czolgosz knew they had to get him quickly out of sight. Cries for a lynching could already be heard. A
nearby anteroom was identified, and the assailant was rushed
inside to await transfer from the Exposition grounds. When
Gallagher checked the room, he saw that Czolgosz's nose was
still bleeding, and that he appeared dazed. "I took a look at
him," Gallagher wrote in his official report, "and felt I ought to
kill him."[11] Meanwhile, police and the uniformed military were
attempting to clear the building of spectators. Not at first
achieving a fast enough response, several fixed their bayonets
to indicate they meant business. The hall emptied promptly,
except for the men gathered about the president.

McKinley, now pale and perspiring, remained in his chair
until a suitable place could be located for him to await the
ambulance summoned from the nearby Pan-American
Hospital. Director-General Buchanan had not been present
when the shooting occurred but was now standing nearby, his
face betraying his horror. Looking up at Buchanan, the president said, "I am truly sorry that this kind of thing happened at
your Exposition."[12]

Still fearful of the temperament of the crowd that was
steadily accumulating outside, the city police were desperate to
get Czolgosz far away from the site, preferably to police headquarters. A patrol wagon parked at the east entrance of the
Temple was already surrounded by a tightly packed mob who
believed it would be the vehicle used to transport the villain.
James Vallaly, chief of the Exposition detectives, surmised that
only a horse-drawn carriage would allow them any chance of
forging a path through the angry mob. James Quackenbush,
who had already called to notify Police Superintendent Bull of
the incident, knew that a large contingent of police were on
their way. He argued that no attempt be made to move the prisoner until Bull arrived. Vallaly refused to wait. He left briefly,
found a hack[13] driver willing to accept the challenge, and

Police photographs of Leon Czolgosz.

Buffalo police headquarters.

instructed the man to bring his carriage around to the building's south entrance, where the crowd was less imposing. Czolgosz, his clothes torn, his nose still dripping blood, and his wrists manacled to detectives positioned on either side of him, was hustled forward. Chief Vallaly jumped up next to the driver and the others piled inside the hack with their prisoner. The driver was given his signal, and the horses lurched forward. Just as predicted, the angry crowd receded before the accelerating team and let the carriage pass. Urging his horses to a full gallop even before leaving the Esplanade, the driver steered the hack over the Triumphal Bridge and headed downtown.[14]

At another doorway, Mexican ambassador Don Manuel Aspiroz managed to talk his way into the building. Rushing up to McKinley, he exclaimed, "Mr. President, is it true that you have been shot?" What could anyone say at a moment like that? The president managed a nod and a polite smile while someone coaxed the ambassador into the background. Meanwhile, the ambulance attendants, who had just arrived, began assisting their patient onto a stretcher. Frederick Ellis, a third-year medical student, carefully drove the electric vehicle away from the Temple of Music, along the west side of the Court of the Fountains, past the Machinery Building, then left on the mall and straight to the Pan-American Hospital.

Buffalo retail merchant J. N. Adam was standing by the Court of the Fountains talking to Peter Van Peyma, a local obstetrician, when the ambulance passed by. They both thought it peculiar that the vehicle was surrounded by a mounted escort. Seconds later the trailing crowd informed them of what had just happened. The two broke into a run toward the hospital.

Word of the tragedy spread quickly throughout the Exposition grounds. A group of Ohioans were waiting patiently at their state's exhibit for the president. He had promised earlier to join them briefly following the Temple of Music reception. When someone ran in and told them McKinley had been shot, most were disbelieving but a few ran towards the Esplanade to seek confirmation.

A 19 year-old cub reporter, Frank Lynch, answered the first call made to the Buffalo Enquirer about the tragedy. "The president has been shot!" he shouted to his city editor, Eli Fouts. Senior reporter Richard Barry ran up, yanked the phone from Lynch, and began taking notes. At the same time, Fouts shouted for the paper's final edition to be held from the presses.

On duty at the Pan-American Hospital that afternoon were an intern, Dr. G. McK. Hall, and a medical student, Edward C. Mann, the son of Matthew Mann, a gynecologic surgeon and dean of the University of Buffalo School of Medicine. Knowing that surgeons were being summoned, he asked that his father be informed, as well. When the message reached Dr. Mann, he was in his barber's chair. Although only one side of his hair had been cut, Mann jumped from the chair and proceeded directly to the Exposition.[15]

Meanwhile, Dr. Van Peyma had completed his short run to the hospital. Dr. Hall and the medical students immediately recognized Van Peyma and urged him to inspect their initial treatment of the victim. The president lay, covered with a sheet, on a white enamel table in the operating room. Moments earlier, as he was being disrobed, one of the bullets had fallen to the floor. It had not penetrated the breastbone but a bruise was visible where it had made contact with the skin. A second wound was located in the left upper quadrant of the abdomen, just below the rib margin. This was clearly an ominous injury. Assisted by the nurses on duty, the medical students had cleansed the bruise above and the penetrating wound below. They then applied gauze dressing and awaited the arrival of the specialists. The president's pulse was strong at 84 beats per minute; he had been given 0.01 grams of morphine for pain, and .001 grams of strychnine,[16] a popular heart stimulant in that day. Dr. Van Peyma approved this initial treatment, spoke reassuring words to McKinley, and then waited so that he might introduce the surgeons to the president as they arrived.

The first to come was Dr. Herman Mynter,[17] whom the president recognized immediately from their brief exchange the previous afternoon. With him came Dr. Eugene Wasdin[18] of the U. S. Marine Hospital Service. Mynter conducted the first detailed examination of the president and took note of the seriousness of his abdominal wound, one that very likely reflected internal injuries. He informed McKinley that an immediate operation would be necessary.

Next, Dr. Edgar Lee[19] pushed his way into their midst, announcing that he was a former medical director of the Omaha Exposition, visiting from St. Louis. He had just learned of the incident and was prepared to take over management of the hospital if necessary. He was politely ignored. Later, when he insisted on joining the surgical team, no one challenged him or even inquired about his surgical credentials.

Missing from the scene and sorely needed was Dr. Rixey. After he had seen Mrs. McKinley safely back to the Milburn residence, Dr. Rixey and his wife had returned to the Exposition to enjoy themselves. Runners were sent to locate the doctor. Also absent and not available, according to initial reports, was Roswell Park, the Exposition's medical director. His housekeeper explained that Park was operating on a patient in Niagara Falls. Efforts to reach the doctor continued. A call went out as well for Dr. Edward Meyer.[20] He too was absent from the city.

Both Courtelyou and McKinley watched ruefully and listened to all that was happening around them. Decisions needed to be made. McKinley reminded his secretary of the obvious: neither one of them knew any of the surgeons in Buffalo or felt confident deciding which one should take charge. Where was Rixey now that they needed him so? Courtelyou took Milburn aside and quietly said that he was depending on him for a recommendation. At 5:10 P.M., Dr. Matthew Mann walked into the operating room and was introduced to the president. In addition to his responsibilities as dean, he was Chairman of the Department of Obstetrics and Gynecology, and a highly regarded surgeon in the community.[21] His colleagues considered Mann a "beautiful operator," noted both for his speed and the orderliness of his technique.[22]

Milburn, who may not have been fully aware of Mann's standing, nonetheless turned to Courtelyou and whispered, "He is the one."

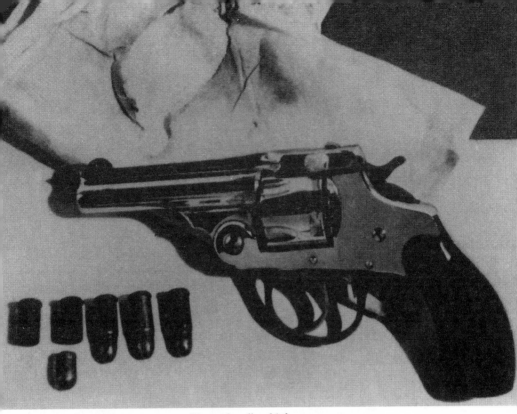

Weapon and ammunition remnants and burnt handkerchief.

Same weapon on display 99 years later.

Matthew D. Mann, Professor of Obstetrics and Gynology, University of Buffalo.

Mann teaching in the operating theater.

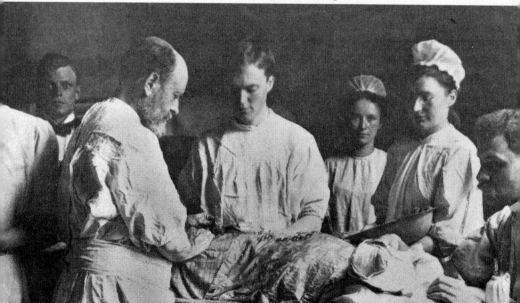

5

OPERATION

"Gentlemen, I am in your hands."

McKinley to his surgeons

Roswell Park was the surgeon most of Buffalo's physicians would have chosen to care for the president's wound. Preeminent among his colleagues, he had been recruited in 1883 from Chicago's Rush Medical College to serve as Chairman of Surgery at the University of Buffalo Medical Department. In addition to being a highly skilled and innovative surgeon, he was a prolific writer. He eventually won greatest recognition for his contributions to cancer treatment, but he also added to the knowledge and understanding of diverse surgical problems, including management of abdominal gunshot injuries.[1]

On the day of McKinley's injury, Park had traveled to Niagara Falls to operate on a man whose malignant neck tumor required a most delicate dissection. Two local physicians, Drs. Chapin and Campbell, were on hand to assist Park.[2] One later recalled that during the procedure, "Someone burst in and said, 'Doctor, you are wanted at once in Buffalo.' Before the man could continue, Dr. Park said, 'Don't you see that I can't leave this case even if it were for the President of the United States?' 'Doctor,' came the reply, "It is for the President of the United States!'"[3]

Dr. Park sent word that he could not return to Buffalo immediately, but with the aid of Dr. Campbell, who knew all the railroad people in Niagara Falls, he immediately began to plan for his transport back to the Exposition. Once he had completed the dissection and controlled the bleeding, he asked Chapin to close the wound. Park then raced to the station, only to find no train ready for him, and no word of a special train being sent from Buffalo. The stationmaster assured him that a regularly scheduled train bound for Buffalo would arrive in twenty minutes. In the interim, Park paced nervously.

More surgeons, among them Dr. John Parmenter,[4]
Professor of Anatomy and of Clinical Surgery at the University
of Buffalo Medical School, had come to the Pan-American
Hospital since Dr. Mann's arrival. John Milburn nevertheless
stood firm on his nomination of Mann as the appropriate doctor to take charge of the case. John Scatcherd, chairman of the
Exposition's executive committee, agreed. Mynter had already
informed the president of the need for immediate surgery; it
would be up to Mann to decide where that surgery would take
place. Courtelyou made clear that he wanted McKinley to be
treated as if he were an ordinary patient, not an important per-
sonage. The memory of the Garfield tragedy lingered.[5] For several weeks after he had been shot, President Garfield's surgeons debated treatment options. One surgeon after another–
more than a dozen were involved before his travail ended–
offered contradictory opinions about surgical exploration.
Eventually Garfield's wound was probed, but by that time, serious infection had set in. He died 79 days after his initial injury,
a victim of the ambivalence and controversy that surrounds any
new method of treatment.

What the nation had deplored most when Garfield died in
1881 was the prolonged indecision displayed by the nation's
finest surgeons. Thus, secretary Courtelyou and every other
government official waiting nearby desperately wanted Mann
and his colleagues to make a decision. Mann did not shrink
from the responsibility thrust upon him, despite his inexperience with gunshot injuries. He weighed his options. The facilities at Buffalo General Hospital were much superior to those at
the Exposition's hospital, but moving the president would
involve its own risks.[6] The Pan-American facility's operating
room had already been made ready for them. McKinley's pulse
was still stable at 84 (blood pressure recordings were not yet an
established practice). Despite little evidence of internal bleeding, Mann elected to stay where they were and proceed with
the operation at once. He asked Drs. Mynter and Parmenter to
assist him; Dr. Lee, perhaps through sheer persistence, also managed to be included on the surgical team. Secretary Courtelyou
turned to McKinley and said he thought Dr. Mann's recommen-

dation should be heeded. Dr. Parmenter, who also had examined the president, agreed, as did Mynter. The president's reply was straightforward:" Gentlemen, I am in your hands."

Compared to Garfield's surgeons, the doctors attending President McKinley knew considerably more about the treatment of gunshot wounds, especially those involving the abdominal cavity. The vulnerability of the abdominal cavity to traumatic penetrations had been well established since antiquity. The abdomen and chest were the favored targets in hand-to-hand combat. With the development of gunpowder and firearms in the fourteenth and fifteenth centuries, the abdominal area became, if anything, even more vulnerable.[7] During the next three centuries, military surgeons managed abdominal gunshot wounds by offering victims temporary comfort, at best; at worst, they simply left the wounded on the battlefield- the prognosis for survival was that bad.[8]

In the 1870s, everything changed. The renowned American surgeon James Marion Sims began treating bullet wounds to the abdomen with laparotomy, the deliberate surgical entry into the abdomen and repair of specific penetrating injuries to the vital organs within. Sims' innovation was facilitated by the simultaneous introduction of anesthesia, as well as the adoption of antiseptic technique. In 1884, Swiss surgeon Theodor Kocher reported the first immediate surgery for a gunshot wound to the stomach.

The decision to operate in McKinley's case reflected the doctors' general awareness of and confidence in these developments in treatment as well as their assessment of the specific case facing them. The site of the president's injury spoke to the near certain penetration of vital organs within, most likely the stomach, perhaps the intestines as well. These injuries needed to be repaired or peritonitis would surely follow. The patient had recently eaten; operating now rather than later might diminish the extent of leakage from the stomach. (The inherent risks of giving an anesthetic to someone who had recently eaten were not yet known.) McKinley's pulse was beginning to grow weaker, and the risk of hemorrhage was always present for penetrating wounds of this kind. The surgical team would not know the extent of the damage until they looked. Adding it all up, they favored immediate exploration.

The Pan-American Hospital was equipped with an operating facility, but it had not been designed for the kind of surgical undertaking about to begin. Dr. Mann would later comment on the particular difficulties that he faced.[9] The only lighting in the operating room was the natural light of that late September afternoon, coming through a window covered with a thin muslin sheet. Although the exteriors of all Exposition buildings had abundant incandescent lighting, the interiors of every structure, including the hospital, were lit with gas lamps. The only exception was the operating room, where gas lamps were banned because of the presence of ether and other flammable gases. On the day McKinley was shot, the limitation presented by the absence of good lighting was compounded by another serious lack: The instruments necessary for an abdominal exploration procedure were not present. Dr. Mynter had only his minor surgical instrument set with him;[10] Mann had come from his barber without any instruments at all. Still, they prepared to proceed with what was available to them. The surgical team felt that they could not risk waiting for Dr. Park since, although they knew he was coming, they did not know when he might arrive.[11] They resolved to serve their president to the best of their capability.

Dr. Eugene Wasdin of the Marine Hospital was asked to administer the ether (ether's safety record made it preferable to chloroform as an anesthetic). Dr. Nelson W. Wilson, the Exposition's sanitary officer, was standing by, prepared to help if needed. Mann asked him to serve as recorder, knowing that every factual detail would soon become historically significant. As these decisions were being made, nursing supervisor Miss Adele Walters and her staff busied themselves with operating room preparations, such as boiling all the available instruments.[12] The nursing team's "sterile nurses" were Miss Morris and Miss Barnes from St. Luke's Hospital, New York; the circulating nurses were Miss Baron from Long Island College Hospital, Miss Shannon from Cincinatti General Hospital, Miss Simmons from Roosevelt Hospital, New York, and Mrs.

Battery powered ambulance used to transport McKinley.

Operating room at Pan-American Hospital.

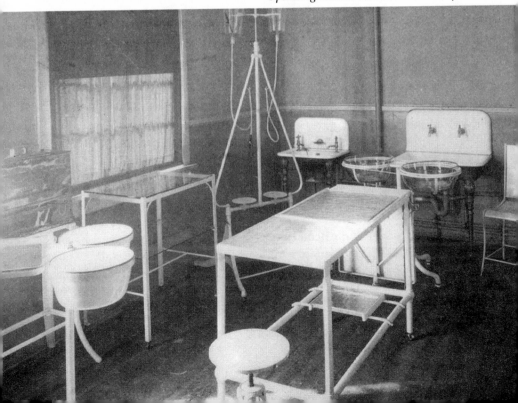

Dorchester from Buffalo General Hospital.[13] Medical student Edward C. Mann was in charge of the needles and sutures, and another medical student, Mr. Simpson, was assigned to pass instruments. Other physicians in attendance included Dr. Van Peyma of Buffalo and Dr. W. D. Storer of Chicago.

As the doctors prepared for the operation, a small crowd of dignitaries and diplomats began to collect outside the hospital, along with a gathering army of newspaper reporters. There wasn't a spare inch of room for any of them inside, so they waited outside in relative silence for any word of the president's condition. A guard standing by the door was periodically assured from within that the president was still alive. He, in turn, would pass word to those near him, and the latest news then would spread like an ocean wave through the crowd. At one point, Senor Edelberto Farres, president of the Cuban commission to the Exposition, appeared, outfitted in his full dress uniform, including medallions. He spotted something to stand upon and proceeded to deliver a brief, emotional oration, noting his nation's sorrow over the day's tragic events.[14]

Police Superintendent William Bull had been informed of the shooting by telephone soon after it occurred. He immediately directed a sergeant to drive him to the Exposition in a police wagon. As they traveled north on Delaware Avenue, a carriage and team came toward them at full gallop, not a customary sight on that fashionable street. As the carriage rushed past, Bull realized that it likely contained the assailant. Urging his driver to turn quickly and follow, the superintendent arrived just as Czolgosz was being taken into police headquarters at Seneca and Franklin Streets.[15] Bull looked back up the street and saw dozens of people on bicycles coming his way, followed by more people, running. (The bicyclists had cried out the grim news to pedestrians as they passed.) Realizing that he would soon have a lynch mob on his hands, the superintendent stepped into police headquarters, issued a general alarm, summoned all off-duty personnel, and placed extra guards at every doorway.

The president's anesthetic was begun at 5:20 P.M. The induction took nine minutes; ether's principle disadvantage was that it was very slow to take effect. The surgical team removed their jackets, donned aprons, scrubbed their hands with soap and water and then soaked them in a basin filled with bichloride of mercury solution. Sterile rubber gloves were experimental at the Johns Hopkins Hospital in Baltimore but not yet in wide use. Most surgeons operated bare handed. The patient's abdomen was shaved, scrubbed with green soap, and then washed with alcohol and ether. At the head of the table, a rack held flasks of warm sterile saline to be used for irrigation. Arranged on another white enamel table were the now-disinfected instruments, ready for use.

Dr. Mann stood at the patient's right-hand side, with Dr. Parmenter to his right; Dr. Mynter stood across from Mann, Dr. Lee to his left. As they waited for Dr. Wasdin's clearance to proceed, they inspected the two injuries. Where the bullet had struck the breastbone, they confirmed with a probe that the skin had not been penetrated. The more serious wound was below the rib margin and two inches (5cm) to the left of midline. When a probe was introduced into this wound, it passed easily into the abdominal cavity, pointing toward the cavity's left lower quadrant. At 5:29 P.M., With the anesthesia now deemed satisfactory, the operation commenced. Dr. Mann made his initial incision parallel to the long axis of his patient's body and extended it from the rib margin through the bullet wound for a distance of five inches. Beneath the skin, they encountered and removed a piece of cloth, most likely a fragment of the president's clothing. Next, the dissection was extended through a generous layer of subcutaneous fat to the muscle layer. After the muscles were divided, the peritoneal membrane was penetrated and the abdominal cavity entered.[16]

As he inserted his index finger into the abdominal cavity, Dr. Mann immediately felt a hole in the front wall of the stomach. Grasping the stomach with his fingers and drawing it part way out through the incision, he could see the bullet wound and also confirm that the stomach was half-filled with liquid food. In order to prevent any further leakage of stomach contents, the bullet wound was immediately closed with a double layer of silk sutures.

In order to examine the back wall of the stomach for a sim-

University of Buffalo Department of Medicine yearbook for 1901 displays its faculty. By coincidence five of seven on this page were on McKinley's medical team: Top left, Matthew Mann; Top right Herman Mynter; Center, Roswell Park; Left center, Charles Stockton; Right center John Parmenter.

ilar injury, Mann lengthened the incision. The stomach was dissected free of its attachment to the large intestine and drawn further out through the incision. The surgeons soon found another wound, larger and more ragged than the first, where the bullet had exited the stomach before plunging deeper into the abdomen. Now they set to work suturing the second bullet wound. The location of the second hole made it a greater challenge, and the lack of appropriate retractors further complicated matters. Ironically, a complete set of surgical instruments lay waiting in the anteroom outside. Dr. Park's housekeeper, knowing that he was needed at the Pan-American Hospital, had on

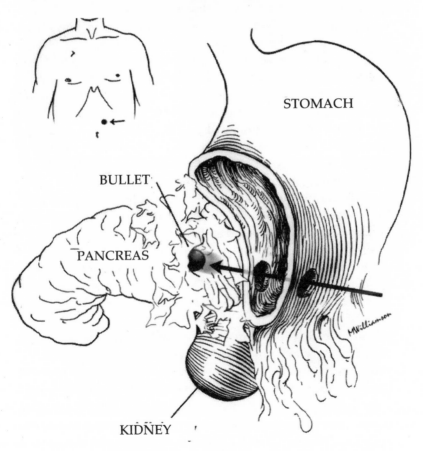

her own initiative dispatched Dr. Park's instruments to the hospital. The bag sat unnoticed and untouched in the medical director's office until the procedure was nearly over.

Dr. Rixey, finally located on the Exposition grounds, arrived moments after the operation had begun. He was overwhelmed with disappointment, not only because of the tragedy itself but also because he had not participated in deciding what was best for the president. When he heard that the surgeons were struggling to see in the waning afternoon light, he found a metal tray and positioned himself where he could reflect light from the window into the operating field. Rixey didn't have to hold his makeshift reflector for long. Someone strung wire that allowed a single electric bulb to be held over the incision. Its power was 8 watts, equivalent to a modern Christmas tree bulb.

With both stomach wounds now repaired, the area was irrigated with the waiting warmed saline solution to minimize the septic effect of spilled stomach contents. Dr. Mann then inserted his right hand deep into the wound to feel behind the stomach and determine whether the bullet had produced further damage. No bleeding was found, and no deeper injury was perceived. At that point, Mann looked up and saw Roswell Park[17] standing in the doorway. The time was 6:00 P.M.

The train Roswell Park had been awaiting in Niagara Falls had indeed arrived, just as the stationmaster had predicted. Park and Campbell boarded and reached the Black Rock station less than an hour later. There, a locomotive waited to take them around the belt line to the Exposition terminal. Park asked the engineer to stop and let him off at the Elmwood Avenue overpass because it was closer to the hospital. Hurrying down the embankment with Campbell running after him, Park hailed a car and pleaded for a ride to the hospital, explaining the circumstances as they proceeded through the West Amherst gate. When their car pulled up to the edge of the crowd, Park jumped out and waved to the guard. "Its Dr. Park," the guard shouted, recognizing the Exposition's medical director. All eyes turned toward the surgeon and a path to the door soon appeared, allowing Park and Campbell to enter the hospital.

Once inside, Park was directed to the operating room. There

he learned for the first time that the operation had begun without him! Furthermore, it was very nearly completed. One can imagine his thoughts. Since the moment he had first learned of the shooting, he had focused all of his efforts on freeing himself to return and serve in the capacity expected of him. Instead, he saw that Mann had taken charge. He recognized only two of the three assisting surgeons, Mynter and Parmenter. Surely stunned by the scene before him, it would not have been surprising if he had aired his frustration and dismay immediately. He did not. In fact, he let nearly ten years pass before he expressed his feelings about the events surrounding the McKinley tragedy. In the operating room that evening, he conferred briefly with the surgical team and then looked for a way he might be of service to the ailing president.

Mann briefly recounted to Park the circumstances of the injury, including the clinical findings, what they had encountered during the surgical exploration, and what had been achieved thus far. Among the surgeons present, opinions varied regarding the need for abdominal drains. These devices, usually fashioned out of stiffened gauze, allowed for the evacuation of body fluids that might lead to infection or corrosion if allowed to pool inside. Mynter said he would definitely use them but Mann's opinion was that there was nothing to drain. Moreover, he feared that a drain site could serve as a portal of entry for bacteria. Park, when asked for his recommendation, desisted, saying that he thought that decision best left to his colleagues who had been present to witness the extent of injury. Mann chose not to use a drain and proceeded to close the incision.

Rixey, still alarmed by how quickly events were unfolding, approached Park in the hallway and asked just who it was doing the operation. "You are the only man here that I know anything about, and I want you to take charge of the case," he added. Park explained that it wouldn't be prudent to change anyone's responsibility at that point. He suggested that he could be of greatest service making arrangements for the president's recovery. Rixey soon agreed.

Mynter urged that McKinley ought not to be moved for several hours, but it had been Roswell Park's firmly established policy throughout the summer that the Pan-American Hospital was not intended for keeping patients overnight. John Milburn, maintaining watch nearby, settled the issue by announcing that he had assured the president his home would be used for the recovery. No further objections were voiced. Park summoned Miss Walters and asked her to begin assembling the personnel, necessary equipment, and supplies. Two nurses were promptly dispatched to the Milburn home, along with a surgical bed and sick room appliances. Observers standing in the courtyard of the hospital saw vehicles pull up to load equipment and concluded that the president was not only alive but also ready for departure. Reporters therefore scurried to available telephones to call in their stories.

The surgeons completed the wound closure at 6:50 P.M. Following application of a bandage, the president's pulse was 122 and his respiratory rate 32. As he slowly awoke, he was given a small dose of morphine for pain control along with strychnine and brandy for the heart. Brandy was another common stimulant used medicinally in that day and administered by mouth or by injection.

After the surgical team had left the operating room, Dr. Park ushered them into a small office and closed the door. He informed his colleagues that, at the request of Cortelyou, they were all under military discipline with respect to communicating their opinions to the press or to the public. All information should represent the collective opinion of those who were caring for the president and would be distributed only through Courtelyou. Dr. Rixey, as McKinley's personal physician, would be in charge of his care. Assisting him would be Drs. Mann, Mynter, Wasdin, and Park. Each one would take his turn staying up with the patient through the night; all would visit the patient every morning and afternoon.

Only Dr. Lee violated the pledge of silence. He left for New York City that same night and soon after arrival there began issuing statements. Park had been suspicious of Lee from the moment he saw him at the operating table, especially after learning from those present that Lee had aggressively asserted himself, even offering to do the operation.

The president was transferred cautiously to a waiting ambulance at 7:32 P.M. Rixey departed earlier in order to inform Mrs. McKinley fully before her husband's arrival. Park removed his jacket, rolled up his sleeves, and stepped into the ambulance. He sat on one side of the president and Wasdin sat on the other. Mann, Mynter, Courtelyou, and the Secret Service operatives followed in another vehicle.

Surrounded by a military escort and local police, the ambulance departed at a pace no faster than men could easily walk; all recognized the need to avoid disturbing the president. Slowly they moved across the mall to Delaware Avenue. Recalling the scene that awaited them that night, Roswell Park wrote, "The passage of that small procession through the crowd and down Delaware Avenue was one of the most dramatic incidents I have ever witnessed. The Fair grounds were crowded that day, and it seemed as though the entire crowd had gathered to witness this event. Every man's hat was in his hands, and there were handkerchiefs at many eyes. I never saw a large crowd so quiet..."[18]

In great numbers, indeed. Police barricades were in place to keep back the thousands who offered their silent respect to the president. All the way down Delaware Avenue they waited, removing their hats as the carriage slowly approached. At the Milburn residence, which was located near the corner of West Ferry Street, workers from the General Electric Company were busy installing special power lines so that silently running fans could keep the entire house cool. When the ambulance reached its destination, Park, Wasdin, and others transferred McKinley, now fully awake, to a stretcher and carried him to a second-floor room that had been prepared for him. Two nurses, Miss Barnes and Miss Simmons, stood by ready to care for the patient until they were relieved the next morning.

Telegraph services throughout the nation had been kept busy ever since the incident. Undersea cables disseminated news of the tragedy to the world. An immediate priority was to notify the vice president. Roosevelt was on Isle La Mont in the middle of Lake Champlain giving an address to his hosts, Vermont Governor Fisk and members of the Vermont Fish and Game Club, when word reached him. Stunned by the news, the vice president asked to be taken by boat to the nearest rail junction. There, he commandeered a train and headed straight for Buffalo.[19]

In New York City, J. P. Morgan, America's unofficial central banker, was preparing to leave his Wall Street office at the close of the financial day. With his hat and cane in hand, he nearly collided with a reporter who ran in with the news. Incredulous, Morgan dropped his cane, slumped into a chair, and sent one of his clerks off at a run to validate the story. Within a few moments, the clerk returned, confirming the news. "This is sad...very sad news...there is nothing I can say at this time," Morgan mumbled. As he departed, reporters already stationed outside his bank began asking about rumors of a meeting with top-level financiers. Other reporters waited at his home on Madison Avenue as well as at Delmonico's, his favorite restaurant. Morgan eluded them. He chose to spend the night secluded on his yacht in New York harbor; he could not yet determine whether the attack on McKinley was part of a larger plot.[20]

In Buffalo, Police Superintendent Bull began conducting the initial interrogation of the president's assailant. Czolgosz had at first identified himself as Fred Nieman but later admitted to his real name. He was fully prepared for the consequences of his act and never raised a hand in defense. Taking in stride all of the blows directed at him earlier, he responded willingly to every instruction given by his captors. When questioned about his intent, he replied simply, "I was doing my duty," and for awhile left it at that. Later, he explained how he had become inspired to take action by listening to the words of Emma Goldman.

Buffalo police had already sent warning bulletins to other police districts to be on the alert for more anarchist attacks. In Paterson, New Jersey, police were jailing all known anarchists. Near Silver City, New Mexico, federal authorities arrested Antonio Maggio, whose crime was predicting that the president would be assassinated before October 1st. In St. Louis, Emma Goldman was standing on a street corner when she heard a newsboy shouting, "Extra edition! President McKinley shot!" With a copy under her arm, she headed for the home of the friend with whom she was staying, and they both read details of the shooting. Neither one recognized the name Leon Czolgosz. "It is fortunate that you are here in St. Louis and not in Buffalo," her friend warned. "They will connect you with this act." Nonsense, Goldman thought to herself.[21]

In Buffalo, two men named Fred Nieman, one a laborer and the other a gardener, both wondered why their telephone had suddenly begun to ring continuously shortly after 4:30 P.M. Police later insisted that they both account for their location at the time the president was shot, even though they held the assailant in their custody. When police arrived at Novak's Hotel, they found that two men with Polish names had registered on the same day as Czolgosz. That was all the evidence the police needed to arrest these individuals and transport them to the same jail where Czolgosz was being held.

The first report of the president's condition was issued by Courtelyou at 7:00 P.M. and transmitted to an anxious nation. The statement read: "The President was shot about 4:00 P.M. One bullet struck him in the upper portion of the breastbone, glancing and not penetrating. The second bullet penetrated the abdomen five inches below the left nipple and one and one-half inches to the left of the median line. The abdomen was opened through the line of the bullet wound. It was found that the bullet had penetrated the stomach. The opening of the front wall of the stomach was carefully closed with silk stitches, after which a search was made for a hole in the back wall of the stomach. This was found and also closed in the same way. The further course of the bullet could not be discovered although careful search was made. The abdominal wound was closed without drainage. No injury to the intestines or other abdominal organs was discovered. The patient stood the operation well. Pulse is of good quality, rate of 130. Condition at the conclusion of the operation was gratifying. The result cannot be foretold. His condition at present justifies hope of recovery. Signed, George B. Courtelyou, Secretary to the President."

The time had now come for Superintendent Bull to deal with the angry crowds outside police headquarters. Their shouts made clear a desire for immediate and violent retribution. The crowd would not have its way. Bull sent his colleague "Big Mike" Regan to confront them; according to a reporter who was present, Regan offered this advice: "If you're good American citizens, go home and let the laws of New York look after this man." Then he added, "Be content with the regular course of justice!" The crowd listened respectfully, remained quiet, and soon began to leave. "Big Mike's" task was made easier by Courtelyou's bulletin, which had been copied onto slates and posted outside a nearby newspaper office. Courtelyou's reassurances would provide the headlines for the next morning's paper.

A second bulletin was issued later in the evening: "10:40 P.M.—The President is rallying satisfactorily and is resting comfortably. Temperature, 100.4°F; pulse, 124; respiration, 24. [signed] Rixey, Mann, Park, Mynter, Wasdin, Courtelyou."

At 11 P.M., Foster, Ireland, and Gallagher made their final security check. There being ample military and police guards stationed around the perimeter of the Milburn residence, the agents returned to their rooms at the Lenox Hotel.[22] Each wrote his own report (on hotel stationary), then retired for the night, ending what had been for each his worst day of goverment service.

❖

Secretary Courtelyou distributing copies of press release to reporters outside Milburn residence

Twenty-eight Pages.

BUFFALO ILLUSTRATED EXPRESS.

Printed by Electric Power from Niagara Falls.

PART 2—PAGES 9 TO 24—16 172 ¼   BUFFALO, N. Y., SUNDAY, SEPTEMBER 8, 1901   PRICE FIVE C

M'KINLEY'S CONDITION CHANGES LITTL

His Physicians report that the President responds well to Medication.

FATEFUL HOURS HAVE BEGUN

Only two Doctors now with him---He sees Mrs. McKinley and tells her to be brave.

CZOLGOSZ TELLS OF HIS PLAN TO KILL

Vice-President Roosevelt and many Cabinet Members arrive at the Milburn Home, but none sees the President.

THE WEATHER.

TODAY'S TOPICS.

Roosevelt's Arrival.

Silence about Czolgosz.

Thought he had killed.

Describe the Sa...

May be lyn...

Conscious all Day.

Prisoner's Trial.

Cabinet Discussion.

His Wife sees him.

Emma Goldman's Talk.

Was here in August.

Czolgosz nerv...

All Eyes on one House.

Absolute quiet.

Went alone to kill.

Plotting the Crime.

WOOD TALKS WITH CAPOTE.

6

RECOVERY?

*"The patient will be at his desk in Washington
within six weeks!"*

Charles McBurney, M.D.[1]

As the first light of dawn appeared on Saturday, September 7th, Buffalo police hurried to complete their overnight security measures. Barricades now surrounded the four blocks adjacent to the intersection of Delaware Avenue and West Ferry Street. Heavy ropes were stretched across Delaware at Cleveland Avenue to the north and Highland Avenue to the south. Similar barriers to general public access had been placed at Linwood Avenue to the east and Tudor Place to the west. Thus, a zone of relative peace and quiet was established for the recovering president. Public entry was limited to medical personnel, necessary support staff, concerned diplomats, and cabinet members, as they arrived from Washington. The War Department ordered the 14th U. S. Army regiment, recently returned from overseas duty, to guard the perimeter of this zone. The soldiers were also charged with maintaining order between the Milburn home and reporters who had settled on the other side of Delaware Avenue in tents erected for their use. Behind the mansion, the Milburn's stable had been transformed into a telegraph office. In the house next door, White House stenographers were in temporary residence, working around the clock in shifts throughout the next week.[2]

The Milburn home had completely lost its ambience as a private residence. The first floor served as a continuous reception area for consultants and dignitaries. The second floor functioned like a hospital. The president's chef and personal servants were brought from his private Pullman car at the railroad yards and put to work preparing and serving as many as 140

The Milburn residence on Delaware Avenue.

Secret Service operatives Ireland and Foster.

meals each day. Mrs. McKinley was relegated to a small bedroom in the adjacent wing. There she waited quietly for any opportunity to visit her husband, even for a few moments. Meanwhile, she tried to write in her diary: "My dearest was receiving in a public hall on our return, when he was shot by a..." Hesitating, she realized that she was uncertain how to even spell "anarchist."[3]

Dr. Rixey spent the night close to his patient's bedside. McKinley had slept a great deal and reported no significant pain. A bulletin issued at 1 A.M. read, "The president is free from pain and resting well. Temperature 100.2; pulse, 120; respiration, 24. Secretary Courtelyou could not sleep and joined Rixey in the middle of the night. After visiting McKinley and checking with the nurses, they issued another bulletin at 3:00 A.M.: "The President continues to rest well. Temperature 101.6; pulse, 110; respiration, 24. Rixey, Courtelyou."

Roswell Park arrived early the next morning to examine the patient and assist Rixey and Courtelyou with another bulletin. They were determined to keep the nation fully informed, especially when the news was so favorable. Park noted that McKinley was already expelling intestinal gas naturally, a good sign indeed. Nonetheless, he ordered a saline enema. At the time, it was widely believed that the body could intoxicate itself (autointoxication) whenever natural passage of bowel contents slowed for any reason. In the case of recovery following abdominal surgery, medications were given to stimulate bowel function, and enemas were administered to remove the feared toxins until normal intestinal activity was restored.[4] Since female nurses were not permitted to assist with the elimination functions of male patients, three male army nurses (Acting Hospital Steward Palmer Eliot, Private Ernest Vallmeyer, and Private John Hodgins) were brought from the nearby Marine Hospital. The next bulletin (and those that followed) omitted these intimate details of the president's care. The doctors shared with the public only the information they deemed most pertinent: "6 A.M.– The president has passed a good night; temperature, 101.6; pulse, 110; respiration, 24. Rixey, Park, Courtelyou." The night nurses were relieved by Miss Maude Mahan and Miss Jane Connolly.[5]

When Dr. Mann arrived, he found his patient alert and in good spirits. McKinley greeted his surgeon with a smile and promptly asked for a newspaper. Thinking that the president wanted to read more about the assailant, Mann suggested that he might like to wait longer. What McKinley actually sought was the public's reaction to the speech he had given at the Esplanade two days before. Everyone present assured him that the response was entirely favorable.[6] When Mann left, he proceeded to his barber to have the previous day's aborted haircut completed.

J. P. Morgan arose very early Saturday morning and returned to his office at 23 Wall Street. A meeting of the Clearinghouse Committee[7] assured support for the markets from Messrs. Rockefeller, Gould, Harriman, Schiff, and Keene, all influential investors on Wall Street. But the reassuring words of Morgan were the most important of all: "The financial situation is absolutely good. There is nothing to derange it. The banks will take care of that. You need not worry about it." His statement was apparently sufficient. During an abbreviated two-hour trading session that morning,[8] the stock market dipped slightly but was stable and remained so for several days afterward.[9]

In St. Louis, Emma Goldman awoke Saturday morning and suddenly remembered the attack on McKinley. Proceeding to a nearby cafe, she purchased the day's newspaper and read its banner: "Assassin of President McKinley an Anarchist! Confesses to Having Been Incited by Emma Goldman. Woman Anarchist Wanted." Reading on, she learned that two hundred detectives throughout the nation were assigned to track her down. Turning to an inside page, she encountered a picture of Czolgosz. "Why, that's Nieman!" she exclaimed, recalling very clearly her recent encounters with the young man. Clearly, her friend's recent warnings were not as preposterous as they had seemed initially. When, reading further, she discovered that several of her fellow anarchists in Chicago had already been arrested, she realized that she would need to give herself up, preferably in Chicago, so that her colleagues might be freed. She departed that night on a sleeper train.[10]

Newspapers throughout the nation announced the tragic incident in Buffalo. Some managed to keep their facts reasonably straight; others offered considerably more fanciful versions. The most frequent factual error was identifying the weapon as a derringer, perhaps on the assumption that all guns small enough to be concealed in the palm of a hand were derringers.[11] In Peoria, Illinois, the *Herald Transcript* reported that McKinley had been "...taken to Buffalo's Emergency Hospital where a bullet, lodged against the breast bone was removed by the well known surgeon, Rosswell [sic] Park." Reporters everywhere sought biographical detail for the actual surgeon and his assistants. In Matthew Mann's hometown of Utica, New York, the editors of the *Herald Dispatch* already knew all about him; the paper devoted more space to the president's surgeon than to the event that precipitated the surgery. Reporters buttonholed surgeons everywhere, asking for their prediction of the outcome. Most were optimistic. Joseph Ransahoff of New York City, who mistakenly believed that Park had been the surgeon, declared the president most fortunate thus far. But, he warned, there was only a one in four chance of survival associated with the type of injury McKinley had sustained.

The search for new angles inspired newspapers such as the *Buffalo Courier* to indulge in "creative reporting," as Secret Service operative Samuel Ireland discovered to his dismay. After answering questions put to him by various government officials Friday evening, he awoke Saturday morning to find the paper printing quotes gleaned from an "interview" with him. It seems that while he responded to the officials' questions, reporters standing nearby were recording his every word. It didn't take long for Director Wilkie to learn about this incident; he sent off a telegram instructing Foster to put a muzzle on Ireland. Keeping the press informed was no more of a Secret Service responsibility in 1901 than it is today. Ireland wrote and then submitted a second report to Wilkie, explaining what had happened and apologizing for the misunderstanding he had created.

The press also happily fed the public's appetite for conspiracy theories. According to the editorial page of the *New York Herald*, "There is reason to believe that other anarchists stand ready to complete the work of Czolgosz if the President recovers...authorities are already in possession of evidence pointing in this direction...other anarchists now under arrest may reveal the substantial plans." A *Washington Post* editor, falsely assuming that Czolgosz was an immigrant, declared, "We open our arms to the human sewage of Europe; we offer asylum to the outcasts and malefactors of every other nation..."His comments were consistent with the general public's feeling of outrage. In sharp contrast to the days of Andrew Jackson, when an attempt on a president's life didn't even lead to conviction of the attacker, now the public demanded not only swift justice but also elimination of a dangerous revolutionary element from their streets.

While most of the nation clamored for action, the man who ordinarily would have added his booming voice was instead deliberately keeping a low profile. The vice president, who arrived at Buffalo's Terrace Station on Saturday at 1:30 P.M., did not wish to appear to be rushing to Buffalo nor did he want to create any hint of unseemly ambition. Prior to the previous afternoon's tragic events, Roosevelt had been entirely frustrated by his subordinate role in American politics. To a friend, he had confided, "The Vice-Presidency is an utterly anomalous office, one that I think ought to be abolished!"[12] As his train carried him across New York state, Roosevelt reflected in silence on the fact that McKinley was not a wealthy man. Rather than being a member of the plutocracy, the president was more nearly among the ranks of the people who were the backbone of America. Any attack on him was a blow at the republic's basis for existence. Later, Roosevelt would lash out against a wide variety of presumed villains, ranging from Tolstoi to William Randolph Hearst.

Reporters were waiting at the station when he stepped off the train, but the vice president had nothing to say to them. Ansley Wilcox, a Buffalo attorney with whom the vice president had worked closely in Albany, intercepted Roosevelt and invited him to stay at his home at 641 Delaware Avenue rather than taking the rooms reserved for him at the Iroquois Hotel. Roosevelt gratefully accepted. First, however, he wanted to be taken to the Milburn residence so that he might pay his respects to the McKinley family, and hopefully to the president as well.

There he encountered cabinet members and other officials who had been arriving from all directions throughout the morning. Secretary of the Treasury Lyman Gage was already in Buffalo. Secretary of War Elihu Root had come promptly from Long Island, Secretary of the Interior Ethan Hitchcock from New Hampshire. Traveling directly from Washington, D.C. were Attorney General Philander Knox, Postmaster-General Charles Smith, and Controller of the Currency Charles Dawes. Within a few hours, a cabinet quorum would be assembled for the conduct of any necessary business. The Buffalo Club, at 388 Delaware Avenue, offered members of the president's cabinet a room where they could meet at their discretion.[13] New York State Governor Benjamin B. Odell Jr. had been in nearby Lockport, and rushed to Buffalo as soon as he learned of the tragedy. Senator Mark Hanna didn't waste any time coming from Cleveland, and he brought with him the president's two sisters.

Telegrams of condolence were received from heads of state throughout the world, including King Edward VII of England, the kings of Portugal, Italy, and Sweden, and the sultan of Turkey. World leaders were anxious as well as saddened. Anarchist attacks seemed to be on the rise everywhere. First there was Austria's Empress Elizabeth, followed by Italy's King Humbert, and now an American president, all attacked within a three-year period. When news of the latest victim reached Russia's Tsar Nicholas II, he and his family were cruising off the Danish coast. A planned rendezvous with Kaiser Wilhelm on Germany's royal yacht was expanded to include a meeting to consider how to avoid further anarchist attacks. Russian and German military leaders were ordered to take every conceivable measure to safeguard the monarchs and their families.[14]

Meanwhile, in the U.S., Leon Czolgosz was under intense scrutiny. All day Saturday, he endured continuing interrogation, now directed by Thomas Penney, the district attorney of Erie County. The prisoner had willingly written and signed the following brief confession: "I killed President McKinley because I done my duty. I didn't believe one man should have so much service and another man should have none."[15] Leaning forward and looking the prisoner straight in the eye,

Penney asked one more time if he had intended to kill the president. "Yes, I did," answered Czolgosz, adding, "I am an anarchist, a disciple of Emma Goldman. Her words set me on fire." Yet, he steadfastly denied having a single accomplice. "I had no confidants, no one to help me. I was alone absolutely." Two alienists, as psychiatrists were called before the influence of Freud, Dr. Carlos F. McDonald and Dr. W. E. Ford, were asked to examine the prisoner. They concluded that he was mentally sane and fully responsible for his act.[16]

Czolgosz related to all who would listen that during his trip to Chicago he had read newspaper accounts of the president's proposed visit to the Buffalo Exposition and that it had seemed to him then that Buffalo probably represented his best opportunity. He hoped to find support for his plan when he returned to Cleveland and called on anarchist leader Emil Schilling. As no support was forthcoming, Czolgosz resolved to shoot McKinley himself. For Penney's interest, he related his three attempts to get close enough to the president to achieve his goal. Not until the third try did he think that he might actually succeed.

Cleveland police began surveillance of the Czolgosz family after receiving word of the assailant's identity from Buffalo police headquarters the previous night. Arriving at the family farm on Saturday morning, detectives questioned Czolgosz's father, Paul, and his oldest brother, Waldeck. Both found it inconceivable that a family member could have committed such an act. Paul Czolgosz kept mumbling, "I can't think it of Leon." Later, when another brother, Jake, was asked if he thought Leon was crazy, he answered, "Peculiar maybe, but not crazy." The stepmother disagreed: "I always thought Leon was crazy! He was never like an ordinary boy. He was timid, a regular coward. He just might have been crazy or he would never try anything like this." In time, every available family member would be thoroughly interrogated, by local police as well as by representatives of the district attorney sent from Buffalo.

Secretary Courtelyou issued four more bulletins that day, none of them reflecting any significant change in the president's condition: "12 P.M. - ...no decided change...; 3:30 P.M. - ...continues to rest quietly...; 6:30 P.M. - ...No change for the worse...; 9:30 P.M. – Conditions continue much the same." The medical record shows that the president's pulse remained within the range of 130 – 140. Normal heart rate is in the 70–80 range; today, doctors would consider a rate as fast as McKinley's cause for concern. Similarly, the president's urinary output of 270 cc.aroused little notice, even though normal daily urine output for an adult male is 1200–1500 cc Today, less than 500 cc in a 24-hour period is considered problematic. When McKinley complained late in the afternoon of intense pain in the pit of his abdomen, he was given another small dose of morphine. At the same time, more saline enemas were administered.

The evening newspaper editions reflected the outrage of people throughout the nation. Numerous clergy were quoted, perhaps because of the irreverence of their language. The president's own pastor, the Rev. H. R. Naylor said that "he could have blown the scoundrel to atoms." Rev. T. Dewitt Talmage wished that " the policemen had dashed his life out with the pistol with which he fired the shot." The Rev. John Floyd Lee of New York's Westminster Church offered the advice that " until a better way is found, lynch him on the spot!"

On Sunday, September 8, 1901, Courtelyou's first bulletin restated the administration's resolve to inform the nation directly of McKinley's progress: "The public will be kept fully advised of the actual condition of the President. Each bulletin is carefully and conservatively prepared and is an authoritative statement of the most important features of the case at the hour it is issued." The restatement of this pledge was prompted by news that Dr. Lee, although he had departed Buffalo Friday evening, immediately after McKinley's surgery, was still offering his own interviews to the press in New York City.

Dr. Mynter had remained with the president the previous night and recorded that McKinley passed a good night. When Mann and Park arrived in the morning, they saw that the president was in exceptional spirits, alert, rested, and comfortable. Examination of the abdomen during a dressing change showed no sign of peritonitis. Following irrigation with hydrogen peroxide, a popular antiseptic agent, no pus was seen issuing from the bullet tract. The pulse was considered strong but remained at 132. Strychnine was continued and another heart stimulant, digitalis, was added to the regimen, a response to the persisting rapid pulse. The next scheduled enema included Epsom salts and glycerin to stimulate expulsion of bowel contents. The rectum was also a popular route for administering nourishment. That afternoon, the president received his first "nutritive enema," a mixture that included egg, whiskey, and water.

Throughout the nation, leading surgeons were monitoring McKinley's progress as it was being described in the news releases. Some forwarded expressions of support to the surgical team. Professor J. H. Musser of Philadelphia, for example, telegraphed to Roswell Park, "We are all so glad you are on hand."[17] But Dr. Rixey still was not entirely confident either of the president's progress or of all the decisions made on his behalf. He summoned the nationally renowned surgeon Dr. Charles McBurney from Roosevelt Hospital in New York City. McBurney arrived in Buffalo Sunday afternoon and was immediately taken to McKinley. After examining the president and consulting all of the surgeons, McBurney issued his report through Courtelyou, declaring unequivocally that the patient would be at his desk in Washington within six weeks. Referring to the surgery performed on McKinley, he added that it was, "The epoch of the century in surgery!" Such was the confidence placed in out-of-town consultants, even in 1901, that a mood of euphoria descended upon the scene soon after Dr. McBurney had spoken. One newspaper embellished the New York surgeon's remarks by saying the bullet rested where it could not have shortened Methuselah's life by a single day.

As her train was pulling into Chicago's Wabash Station, Emma Goldman removed her glasses and donned a small sailor hat with a blue veil. The disguise was so effective that her waiting friend failed to recognize her. Taken by surprise when Goldman approached him, he urged that they depart quickly to avoid any chance of recognition. They spent several hours discussing their options. An offer had come from the *Chicago Tribune*, a $5,000 scoop fee if she would grant an exclusive interview. Unfortunately, the police reached her first, and she was jailed without charge, presumably to await extradition to

Dr. Presley Rixey

James Parker

Dr. Charles McBurney

Secratary of State John Hay

Buffalo. In the meantime, she was questioned for several days, around the clock, by a relay of more than fifty detectives. Finally, Chicago Police Chief O'Neill appeared. He sat down in her cell and asked for a quiet talk. "I have no wish to bully or coerce you," he said. Wary at first, Goldman told him her story, the same story she had repeated many times over for his detectives. He chose to believe her, and from that moment forward, conditions improved significantly for her. She even discovered that many of the matrons and guards in the jail were sympathetic to her political grievances. "We're all Democrats in here, not Republicans!" one of her guards whispered.

Over the weekend, angry crowds in Paterson, New Jersey, willingly aided by the police, captured and jailed dozens of suspects, also without charge. It was the worst kind of vigilantism. Meeting under cover of darkness, anarchists who had not yet fled quietly drank their toasts to a man unknown to them, Leon Czolgosz, who had achieved something that most of them had only talked about.

At the same time, Czolgosz's victim seemed to be growing steadily stronger. By Sunday, President McKinley was beginning to believe that the future might hold promise for him. He had been hearing nothing but good news from all of his visitors. It was the best kind of mental reinforcement for anyone recuperating from such a serious injury. Late Sunday afternoon, his doctors were sufficiently pleased with his progress to recommend the first sips of water. Courtelyou kept the good news coming frequently, first to the press tent and then over the telegraph wires: " 4 P.M. - The President since the last bulletin has slept quietly - four hours altogether since 9 o'clock; 9 P.M. - The President is resting comfortably and there is no special change since the last bulletin." The surgeons continued to ignore their patient's rapid pulse (it had not dropped below 128 all day). His urinary output, which totaled 420 cc, apparently was considered sufficient.

When the nation awoke on Monday morning, September 9, 1901, they found their newspapers filled with reassuring news, including Dr. McBurney's pronouncement. The president's progress, coupled with still more reassuring words from J. P.

Morgan, resulted in an upturn in the stock market; most traders seemed very willing to keep their funds invested. Furthermore, there had been no further evidence of violence anywhere in the world. While many still believed that a conspiracy had produced the tragedy, the world appeared free of additional victims for the moment.

Monday morning also brought the arrival of an x-ray machine, courtesy of Thomas Edison, who wanted to make certain that the latest technology would be available to the president's surgeons. He dispatched the machine from his laboratory in New Jersey, and he arranged for a technical expert from New York City to be present in Buffalo to assure the machine's proper use. Observation of the apparatus being carried into the Milburn home Monday morning led to rumors that more exploratory surgery was contemplated. Mr. Milburn, who would appear on his porch from time to time to hold informal press conferences with reporters nearby, explained that installation of the apparatus was precautionary. Coincidentally, physicians specializing in the use of x-rays were meeting in Buffalo at that moment. The Roentgen Ray Society, a newly formed professional association, sent a delegation to visit Roswell Park and urged that their technique be considered for the benefit of President McKinley. Dr. Park tried to explain why retrieving the bullet was not considered important for McKinley's recovery. After the meeting, he decided that it might be wise to rehearse an x-ray search for the missing projectile. Dr. Kenersen, public health officer at the Exposition, weighed 200 pounds, as McKinley did, and his abdominal girth of 56 inches was identical to the president's. Kenersen agreed to stand in for McKinley while trial runs with the apparatus were practiced at the Milburn home. Unfortunately, the machine Edison had sent arrived with an essential part missing. and no x-rays of the president were taken.[17] Surgeons held to their position that the bullet's location was not a critical issue.

The bulletins on Monday reflected further improvement in McKinley's condition: "9:20 A.M. - ...becoming more and more satisfactory. 3 P.M. - ...steadily improves. 9:30 P.M. - ...continues favorable." His pulse had diminished somewhat but remained in the range of 112-122. His urinary output of 540 cc was only slightly greater than the previous day's. Although Courtelyou preferred that the public information responsibilities be left to him, John Milburn appeared briefly on the front porch of his home to let reporters within earshot know were that "Everything at the seat of Government was as smooth as silk." The assembled press noticed that bulletins were becoming less frequent and complained. Courtelyou reminded them that consistent good news didn't need to be repeated too often; he probably believed the opposite. Reporters, abhorring a vacuum, began to write about each other's coverage of the story, or they made bets on who would be accompanying Mrs. McKinley on her daily carriage ride and then reported the results as news. News of the president was so scarce that even the marching habits of the troops guarding the zone around Delaware Avenue and nearby streets were considered newsworthy. Because the paved sidewalks had taken a toll on the soldiers' feet, they were now treading visible paths in the softer lawns nearby. One reporter speculated about the need to replant the lawns in order to obscure the damage being done by sentries.

Anyone departing the Milburn residence was fair game for an interview but most had little to say. The vice president visited twice each day, but he went out of his way not to distract attention from the president. Except for enjoying a visit to Buffalo's zoo, where a newly acquired white polar bear was attracting crowds, Roosevelt stayed out of sight and avoided the press. The surgeons continued to abide by their prior agreement and spoke only through Courtelyou's periodic bulletins. Once, reporters did manage to extract a comment from Dr. Mynter as he left the Milburn home. He seemed in disagreement about what to feed McKinley. "The President is getting very little nourishment," he unthinkingly blurted out to the eager reporters. Then, realizing what he had done, he tried (unsuccessfully) to reverse the impression of dissension in the ranks that his remark conveyed, "Oh, he won't starve to death...can't starve a man in six days." Of course, every newspaper that had a reporter in the press tent printed his comments the next day.

Ansley Wilcox mansion, site of inauguration.

Roosevelt and Hanna confering as they walk.

By Tuesday, September 10, 1901, the consistently reassuring news led to numerous departures from Buffalo. The vice president prepared to join his family for a scheduled vacation in the Adirondack Mountains; he planned to depart the next morning. Treasury Secretary Knox and Secretary Root left for Washington. Secretary of State John Hay, on the other hand, finally made his appearance in Buffalo that day, arriving by train from Washington. When Louis Babcock picked Hay up, he was stunned to hear his passenger ruefully declare that the president would not likely survive his injury. Hay was known for his pessimistic outlook on life. He had been close to both Lincoln and Garfield, and he still grieved the loss of his son who recently had died in an accident. As the men traveled up Delaware Avenue to the Milburn home, Hay explained to Babcock, "I was one of the secretaries of President Lincoln. He was shot and died. I was a close friend of Garfield, who tendered me a post under him. He was shot and died. Now I am Secretary of State under President McKinley. He will surely die for it has been the fate of the Presidents with whom I have been associated to be assassinated." Babcock expressed his sorrow that an event so tragic had happened in his own city. "Don't take that to heart," Hay replied. "Anyone can shoot the President if he does not wish to escape."[19]

Secret Service operatives kept themselves busy pursuing investigations prompted by letters from individuals reporting evidence of a conspiracy. Mr. Charles Brown, a Canton, Ohio florist, had written to Courtelyou that he had observed the assassin in Canton, together with a woman and another man. Foster and Gallagher pursued the lead and then reported that on the day the florist said he had seen Czolgosz in Canton, McKinley's assailant was definitely known to have been in Buffalo. Furthermore, everyone who reported seeing Czolgosz in Buffalo confirmed that he was always alone, never accompanied by anyone.

The stenographers handled an unprecedented volume of mail received each day. There were simple greetings, and thoughtful poems, plus an ample supply of security advice. In order to prevent occurrences of this kind in the future, one man urged that cameras be installed on top of all the Exposition towers to spot anarchists in advance of tragedy. (The writer offered no hints regarding the distinguishing characteristics of anarchists.) Plenty of recipes for guaranteed recovery or the rapid healing of wounds were received each day. A jar of liniment that smelled of carbolic acid was sent with a note urging that it be rubbed into the wound daily.

The 10:30 P.M. bulletin on Tuesday broke precedent by offering a lengthy and defensive explanation for that afternoon's surgical manipulation of the incision site. Where the bullet had entered, some sutures were released to allow for removal of unhealthy tissue just beneath the skin. Nevertheless, the president's overall condition was unchanged and he had begun to take nourishment by mouth in the form of beef juice. Nutritive enemas were still being given three or four times each day, and an enema containing soap was later administered, once again to stimulate passage of stool.

Wednesday, September 11, 1901, was for McKinley much like the previous day, except that he was experiencing considerable irritation of his rectum and an inability to retain the enemas given him. Little wonder! More stitches were removed and the surgeons acknowledged that the president did have a superficial wound infection although these exact words were not included in the bulletins. Instead, the public was told that his wound was healthier, and that the patient's stomach was tolerating beef juice in larger quantities. Temperature remained 100.2 throughout the day; the pulse was still elevated at 116-120; urine output was 750 cc.

At a time when the president appeared to be suffering the complications of his treatment rather than the outcome of injury or his surgery, a letter sent by Buffalo shoemaker H. R. Burt to McKinley's physicians offered some interesting advice. "Dear Sirs, Please allow me to say that milk not cream given to the President will stop the posin [sic] that may be in his system from the bullet. Also, warm water interjected into the bowels will not injure him like oil or calomel." Everybody had their own enema theories. Moreover, his reference to a poisoned bullet was not the last to be heard. Mr. Burt closed by urging therapeutic restraint:" If the President is not doctored too much and let nature take its time, his chances of recover[sic] will be greater than if he is given too much medicine. He is not a sick man but a wounded man." The writer, like McKinley's best consultants, did not realize how sick the president was becoming.

Wednesday night found only Rixey with the president. Runaway optimism had dispersed the rest of the medical team. Even Courtelyou managed to enjoy his first full night of rest since the incident. Reporters were more desperate for news than ever. One covered the breaking news that a gust of wind had swept through the telegraphers' tent, taking dozens of pages of unsent news copy with it. Another reported the results of his interview with "Big Jim Parker," as the man who joined the melee that brought Czolgosz to the floor was now known. Parker's notoriety had prompted many far-fetched rumors, such as that the man was being wined and dined at the Buffalo Club. The reporter had easily found Parker at his post as a waiter at an Exposition restaurant. "What are you going to do next?" Parker was asked. "Do nothing!" he replied. "Ain't I working?"

Dr. McBurney had remained all week in Buffalo, visited the president each day, and participated in all decisions as well as in Courtelyou's preparation of the periodic bulletins. He had also managed to work in a tour of Niagara Falls. His plan for Thursday, September 12th, was to examine the president one more time, then tell Rixey that there was no further need for him in Buffalo. At the daily 8:30 A.M. surgeons' meeting, nurses reported that McKinley was now being fed solid food. The president had relished his broth and coffee but did not care for his toast. The open portion of the wound was being cleansed with a dilute iodine solution and hydrogen peroxide. McKinley now seemed at his best, and everyone present believed that any remaining risk of peritonitis had passed. He was expelling gas freely and his bowels were moving. Pain was no longer an issue. The pulse was still rapid and the urine output barely more than previously noted, but these anomalies did not seem to worry McBurney or anyone else.

Thus, it was easy to conclude that McKinley had reached a point in recovery that justified their highest expectations. Dr.

McBurney shook the president's hand one last time and extended his farewells to everyone in attendance. Then he took Mann and Park aside and promised that he would return promptly if they needed him. As he left the house, he paused before a cluster of reporters to announce, "It is the first time that he had solid food since he was shot and it did him good. He wanted a cigar too but he didn't get it!" McBurney gave a final wave to the reporters. Knowing just what to make of the surgeon's departure, they all rushed to their typewriters and telephones. President McKinley was certain to recover!

❖

EXTRA! BUFFALO EVENING NEWS. 5°

VOL. XLII—NO. 132.   BUFFALO, N. Y., FRIDAY, SEPTEMBER 13, 1901.   PRICE O

EXTRA! EXTRA! EXTRA! EXTRA

HIS CONDITION CRITICAL;
HOPE NOT ABANDONED!
CRISIS FEARED TONIGH

His Heart Has Been Weak All Day and Frequent Injections of S Solution Have Been Given---Oxygen Apparatus Ready.

OFFICIALS AND PHYSICIANS COMING BACK IN HASTE.

Vice President Coming as Fast as Special Train Can Bring Him.

'y Root — McBurney and Party Come to Buffalo With All Haste, The Latter a Noted Heart Specialist.

SENATOR DEPEW ARRIVES HERE.

As Soon as He Got Off Train He Was Driven to Milburn House.

COL. ROOSEVELT.

Foreigner Alleged to Have Started for Washington on Mission of Murder.

The Latest Bulletin Issued This Afternoon Says the President is Better.

Friday, September 13 1901

7

DEATH!

"That's all a man can hope for during his lifetime - to set
an example, and when he is dead, to be an inspiration for history."

William McKinley, 1899[1]

On Thursday, September 12th, almost as soon as Dr. McBurney had left Buffalo, the basis for everyone's optimism began to crumble. First, the president made clear that he wasn't feeling nearly as well in the afternoon as he had in the morning. Moreover, his pulse was 130 again and significantly weaker, an ominous change. He had passed no intestinal gas since early in the morning. His doctors, every one of them, made the same diagnosis: intestinal toxemia. In compliance with the beliefs of the day, they ordered another enema. It yielded little.

Dr. Charles Stockton, professor of medicine at the University of Buffalo School of Medicine and noted diagnostician, had returned from his summer home in Stockbridge, Massachusetts, and was summoned for consultation. His primary concern was the president's weakening pulse. Digitalis was given again, along with more strychnine to stimulate what Stockton believed was a failing heart. Noting also that enemas were not producing the desired result, he prescribed calomel, a powerful laxative.[2] This in combination with another enema did result in passage of a limited volume of semi-fluid stool. No more solid food, not even beef juice, was fed to the patient.

At 11 P.M., one pint (480 cc) of saline was administered by clysis, meaning via needle injection into the fatty tissue under the skin. Ida McKinley had received salt solutions administered this way several months before when she was seriously ill in San Francisco. Regrettably, the president failed to respond as she had. The bulletin at 3:00 P.M. was purposely misleading: "The President's condition is very much the same as this morning. His only complaint is of fatigue. He continues to take a suf-

ficient amount of food." It might have been difficult for
Courtelyou to admit to anyone, himself included, just how bad
the situation appeared. For the 8:30 P.M. bulletin, he chose his
words very carefully, disclosing that " The president's condition
this evening is not quite so good. His food has not agreed with
him and has been stopped. Excretion has not been properly
established...his pulse is not satisfactory[3], but has improved in
the last two hours."

The press did not need this last bulletin to realize that
something was amiss. More than one hundred reporters were
assembled in and around the press tents. Many were scattered
along the sidewalks, and some stood in the middle of Delaware
Avenue, where their view of the Milburn home was less
obstructed. Most obvious to all was the increased frequency of
visits from surgeons and other consultants. Furthermore, these
visitors all wore expressions of deep worry on their faces and
they lingered inside. Late editions of the newspapers cited an
unfavorable turn in the president's health. Through the night,
McKinley's pulse grew even weaker, despite frequent injections of strychnine.

Leon Czolgosz had not been moved from police headquarters, where he had been sequestered after the shooting. The
more secure city jail was undergoing renovation. In addition,
keeping Czolgosz at police headquarters made it easier to com-
ply with the orders of Dr. Joseph Fowler, police surgeon, who
had insisted that the prisoner be observed at all times for evidence of insanity. In fact, Czolgosz consistently displayed only
the most cooperative behavior. Now, as word filtered into headquarters that the president's condition had worsened, the
police began to worry about their captive's safety. In the event
of the president's death, the assailant would become an assassin, and once again the streets would likely fill with angry people ready to take justice into their own hands. Superintendent
Bull doubled the guard at every door of the stationhouse and
made plans to transfer the prisoner to the Erie County penitentiary if the news from Delaware Avenue wasn't more
encouraging in the morning.

Meanwhile, telephone calls were placed to all members of

the president's cabinet, most of whom had just recently departed, suggesting that their presence might be needed again in
Buffalo. Ansley Wilcox offered to contact the vice president's
secretary William Loeb, who would most likely know exactly
where in the Adirondack Mountains Roosevelt could be found.
Dr. McBurney had not reached New York City yet but would be
incredulous when he arrived home and learned of the president's worsening condition. For everyone standing by at the
Milburn home, there was an overwhelming sense of impending
tragedy. Laymen and professionals alike recognized that the
limits of medical knowledge had been reached.

Roosevelt was staying with his family at the Tahawus
Hunting Club, thirty-five miles beyond North Creek, the closest railroad junction. A message from Loeb was hand-carried to
the club from the nearest telephone link. "Courtelyou wires
President's condition causes gravest apprehension," Loeb had
written to Roosevelt, adding, "Ansley Wilcox telephoned...slight
improvement. Advise your coming here immediately...will
send special engine to bring you in..." The vice president had
left that morning to climb Mt. Marcy. A guide brought the note
up to him as he was descending the mountain trail. Later, he
would recall sensing the worst possible outcome for McKinley
when he saw the messenger approaching. He did not react visibly, however. He took his time returning to the club; then,
while he lingered there with his family, a second message
arrived. This missive, sent by Secretary of War Root, was unmis-
takably a summons: "Hon. T. Roosevelt, The President appears
to be dying and members of the Cabinet in Buffalo think you
should lose no time in coming." Four drivers with carriages and
teams already positioned along the departure route were prepared to function in relay. Roosevelt bade farewell to family
members and began his nighttime ride to the presidency.[4]

Reporters still maintaining a night vigil in the press tent
realized how grim the situation was when they received
Courtelyou's bulletin at 2:50 A.M.:

"The President's condition is very serious and gives rise to
the gravest apprehension." Presses were held so that the morning headlines would accurately reflect the worsening situation.

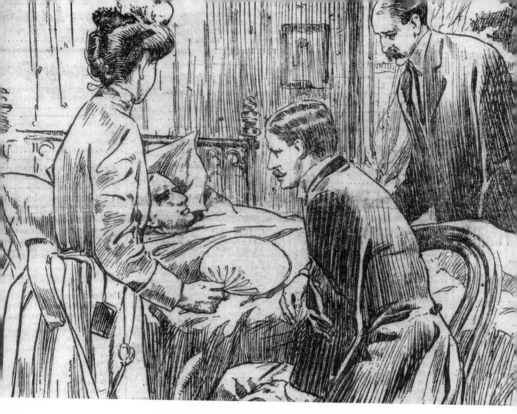

Two Artist's renderings of the death scene.

Beginning at 8:30 A.M. on Friday, September 13th, McKinley was given injections of adrenal gland extract[5] in hopes of stimulating a stronger bodily response. Two more pints of salt solution were infused in the subcutaneous fat, and then a combination of adrenaline mixed in salt solution. The president's pulse was now barely palpable. Subsequent bulletins on Friday included words that implied faint hope but fooled no one: "9 A.M....condition has somewhat improved...2:30 P.M....has more than held his own since morning...4 P.M....only slightly improved."

At 11 A.M. on Friday morning, Leon Czolgosz was transferred under heavy guard to the Erie County penitentiary. He was placed in an empty cell in the otherwise vacant women's dungeon. No one at the facility was told his name or his offense. By coincidence, the coach driver who had brought him from the Exposition to police headquarters also transported him to the penitentiary. Police authorities intended to keep the prisoner secluded until the fate of the president was known. Czolgosz had not yet been officially charged with any crime.

Charles McBurney boarded a train bound for Buffalo as soon as he learned of the president's deteriorating condition. When he reached the Milburn residence late Friday afternoon, McBurney could tell by looking at the faces of those in attendance that little hope was left. Drs. Edward Janeway, also from New York City, and W. W. Johnston from Washington, D. C., both heart specialists summoned by Rixey, examined the patient but could do nothing more. Mrs. McKinley remained close at hand, visiting her husband for very brief periods at more frequent intervals. While the president was still alert, he acknowledged her presence with a faint smile. His final audible words were whispered to those standing close to him: "God's will be done, not ours." Someone heard him faintly humming his favorite hymn, "Nearer My God to Thee." Soon after, he lost consciousness. As the evening passed, various people entered the room. His old friend Mark Hanna tried to rouse the president, imploring, " William, William, don't you know me?" McKinley did not respond to Hanna or anyone else. He never regained consciousness.

The bulletin at 9:30 P.M. confirmed the obvious, "The President is dying." Rixey maintained a bedside vigil until the very end. On Saturday, September 14, 1901, at 2:15 A.M., eight days, ten hours, and eight minutes after a lone anarchist took the course of history in his own hands, William McKinley, 58 years old and 25th president of the United States, was pronounced dead. The 39th and final bulletin read simply, "The president is dead."

Roswell Park would later pay homage to McKinley with these words: "...he bore his illness and such pain as he suffered with beautiful, unflinching, and Christian fortitude, and no more tractable or agreeable patient was ever in charge of his physicians. No harsh word of complaint against his assassin was ever heard to pass his lips... Up to this time, I had never really believed that a man could be a good Christian and a good politician."[6]

Not until dawn Saturday did William Loeb, waiting impatiently beside the president's special train for almost twenty hours, finally recognize a lone carriage approaching with Roosevelt bundled inside. "Complicated, complicated!" the driver heard his passenger mutter as they descended a slippery mountain path barely wide enough for the carriage. Later, Roosevelt would recall that he was filled with remorse over "...becoming President through a graveyard." He preferred to earn his own right to the office. Loeb handed him the latest wire: "Hon. Theodore Roosevelt, The President died at 2:15 this morning. John Hay, Secretary of State." According to the Constitution, the office had automatically passed to him at the moment of McKinley's death, several hours before. When Roosevelt's train reached Albany, the new president transferred to another, consisting of a locomotive and one car, which awaited him on a siding. Reporters standing nearby asked for a comment but he declined. Shutting himself inside a compartment, Roosevelt sat alone in reflective thought as he sped towards Buffalo on tracks cleared for him by the New York Central Railroad.[7]

The entire world was stunned by the news of McKinley's death, largely because only two days before, reports from Buffalo had been so promising. Tributes to the late president were soon heard from loyal supporters and rivals alike. Andrew Carnegie said of McKinley," He stands forever with Lincoln and Garfield in the 'Temple of Martyrs,' wearing like them the

Buffalo Courier.

FEARLESS and HONEST.

...VI—NO. 257. BUFFALO N. Y.—SATURDAY MORNING, SEPTEMBER 14, 1901. 12 PAGES—ONE CENT

...UFFALO COURIER HAS A LARGER CIRCULATION IN BUFFALO THAN ANY OTHER NEWSPAPER

...XTRA!

M'KINLEY'S LAST WORDS.
"Good-bye, All; Good-bye. It is God's Will—His Will Be Done. Not Ours."

EXTRA!

..'KINLEY IS DEAD!

...SSED AWAY AT 2:15 THIS MORNING

...S. M'KINLEY BREAKS DOWN AND SHE IS TENDERLY CARRIED FROM THE BEDSIDE

...OOSEVELT IS HURRYING TO CITY

The last coherent statement made by the President was between 10 and 11 o'clock last night. He was then ...ed by Drs. McBurney, Stockton, Mann and Mynter that there was no hope of saving him, and he was told to ...e for the worst. At that time the family was called into the room.

...Mrs. McKinley was brought in, and for a moment sat on the edge of the bed, but the doctors removed her. ...she held his hand he said: "Good-bye all, good-bye. It is God's will. His will be done, not ours."
...During the last three hours the President mumbled words from the hymn "Nearer, My God, to Thee."

City of Buffalo—Bureau of Vital Statistics.

CERTIFICATE AND RECORD OF DEATH,

89

...OF ERIE, ...NEW YORK.

OF

William McKinley

...eby certify that I attended deceased from .... 189.. to .... 189....., that *he* died on th ...st saw .... alive on the .... day of .... 2 ⁷⁵ .... 189..., that *he* died on th ...ʰ day of *Sept* 1901, about *2* o'clock, A. M., or P. M., and that to best of my ...ge and belief, the cause of *his* death was as hereunder written.

Duration of Disease

...ause, *Gangrene of both walls of Stomach and Pancreas*

...ting Cause, *following Gun shot wound*

Witness my hand this *14th* day of *Sept* 1901.

Burial, *Canton Ohio* (SIGNATURE)

Burial, DRULLARD & KOCH, *H R Gaylord* *W G Waring*, D

...aker, *56 E Delaware Ave*

...ce, *N. Niagara St* *Buffalo James F Wilson*

...ion is given to embalm the above named body. *H R Gaylord* M. D holy crown of sacrifice for the Republic. "Former political opponent William Jennings Bryan offered only kind words:"His life was remarkable, and his personal character above reproach." From abroad, a flood of praise and sympathy arrived from heads of state. "Most truly do I sympathize with you," wrote Edward II of England, "and the whole American nation."

Mrs. McKinley did not want to hear about an autopsy, much less grant permission for one. She was prevailed upon to reconsider her strong objections, however, so that the nation might know the full effects of the assassin's bullet and surgeons might learn more about saving others similarly wounded. Reluctantly, she compromised, agreeing to an autopsy limited in both its duration and scope. The heart and lungs could be examined, and the intestinal organs studied in place. Nothing could be removed, however, save for minute samples to be studied microscopically. Commencing their work at noon on Saturday, in the presence of District Attorney Thomas Penney and Erie County Coroner James Wilson, Drs. Harvey Gaylord and Herman Matzinger of the New York State Pathological Laboratory continued examining the body for nearly four hours. Also present at the procedure were the physicians who had fought to preserve their patient's life and failed.[8]

When the autopsy was over, Coroner Wilson surveyed the notes made by the pathologists (eventually the notes would be made into a final report) and recorded the following cause of death in the police blotter: "...gangrene of both walls of the stomach and pancreas following gunshot wounds." The same words would be used to complete a death certificate. As a final conclusion, this statement left much to be desired. It raised more questions than it answered. Misinterpreting the meaning of gangrene, reporters immediately assumed that McKinley had died of an infection. After all, President Garfield's gangrenous wound had been the result of a septic process. In McKinley's case, however, gangrene simply meant the death of tissue, admittedly a very extensive zone, covering much of the pancreas and adjacent organs, including the stomach and intestines. What caused the gangrene became a matter of conjecture, even among the learned medical professionals present.

When the results of the autopsy were made public and disagreement immediately followed, the pathologists defended
themselves. "A matter of no inconsiderable embarrassment to
us arose," they explained, "in the objection to our removing sufficient portions of the tissues for examination."[9] They were
voicing a perspective that pathologists maintain to this day,
namely the belief that a larger sample of examinable tissue
would yield definitive results. Roswell Park focused on the pancreas and held little doubt that its injury, unrecognized by the
operating surgeons, was the key to explaining everything that
followed. Matthew Mann, on the other hand, expressed little
interest in the pancreas. He chose to focus instead on revealed
changes in the heart, whose muscle was pale and thin and partially replaced with fat, the result of that organ's failure in the
end. Mann attributed these changes to McKinley's sedentary
life, apparent to all even before his wound increased demands
on cardiac function. None of the doctors conceived of a possible relationship between a failed heart and an inflammatory
process that lay unresolved within the abdomen.

Out of left field came one more theory, poisoned bullets!
This possibility was offered by Dr. Wasdin, the anesthesiologist.
How else, he asked, can such a rapidly advancing degenerative
process be explained satisfactorily, if not by the action of some
powerful corrosive poison? The utter lack of supporting evidence
for Wasdin's contention did the theory no harm. Journalists
instantly embraced the poisoned bullets theory. It made for sensational copy in newspapers throughout the nation.

Ansley Wilcox once again stood waiting for his friend
Roosevelt's arrival, this time at the Terrace Street Station, and
this time in the company of a mounted police escort prepared
to lead the new president safely to the Wilcox residence.
Roosevelt stepped from the train at 1:30 P.M., barely acknowledged cheers from the assembled crowd, and urged Wilcox to
take him to his home without delay. Still showing the effects of
the long, damp ride out of the Adirondacks, he needed to borrow a jacket and pinstriped pants, clothing more appropriate
for the events awaiting him than his travel-worn costume.
Secretary Root and other cabinet members were waiting in the

drawing room of the Wilcox mansion. Roosevelt greeted them hastily, then went upstairs and readied himself. Everyone present wanted him to pause for swearing the oath of office, but Roosevelt would not hear of it. He insisted that he must first pay his respects to Mrs. McKinley as a private citizen. A carriage awaited him but when he saw that it was to be accompanied by cavalry, he waved the escort aside and asked the driver to proceed quickly to the Milburn home.

Meanwhile, Louis Babcock had just returned from the Buffalo library where he had consulted an 1881 *New York Herald* for the exact wording of the presidential oath of office, administered to Chester Alan Arthur shortly after Garfield's death. It was Secretary of War Root who had suddenly realized a few hours earlier that they didn't have the oath's wording. A newspaper dating from the nation's last experience with a presidential assassination was deemed the most likely available source for the missing information.

Returning from his visit to Mrs. McKinley, Roosevelt met briefly with Root, then turned his attention to other cabinet members. The Wilcox mansion was considered ideal for the ceremony, so Roosevelt waited for all the necessary participants to gather in the front parlor. Reluctantly, he also agreed to admit a reporter or two as observers, but when the lone photographer present experienced difficulty with his equipment, the president refused to admit others. The historical record of this event therefore includes no illustration other than an artist's imagined rendering. Roosevelt's impatience was legendary, but at this moment, his nervousness prompted him to suddenly announce that "...in this hour of deep and terrible bereavement, I wish to state that it shall be my aim to continue, absolutely unbroken, the policy of President McKinley for the peace and prosperity and honor of our beloved country." Secretary Root began a short introduction but soon became emotionally overwhelmed and curtailed his remarks. He called upon 41 year-old U.S. District Judge John R. Hazel, the youngest member of the federal judiciary, to administer the swearing in. At 3:30 P.M., September 15, 1901, Theodore Roosevelt stepped forward, raised his right hand, and repeated the oath to serve

Twenty-eight Pages.

BUFFALO — THE ILLUSTRATED — EXPRESS.

Printed by Electro Power from Niagara Falls.

-PAGES 9 TO 28—74. 1721. No. 58. BUFFALO, N. Y., SUNDAY, SEPTEMBER 15, 1901. PRICE FIVE CENTS

[ROO]SEVELT QUICKLY SWORN IN AS PRESIDENT--
M'KINLEY'S BODY TO LIE IN THE CITY HALL

The new Chief Executive declares he will follow in the Footsteps of McKinley.

TOOK OATH AT WILCOX HOME

Brought to Buffalo at utmost Speed from Mount Marcy in the Adirondacks.

NO EXTRA CONGRESS SESSION

After consulting the Cabinet the President decides such a Course is not necessary—Talk with Secretary Root.

Public may View the dead President from Noon to 5 O'Clock this Afternoon.

FUNERAL SERVICES AT 11 O'CLOCK

Only Relatives and close Friends will be admitted to the Home of Mr. Milburn.

ENTIRE CITY IS IN MOURNING

Tomorrow Morning the funeral Train will start for Washington—The President's last Moments.

Theodore Roosevelt - 26th U.S. President.

Wilcox Mansion - the inaugural site.

as President of the United States. He was 42 years old and the youngest ever to serve as the nation's chief executive.

Roosevelt asked the cabinet members present to remain for a few moments. Attempting to reinforce his earlier comment, he told them again that he needed their continued public service. Then he departed for a private walk with Root. Remaining members of the cabinet elected to return to their meeting room at the Buffalo Club. There, they quickly decided it was their duty to submit undated resignations and await the president's more carefully considered wishes. Within a few months, Roosevelt would replace them all.

Mrs. McKinley preferred the simplest of funeral arrangements but she was granted that wish only for the closing service that would be held in Canton. The days of mourning and ceremony were prolonged; in the end, they exceeded in length and elaboration the recent funeral of Queen Victoria. The nation's homage began on Sunday morning, September 15, 1901, when a funeral hearse draped in black and drawn by four coal black horses drew up to the Milburn residence. Inside the house, a brief service limited to cabinet members, local officials, and family members was being conducted. The late president's casket was open; his body was dressed in a black suit, and a lone button, designating membership in the Grand Army of the Republic, adorned his lapel. His facial expression still bore the signs of great suffering. His closest friend, Mark Hanna, was the last to approach the casket. He knelt, and then wept.

The funeral procession, escorted by dressed units of the Army, Navy, and Marines, advanced slowly down Delaware Avenue. Spectators stood ten deep, many wearing badges that bore a picture of McKinley. Scattered in the crowd were men who had donned the uniforms and medallions of their Civil War units. They came to honor both a fallen president and a decorated war hero. The hearse circled the square that would later serve as the site of a monument to McKinley, then progressed to the city concourse, where the president's body would lie in state for the afternoon. Thousands passed the casket in two lines; among the mourners was James Parker, the next man in line at the Temple of Music, who had helped to subdue the assassin. At 6:00 P.M., the hearse carried McKinley's body back to the Milburn residence.

Another important event took place that day, quietly, and beyond the scrutiny of the press. The sole meeting of a grand jury specially appointed to deal with the case of assassin Leon Czolgosz was called to order at 10:15 A.M. District Attorney Thomas Penney sat at a table in the courtroom, flanked by four of his assistants. The earliest witnesses to testify were Drs. Mynter, Gaylord, Matzinger, and Mann; they wished to depart for the services honoring the late president. Next came Secret Service operatives Gallagher, Ireland, and Foster; they needed to return to their protective duties. Attorneys Quackenbush and Babcock, who had organized the Temple of Music reception, followed. These two men proved to be the most valuable witnesses because they could describe accurately what happened immediately prior to and following the shooting. There were twenty-eight witnesses in all; yet the entire proceeding took less than five hours. The verdict, "The grand jury of the County of Erie, by this indictment, accuse Leon F. Czolgosz, alias Fred Nieman, of the crime of murder in the first degree."[10]

District Attorney Penney, with Superintendent Bull's cooperation, had planned Czolgosz's arraignment to occur while crowds and reporters were diverted by funeral events nearby. The prisoner had been transported from the penitentiary back to the jail at police headquarters and then by underground passage to a courtroom not far from where his victim's body lay in state. When Penney asked if he had counsel, Czolgosz simply shook his head no. Penney next asked if he wished to have counsel defend him. The assassin remained silent. The district attorney turned to presiding Judge Edward Emery and asked for the court to assign legal counsel. Emery, anticipating the assassin's refusal to cooperate, announced that two retired state supreme court justices would be asked to defend Czolgosz, Loran Lewis and Robert Titus. The arraignment was adjourned, and Czolgosz was returned to his cell.

The funeral train departed from the Pennsylvania Railroad Terminal at 8:30 on Monday morning, September 16th, bound for Washington, D. C. The president's flag-draped casket was positioned in an observation car surrounded by a uniformed military guard of honor so that mourners standing alongside the railroad tracks could view it easily. The train slowed for each community as it passed, advancing south through western New York State, then into the oil and coal fields of Pennsylvania, down the valley of the Susquehanna River, through Harrisburg and Baltimore, then on to the capital. Along the way stood mourners in small groups and large, men removing their hats as the train passed. Several towns provided musical background, including the tolling of church bells and a choir singing "Nearer My God to Thee." Some people thought they saw Mrs. McKinley weeping for her husband; in fact, she remained in her compartment, out of view for the entire journey.

In Washington, the rain fell steadily and continued to do so for the duration of the ceremonies held there, leading one reporter to observe that even the heavens wept for McKinley. Overnight, the casket lay in state in the East Room of the White House, protected by a military honor guard. The next morning, the procession advanced down Pennsylvania Avenue to the Capitol, led by cavalrymen with their sabers raised in salute, followed by military commanders and diplomats, legislators and justices. People of all classes and conditions had assembled along the way in numbers considered unprecedented for any public event yet held in Washington. At 10 A.M., the casket was placed upon a catafalque in the Capitol's rotunda, a choir sang softly nearby, and the memorial service began. At its completion, thousands of mourners who had waited hours outside in the rain began to file past the casket and continued to do so until evening came. The casket was borne back to the waiting train and once again placed in the observation car, now illuminated so those who waited to watch the train pass in darkness could see the casket.

Throughout the night, passing by way of Baltimore, then Harrisburg, then Pittsburgh, the train encountered thousands more citizens who, like their counterparts in the capital, had stood for hours in the rain waiting to offer their respect to a fallen hero. As the illuminated casket passed them, the upturned faces were bathed in tears, as noted by observers on board. At dawn, the train entered Stark County, Ohio where McKinley had begun his public service, and where crowds now assembled to see one of their own come home for permanent rest. The funeral train arrived in Canton at noon, on Wednesday, September 18th, exactly two weeks after the president had departed for Buffalo in the vigor of complete health. Many who now stood waiting silently had been there to cheer him as he departed. The casket was borne to the Stark County courthouse and there it remained while many more visitors streamed past. At the close of the day, the casket was brought to the McKinley's North Market Street home. Close family members maintained a vigil through the night.

On Thursday, at the Methodist church in Canton, Dr. C. E. Manchester, the president's closest Civil War companion in arms, conducted the final memorial service. In his eulogy to the late president, Secretary of State John Hay highlighted the growth of McKinley's international and strategic perspective: "He was gratified to the heart that we had arranged a treaty which gave us free hand on the Isthmus (of Panama). In fancy, he saw the canal already built with the argosies of the world passing through in peace and amity."

The procession to West Lawn Cemetery was escorted by the Army's highest-ranking generals and Cleveland's Infantry Troop A, dressed in black hussar uniforms and riding black horses. It was the same unit that had accompanied McKinley from the White House to the Capitol during two presidential inaugurations. The entire Ohio Militia, 8,000 members strong, also was present in Canton that day, along with members of the Knights Templar, Masonic orders, Odd Fellows, and the Grand Army of the Republic. In each, the late president had been an active participant.

President Roosevelt designated September 19th as a day of mourning throughout the nation. The exact hour of the final service had been pre-announced, along with the closing moments when the president's body would be lowered into the ground. During that five-minute interval, telephone service throughout the nation ceased, factories shut down all machinery, and several million people silently bowed their heads in reverence. There had never been a moment like it, when the citizens of an entire nation were brought so close in sentiment at the same instant.

McKinley's body was only temporarily interred in Canton's West Lawn Cemetery. Plans were already underway for construction of a memorial that would befit America's twenty-fifth president. The site eventually selected was a hilltop knoll adjacent to West Lawn and visible from central Canton. Ida McKinley settled in Canton, not at the North Main Street house, which she sold, but in the Saxton family home where she had spent her childhood. There, she established a modest shrine to her late husband in a small room next to her second-floor bedroom. President McKinley had drafted his tariff bill there during the summer of 1890. Thus, she placed a copy of the manuscript on a small writing table, surrounded by several of his medals and a favorite photograph. She visited that room for a few cherished moments each day for the remainder of her life. All the rest of the time, she stayed in her bedroom next door, lost in thoughts of her late husband. In her final days, she commented to a friend, "He is gone and life is dark to me now." Ida McKinley died on May 26, 1907. Her remains and those of daughters Katie and Ida are also interred at the McKinley Memorial in Canton, Ohio. Today, the Saxton family home serves as the First Ladies Museum. Mrs. McKinley's bedroom and adjacent shrine to her husband have been preserved.

❖

September 15, 1901: Funeral procession leaves Milburn residence.

Casket with McKinley's remains carried from train in Canton, Ohio.

Leon Czolgosz

8

PUNISHMENT

"The power of punishment is to silence, not to confute."

Samuel Johnson

For nearly seven days, the entire nation had celebrated McKinley's surgeons as heroes. With the president's death, these same men were viewed as backwater bumblers, or worse. Criticism came first from the press, then from Congress, and in time from professional colleagues as well. The drive to punish Dr. Mann, the assisting surgeons, and the many consultants who had participated in the president's care continued for several weeks. Surgeons in Boston, New York City, and Philadelphia were especially derisive, noting how unfortunate it was that the president had sustained such a serious injury in a backwater community like Buffalo. Any recollection of the fact that New York City's own Dr. McBurney had participated was already forgotten—except in Buffalo, where reporters countered by ridiculing "...big city physicians who couldn't supply a better consultant."[1]

Some in the medical profession preferred to level their attacks on the late president's doctors covertly. One Chicago reporter clearly benefited from expert assistance. "The coroner's investigation points to the responsibility of the surgeons who gave the wounded president solid food prematurely," the story stated authoritatively. Moreover, readers were informed that " Mr. McKinley did not die as a direct result of the assassin's bullet, but was killed by toxemia of the intestinal tract, all of which shows that some of the most distinguished surgeons exercising their highest intelligence can make blunders that seem almost childish to the lay mind." Other opinions expressed in print were based on far less medical erudition. One author explained the president's death as"...an overpowering of life principle by violence and exhaustion!" A physician in Arlington, Vermont proposed the cause to be "adrenal gland destruction resulting in lack of secretion...a fall of vascular tension, a weakening and rapidity of the heart." Few critics, however, were willing to propose an alternative therapeutic strategy.

The intensity of public censure led Ansley Wilcox to suggest that Drs. Mann, Park, and the others consider filing a suit for defamation. Accordingly, a meeting was convened at Wilcox's residence. Rather than undertaking litigation, however, the surgeons decided to issue a joint statement that summarized their position: "The undersigned, surgeons and physicians who were in attendance on the late President McKinley, have had their attention called to certain sensational statements recently published in the daily papers...indicating dissension and mutual recriminations... We say again that there was never a serious disagreement among the professional attendants...The unfortunate result could not have been foreseen before the unfavorable symptoms declared themselves late on the sixth day...pending completion of the reports of the post-mortem examiners, we shall refuse to make any further statements for publication."[2] The signers were Mann, Park, Mynter, Wasdin, and Stockton. They also declared that all alleged interviews with any one of them could be considered fictitious. In other words, they opted for silence, a decision each one honored for several years.

Within a few weeks, editorials in recognized medical journals offered a spectrum of opinions, most supportive of the clinical decisions made on behalf of the president." The entire conduct of the case was upon modern scientific medical and surgical principles," Dr. William Potter, editor of the *Buffalo Medical Journal*, wrote, "and no intelligent observer can gainsay this fact." The official position of *The Medical News* was similarly supportive:" It is clear that no human skill could have saved the President's life and that everything that modern scientific medicine could possibly suggest was done for him." In *American Medicine*, the editor asserted," We think that the best professional opinion will still entertain the theory that the pancreatic secretions may be a factor in the causation of necrosis." He went on to question why necrosis of an entire organ like the pancreas would cause death, a mystery to every physician in 1901.

In sharp contrast, Dr. George Schrady commented critically in *The Medical Record*: "It is a pity, indeed, that such an evident failure in diagnosis should have been so conspicuously demonstrated to the general public." It was his opinion that the operation had been tragically incomplete; specifically, the finding of gangrene behind the stomach proved a need to find and remove the elusive bullet. There would be a continuous stream of criticisms like Schrady's for several years, and a persisting trickle over the span of several decades.

Concern for the conduct of McKinley's surgeons influenced official policy regarding compensation for their services. When President Garfield's surgeons had submitted their claims, Congress had responded by engaging in prolonged and distasteful bargaining. During the months following McKinley's death, a similar scenario began to unfold. Congress first declared that it would need to resolve a debate over whether the president's expenses should be paid from his estate or from the nation's treasury. The prevailing public opinion was that the president had been struck down while serving as a public official, not as a private citizen; responsibility for any claims must, therefore, be assumed by Congress and not the family. Senator Mark Hanna was sufficiently irritated by the government's procrastination that he threatened to pay the bills himself, rather than allow the burden to be placed on Mrs. McKinley. Even Dr. Mann was drawn into the controversy when he was asked to confirm that the surgical team had in fact been called into service by government authorities. Several more months of fierce debate ensued before the bills were finally approved for payment.

There were no delays in resolving the fate of Leon Czolgosz, however. Only forty-three days passed between the grand jury's indictment and the assassin's execution, a pace of justice that would be unthinkable today. Those who examined Czolgosz prior to his trial were still pondering his sanity. Throughout the trial, however, the uniform opinion of the few witnesses who addressed the sanity issue was that Czolgosz had been in full command of his mental faculties when he took the life of the president. Debates over the prisoner's mental competence persisted long after the execution. National sentiment effortlessly merged two contradictory perspectives, at once blaming the prevailing mood of the times and also holding assassins fully accountable for their actions. Thus, Lincoln met death in an age of hate, Garfield in a period of intense partisan division, and McKinley in an era of anarchy. Popular opinion held that Czolgosz had been under the influence of the anarchist movement, a derivative of the expanding foreign element in America. No one, however, wanted to see violence rewarded by acquittal.

Emma Goldman, who had for some time wanted to go to Buffalo in order to "...help the boy," as she dubbed Czolgosz, was at last in a position to do so. The judge presiding over her extradition hearing proved to be a stickler for rules of evidence. From the beginning, he had been suspicious of the case being made by the Buffalo attorneys. They held no evidence for her complicity in the shooting and thus failed to make a convincing argument. Goldman was set free to do as she wished. Her Chicago friends urged her to refrain from traveling east until the witch-hunts for every alleged conspirator had run their course. She had been fortunate to receive justice in Chicago; a similar outcome could not be depended upon in any other city.[3]

Goldman departed nonetheless, thanking her many colleagues for their solace during one of the most trying episodes in her life. She kept her face hidden behind a newspaper when her train paused briefly in Buffalo. Police did not board and haul her away as she had been warned that they would. When she arrived in Rochester to visit her sister, Goldman learned that every family member had been ordered to appear at police headquarters for questioning soon after the attack on McKinley. Her young niece's schoolmates had taunted her by chanting "Aunt Emma is a murderess!" Suspecting that the police were still watching her sister's home, Goldman remained there only for a short time. Family members agreed that she could better assure her safety by blending into one of the larger urban centers to the east.

As for "the boy," she remained highly sympathetic to his

predicament. Her persistent loyalty to Czolgosz probably reflected Goldman's basic opinion of McKinley, whom she considered "...the willing tool of Wall Street, and of the new American imperialism that flowered from his administration." She had been completely misinformed, however, about Czolgosz's access to an attorney. Believing that he had been denied counsel, she tried to raise funds for his defense. She quickly discovered how divided her fellow anarchists were about the assassin. Many adopted the same position Schilling and Isaak had taken earlier; namely, that Czolgosz knew nothing about the movement and had not worked for it. Thus, he deserved no support from them. The fact that he had actually performed the decisive act that many of them dreamed, talked, and wrote about made little difference to them and reflected their own ambivalence about what anarchists should stand for. Many who objected to supporting Czolgosz were simply being pragmatic: Why risk further misery at the hands of a vigilant police force? They preferred to hide rather than to defend their ideological position. Goldman's eventual realization that she stood nearly alone from other revolutionaries in the aftermath of McKinley's death was perhaps the severest punishment of all for this stubborn propagandist who had rarely compromised her political beliefs. Meanwhile, she needed to decide where to go next, and where to establish a base for pursuing her smoldering revolutionary ideals.

Goldman's failure to secure funding for "the boy" in Buffalo may have troubled her but it did not distress Leon Czolgosz. He already had more legal assistance than he wanted. The Erie County Bar Association had proposed the retired state supreme court justice Loran Lewis, who had been present at the arraignment, as defense counsel for the assassin. Visiting the prisoner after Czolgosz had been formally charged with first-degree murder, Lewis announced his role and discovered that the defendant would not even talk to him. A second judge Robert Titus, was asked to assist Lewis. Titus had been traveling in Wisconsin and was not aware of his assignment until he returned home. Astonished, he declared he no intention of defending the assassin. Pointing out to Lewis that he still had

political aspirations, including the governorship, Titus wondered aloud how participation in the trial of this despicable
man would likely affect his future. In the end, though, Lewis
prevailed and both judges agreed to serve the court as well as
the defendant. As distinguished local jurists, they recognized
their duty to demonstrate that every person accused of a crime
deserved an adequate defense. Although their change of heart
impressed many, it made no difference to Czolgosz. He steadfastly refused to speak to either one of them. On September
17th, the prisoner appeared again before District Attorney
Penney, this time in the presence of his attorneys. When asked
how he pleaded, he remained mute. A plea of not guilty was
recorded and notice given that the trial would begin the following Monday, less than a week away.[4]

On the morning of Monday, September 23rd, Czolgosz was
brought before Judge Truman White of the Superior Court of
the State of New York. When asked again how he pleaded, the
prisoner replied, "Guilty." Because defense counsel had already
been assigned, a prior not-guilty plea entered, and a jury
already selected, Judge White ruled that a changed plea could
not be accepted. Czolgosz looked puzzled but unconcerned.
The clerk of the court was instructed to record a plea of not
guilty and the judge announced that jurors had already been
examined for selection. Unlike jury selection today, each prospective juror had been allowed to admit that he had already formed
an opinion on the matter, but each pledged that all preformed
opinions would yield to any new evidence presented at trial.
Czolgosz was asked if he objected to any of the jurors. He ignored
the question. So, the twelve, all men, were sworn.

The prosecution began its case by recounting the defendant's specific act of murderous intent against a sitting president. Initial witnesses described the scene, the reception hall
arrangements, McKinley's position, and the movement of people into and out of the Temple of Music. Next, Dr. Gaylord recit-
ed the findings at autopsy, attempting to explain what he had
seen in terms that the jury might understand. During cross-
examination, the defense counsels never questioned whether a
causal relationship existed between the assassin's bullet and

the president's death, a standard procedure in homicide defense. Neither did either counsel introduce the possibility of death from surgical misjudgment or error. Instead, cross-examination reinforced the alleged causal link between the bullet's passage through the pancreas and the president's death. This led attorneys observing the trial to conclude that defense counsel seemed to be helping prosecute the people's case. Dr. Mynter, the first surgeon to provide testimony, explained his initial examination and findings as well as the reasons he believed immediate surgery was necessary. Dr. Mann followed with a detailed description of the operation he performed. Next, Grand Marshal Louis Babcock took the stand in order to place the accused inside the Temple of Music at the time of the attack on McKinley. Babcock once again described in detail what he had seen seconds after hearing the loud report of gunfire.

When James Quackenbush testified, he chose to omit any reference to his offhand comment to Babcock about the possibility of an assassination. Instead, he recalled the content of the interrogations conducted with Czolgosz when the assailant had first been brought to police headquarters (Quackenbush had participated in these sessions). The accused had willingly told his life story to everyone present and then had freely admitted his crime. After Quackenbush affirmed that Czolgosz had given his statement without any duress from police authorities, the accused's confession was placed in evidence before the court.

The jury now had listened to everything it needed to hear in order to reach a verdict. The testimony had been presented in less than a full day. Czolgosz sat motionless through it all, looking neither to the left nor right, and displaying no emotion. Nevertheless, Penney pushed on, not wishing to overlook any detail; the proceedings continued well into the following day.

Secret Service operatives Gallagher and Foster were asked to describe their roles in protecting McKinley on the fateful day. Foster admitted that, carried away by his anger, he had struck the gunman's face. Artilleryman Francis O'Brien described his capture of the smoking revolver, an account which differed significantly from Gallagher's, but no one in the courtroom seemed troubled by the discrepancy. After hearing sworn testimony from Superintendent Bull that the prisoner had never been coerced, that he had admitted his crime freely and with full understanding of the consequences of his actions, District Attorney Penney rested his case and sat down.

Judge White then turned to Judges Lewis and Titus. Lewis stood slowly, turned to Czolgosz, and asked if he would go to the witness stand. The prisoner silently indicated that he would not and remained in his seat. Looking back at Judge White, Lewis announced that he would not be calling any other witnesses. He added that given the persistent refusal of the accused to speak on his own behalf, all further testimony was necessarily closed. He asked, however, that he and his colleague be granted the privilege of making personal statements to the jury. White urged them both to proceed.

Admitting that it had been more than twenty years since he had last addressed a jury as defendant's counsel, Lewis proceeded to explain that, if the prisoner's crime was an act of insanity, then he must be first acquitted and then confined to an asylum. He emphasized how important the judicial process was in America, and how damaging a lynch mob would have been in this case. He devoted additional time to justifying his own participation in the trial. What he did not do was offer any information regarding Czolgosz's mental status at the time he shot President McKinley, an omission that would later draw criticism.[5] Lewis closed with a eulogy to the late president and a display of emotion that forced him to pause intermittently and then to sit down. When Judge White asked if co-counsel wished to make a statement, Titus stood, paused, indicated that it seemed unnecessary for him to restate what had already been said, and sat down. Perhaps he was still contemplating his re-entry into the political arena.

In a forceful closing statement, Thomas Penney appealed to the emotions of the jurors and all others present, describing in excruciating detail an image of McKinley's suffering as represented in the late president's recent funeral. He closed with the exhortation, "...no man, no matter who he is or where he hails from, can come here and commit such a dastardly act, not only against such an individual, but against our laws and institutions, and not receive the full penalty of the law." Judge White issued his charge to the jury, and they retired for deliberation at 3:50 P.M.

Thirty minutes later, the clerk announced that the jury was prepared to return. The jurors filed back into the courtroom at 4:25 P.M. When the judge asked if the jury had been able to reach a verdict, the foreman stood and said, "We have...Guilty of murder in the first degree as charged in the indictment." Asked if the verdict was unanimous, the foreman said that it was. Judge White thanked the jury members for their service and excused them. As the twelve men slowly left the courtroom, some glanced furtively toward Czolgosz, who remained seated, motionless and impassive.

Two days later, on September 26th, Judge White reconvened the court for the sentencing. District Attorney Penney began by ordering Czolgosz to stand. Startled by Penney's tone, the defendant complied. In fact, he proved as willing to answer Penney's questions that day as he had been during the interrogation at police headquarters. Many of the questions had been asked before: his age, city of birth, place of last residence. Czolgosz answered every question until the clerk of the court interrupted with a query of his own. Turning on him, the defendant snapped back that he would speak only to Penney. The District Attorney continued with the most pertinent question of all; namely, whether Czolgosz had any legal cause why sentence of the court should not be pronounced against him. The prisoner answered that he did not. Did he have anything to say to the judge? Czolgosz replied that he did not.

Judge White, leaning forward, asked the prisoner if he felt that he was insane, or if he had any cause for a new trial. Czolgosz answered that he had nothing to say about either point. Turning to Judge Titus, White asked if he thought his client had anything more to say to the court. Titus, looking at Czolgosz, suggested that something be said to free his family of any associated guilt. For the first time, the prisoner responded with emotion. "I would like to say this much," he stated, suddenly and surprisingly breaking his customary silence, "that the crime was committed by no one else; no one told me to do it, and I never told anybody else to do it."

This unexpected demonstration of feeling caused a stir in the courtroom. When quiet was reinstated, Judge White issued his sentence. "Leon Czolgosz, in taking the life of our beloved President, you committed a crime which shocked and outraged the moral sense of the civilized world. The sentence of the court is that in the week beginning October 28, 1901, at the place, in the manner, and by the means prescribed in the law, that you suffer the punishment of death." Every reporter present and every other observer in the courtroom watched intently for any sign from Czolgosz that Judge White's chilling words had disturbed him. They were all disappointed. The convicted assassin did not even blink.

Police reports show that the prisoner returned to his cell that afternoon, ate a hearty dinner, spoke openly with his guards about general topics (excluding the trial), and slept soundly through the night. The next day, he was transferred to a state prison outside the modest community of Auburn, New York. There, he was placed in a cell designated for prisoners assigned the death penalty.

On October 12th, Albert Gallagher wrote Secret Service Director John Wilkie to ask permission to attend (at his own expense) the execution of Czolgosz. "I would like to say more about the villain, but I am familiar with the postal laws. I still have the marks of the kicking I received, to say nothing about the choking and I feel that the only satisfaction I can get out of it will be to see the curr[sic] in the chair." The record does not show whether Gallagher was given the necessary time off.[6]

Very early on the morning of October 29th, Leon Czolgosz was escorted into the execution room at the Auburn state prison. Officially designated witnesses included the superintendent of state prisons and several physicians, among them Dr. Edward Spitzka, who was assigned to perform the mandated autopsy (it was hoped that the autopsy would resolve debate over the nature of the assassin's brain[7]). Representatives of the press were also present. Guards firmly guided the prisoner into a chair carefully wired to inflict a lethal electrical current. This would be the first time in history that alternating current was used for a criminal execution. Straps were adjusted to his arms, legs, body, and head, followed by attachment of the electrodes that would send the current through his body.

Czolgosz offered no resistance to these manipulations. But, apparently worried that he would be executed without being allowed to speak one last time, he suddenly shouted out, "I killed the President because he was the enemy of the good people - the good working people. I am not sorry for my crime!" Warden Mead had fully intended to call on the assassin for his final words; that was a part of his customary routine. Not wishing to hear anymore of this man's protest, however, the Warden silently gestured to the electrician, who in response obediently turned the lever. Instantly, 1,800 volts[8] were delivered. Witnesses, caught by surprise, were astounded as Czolgosz was suddenly thrown into a spasm affecting every visible muscle group in the current's path. Hidden from their direct view was that most critical of muscles, the heart, now transformed into purposeless fibrillations.[9]

When the circuit was reopened, the assassin's entire body fell limp before the spectators. Each physician present was asked to step forward to examine the corpse. The first to approach hesitated visibly before feeling for the corpse's pulse; others approached the task with equivalent reluctance. The image of the victim's spasm etched upon their retinas would not soon fade. Once all the physicians had completed their examinations, Leon Czolgosz was officially pronounced dead. He was twenty-eight years old.

The autopsy immediately followed the execution. Dr. Spitzka was assisted by Dr. Carlos MacDonald, one of the alienists who had previously examined Czolgosz in Buffalo. Initially, the two took note of the assassin's physiognomy, i.e., the physical features of his face and skull. They described him as "youthful, good looking, with a pleasant expression." Blistered skin was noted at all of the sites where electrodes had been attached to the body surface. With a saw, Dr. Spitzka divided the skull to expose the brain, and then carefully removed that organ from the cranial vault. Newspapers would later make much of the fact that the brain was found to be "above normal." What this meant was that according to

Spitzka, Czolgosz's brain was slightly heavier than averages recorded for other "Polish brains."[10] Small hemorrhages were noted throughout the organ, a result of the recently administered electrical current.

After examining every surface feature of the brain, the pathologist concluded that "...nothing has been found in the brain of this assassin that would condone his crime for the reason of mental disease due to intrinsic cerebral defect or distortion." In other words, the brain did not look abnormal. The pathologist went on to explain, however, that some forms of psychosis have no anatomical basis but may depend instead upon circulatory and chemical disturbances.[11] The doctors' final conclusion was that their subject was "socially diseased and perverted, but not mentally diseased." Spitzka continued on a philosophical note, "The wild beast slumbers in us all. It is not always necessary to invoke insanity to explain its awakening." Members of the press were chagrined. They weren't looking for philosophy or poetry. They needed to know whether the assassin harbored a criminal mind. The autopsy report could not be used to either confirm or deny that popular allegation.

Warden Mead had received his orders: execute the assassin and then destroy his body. Prior experience had shown that the standard prison burial practice of adding a layer of quicklime before sealing the grave would not result in the desired goal for several weeks. Taking his responsibility seriously, Mead directed that instead of quicklime, a carboy of sulfuric acid be poured over Czolgosz's remains at burial, and so it was. No one ever questioned the order or its intended purpose.

❖

THE AUTOPSY.

___

Physicians Found the Brain Normal, or Slightly Above—The Body Quickly Destroyed.

___

Auburn, Oct. 29.—Naturally, almost the entire attention of the physicians assigned to hold the autopsy was directed towards discovering if possible whether the assassin was in any way mentally irresponsible. The autopsy was conducted by Dr. Carlos F. MacDonald, an expert alienist and former president of the New York State Lunacy Commission, Dr. E. A. Spitzka of New York and Prison Physician Gerin.

The top of the head was sawed off through the thickest part of the skull, which was found to be of normal thickness, and it was the unanimous agreement after microscopical examination that the brain was normal or slightly above normal. This demonstrated to the satisfaction of the physicians that in no way was Czolgosz's mental condition, except as it might have been perverted, responsible for the crime. The autopsy was completed shortly before noon.

The body was placed in a black-stained pine coffin, every portion of the anatomy being replaced under the supervision of Dr. Gerin and Warden Mead. Shortly afterward it was taken to the prison cemetery and an extraordinary precaution taken to completely destroy it.

A few days ago, under the warden's order, 12 pounds of meat was placed in a glass jar and the same proportion of quicklime which would be used to consume a human body was placed in the jar. It was found upon examination this morning that the meat had shown little sign of disintegration.

Warden Mead at once conferred with some of the physicians present and determined, in conjunction with Supt. Collins, that as the purpose of the law was the destruction of the body it was not necessary to confine themselves to the use of quicklime.

9

AFTERMATH

"...We should war with relentless efficiency not only against the anarchists, but against all active and passive sympathizers..."

President Theodore Roosevelt, 1901[1]

Emma Goldman chose New York City as her destination after visiting family members in Rochester. Friends and collaborators were plentiful in Manhattan, and the population density should have permitted her to hide from the still-watchful police. But nearly every newspaper in the nation had published her photograph, usually on the front page, and this heightened notoriety soon deprived her of her independence. Potential landlords refused to consider her tenancy, insisting that she leave at once, before police descended on the neighborhood. Potential employers would not even think of hiring her. Humiliated, she was forced into seclusion with friends, moving frequently to avoid recognition.[2]

Meanwhile, the anarchist movement had effectively moved its operations underground. No longer could raids on the favorite anarchist gathering places in Paterson, New Jersey yield known sympathizers. Circuit-riding propagandists cancelled their speaking engagements. Vigilante raids in numerous communities forced the evacuation of suspected anarchist families. Meetings of the Liberty Association in Cleveland, where Czolgosz had been inspired by Emma Goldman's oratory, were shut down. The publication of revolutionary pamphlets and newsletters also waned. A few days before McKinley was shot, Johan Most in New York City had forwarded a regularly scheduled edition of *Freiheit* to his printer. The issue featured the incendiary words of German revolutionary Karl Heizen: "Despots are outlaws...to spare them is a crime. We say murder the murderers. Save humanity through blood, poison, and iron!" Learning of

Czolgosz's deed, Mr. Most made a frenzied effort to withhold circulation of the issue. He failed. One copy was all the police and
a judge needed for evidence. New York had passed laws specifically applicable to the activities of radicals like Most. Section 675
of the New York State Penal Code made it a misdemeanor "...to
commit an act which seriously disturbed the public peace or
openly outraged public decency..."[3] Arrested a few days after
McKinley's death, Most was tried, convicted, and sentenced to
one year in prison.[4]

Little sympathy existed for professed revolutionaries. Police
and judges who acted to suppress propagandist organizations
enjoyed the full support of the public. Yet there were no federal laws
to deal with assassins, only criminal statutes in most states. Public
pressure grew for congressional legislation to deny U. S. entry to the
"foreign element" that many considered a principal source of all
domestic revolutionary activity. This plea would be spoken loudest
and most eloquently by President Roosevelt himself.

* * * *

When he first spotted the courier approaching him on Mt. Marcy
trail, the vice president had experienced an immediate premoni-
tion of disaster. Roosevelt was no stranger to the political impact
of presidential assassination. As a youngster, he had joined his
brother Elliott to watch the funeral cortege of Abraham Lincoln
as it passed through Union Square, near their home in New York
City.[5] Now, as he rode in a train making its way across New York
State and bringing him steadily closer to his new role as president, Roosevelt reflected on his working relationship with
McKinley. He acknowledged to himself that "the President in a
cold-blooded way has always rather liked me, or at least has
admired certain qualities in me. There are certain bits of work he
would be delighted to have me do. But at bottom, neither he nor
Hanna sympathize with my feelings or are comfortable about
me, because they cannot understand what it is that makes me act
in certain ways at certain times, and therefore think me indiscreet
and over-impulsive."[6]

Roosevelt was used to commanding his own fate and had
never shied from taking the initiative. Having suddenly been

granted the opportunity to lead the nation, he set about trans-
forming the office of the presidency. Those who had come before
him, including McKinley, had not presupposed that the executive
branch should be responsible for setting the legislative agenda of
Congress. Roosevelt thought otherwise. He proved so effective in
directing Congress that his model would influence every president who followed. The new president chose to begin with an
issue that was already prominent in the minds of congressional
leaders and the public—the compelling danger of anarchism and
the need to punish as a federal offense all assaults on high-rank-
ing officials, regardless of where those attacks might occur.

In the first message he delivered to Congress, Roosevelt proposed that "...we should war with relentless efficiency not only
against the anarchists, but against all active and passive sympathizers with the anarchists." He believed that both advocates and
apologists for anarchism were accessories to murder. And, liken-
ing anarchy to piracy and the slave trade; Roosevelt proposed
that treaties be signed making each of these offenses unlawful in

President Roosevelt addresses Congress after his inauguration.

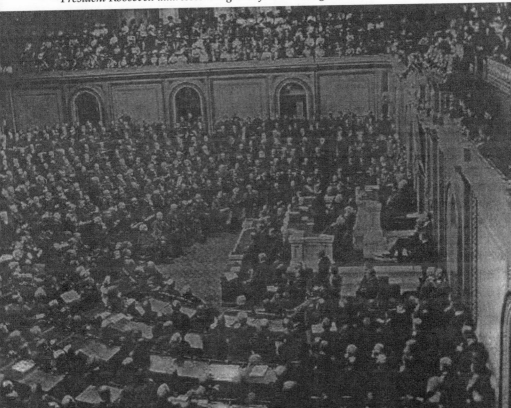

every civilized nation. (He seemed not the least concerned about the absence of any precedent for international agreements of this kind.) Furthermore, he urged Congress to exclude from the United States all who promoted assassination, and to deport any alien who had ever espoused these views. Like so many others, Roosevelt overlooked the fact that the assassins responsible for the deaths of U.S. presidents had all been Americans–John Wilkes Booth, Charles Guiteau, and Leon Czolgosz were native sons, as were many of the vocal advocates of revolutionary principles. The bills submitted to the Senate and the House of Representatives failed to address this reality. Most advocated some form of alien exclusion or deportation; none dealt effectively with native-born revolutionaries. Pending legislation also failed to assure the rights of the vast majority of immigrants, who had no interest in political insurrection.[7]

Debate continued in both houses of Congress for more than a year. What finally passed on March 3, 1903, was a measure limited to forbidding the naturalization of those who advocated forcible overthrow of the government. Fines would be levied against individuals who assisted the entry of aliens considered dangerous to the nation. Roosevelt eagerly signed the bill the morning after it passed both houses of Congress. It remained for individual states to attempt control of domestic anarchists. New York State promptly passed its own legislation declaring that the advocacy of "criminal anarchy" by written or spoken word was a felony punishable by imprisonment for as long as ten years. Although the law was rarely used as an anti-anarchist measure, its constitutionality was eventually challenged and then later upheld by the United States Supreme Court.

* * * * *

An acute need for better presidential protection was recognized by nearly everyone except Roosevelt himself. Like McKinley, he was annoyed whenever guards or troops were deployed within range of his view. Once again it was George Courtelyou's task to convince the president to acknowledge the potential danger that existed in any assembled crowd.[8] On October 4, 1901, Courtelyou convened a conference on presidential security at the White

House.[9] Those attending were Mr. W. H. Moran of the Secret Service, Major Richard Sylvester, superintendent of the District of Columbia police, and Mr. W. E. Cochran, post office chief inspector. Surprisingly, on the morning the conference began, President Roosevelt formally approved the planned discussions and authorized Courtelyou to tell all assembled that they had the president's blessing to "go ahead and do whatever you think best in this direction." It was a major concession on Roosevelt's part, and Courtelyou intended to make the most of the president's unexpected charge to those assembled.

The group formulated a coordinated security plan that each of the participating services could support. Mr. Cochran agreed to establish a systematic review of all letters of aggressive intent sent to the president, to record their geographic origin, and to make that information available to personnel in the other two agencies so they might take these threats into account when planning security for the president's frequent journeys. Major Sylvester defined the parameters to be used by the mounted guards who would accompany Roosevelt everywhere he went in the Capital. Mr. Moran noted that the Secret Service's mandate for protecting the president still lacked congressional approval. Moreover, the existing appropriations for the Secret Service would not cover the scale of security that Courtelyou had in mind.

When Congress had convened after the death of McKinley, no less than seventeen proposals for expanded presidential protection were introduced. The sticking point for Congress was a need to establish a federal police force. This step had been avoided for more than a century, and there were many who still resisted the move, even in the wake of a third presidential assassination in thirty-six years. Furthermore, the legislators' attention was divided. They had a great many bills to consider on related questions (e.g., whether assaulting a president should be made a federal offense). The debate over expanded presidential protection would persist for five more years. Meanwhile, the Secret Service continued to do its best on an ad hoc basis. All presidential protective activities were recorded under the counterfeiting control budget. Director Wilkie soon found himself under congressional investigation for this deception, but Roosevelt came to his defense and forced a decision regarding the expansion of Secret Service responsibilities.

The president eventually became outspoken in his acknowledgement of the benefits of Secret Service protection, although not for the agents' ability to deter prospective assassins. "The Secret Service men are a very small but necessary thorn in the flesh," Roosevelt asserted, noting that "...of course they would not be the least use in preventing any assault on my life...but it is only the Secret Service men who render life endurable, as you would realize if you saw the procession of carriages that pass through here, the procession of people on foot who try to get into the place, not to speak of the multitude of cranks and others who are stopped in the village [of Washington]."

During the closing days of 1906, Congress finally voted to enact legislation assuring the Secret Service's protective function. The law, which left the agency within the Department of the Treasury, assigned the Secret Service full responsibility for guarding all future presidents. Congress appropriated the necessary funding early in 1907. When Theodore Roosevelt visited Panama's Canal Zone in 1908 (the first sitting president to officially travel beyond the nation's borders), the Secret Service accepted its first international responsibility. The agents' first duties guarding a president-elect began later that same year, following the election of William Howard Taft. In 1917, the agency's protective function was extended to include the president's immediate family, and a new statute made it a federal offense to use the mail to threaten a president. Not until 1965 was assault on or assassination of a president declared a federal crime.[10]

* * * * *

If that glorious day prior to McKinley's mortal injury was Buffalo's finest, then the closing days of the Exposition represent some of its worst times. The mood of the city throughout the rest of September and October remained as somber as it had been on the dark, rain-filled day of President McKinley's funeral. Nothing that Mr. Milburn and his executive committee could conjure or attempt proved sufficient to rekindle interest in the Exposition's many exciting technical displays or midway attractions. The attendance record had been broken on President's Day, but the crowds never again came close to that achievement. During the week leading to McKinley's arrival, 168,000 paid admissions were recorded. Thereafter, weekly attendance rarely exceeded 100,000. Concessionaires and exhibitors complained bitterly throughout the week of McKinley's apparent recovery that the public had abandoned "The Pan." They prayed it was only a brief pause, perhaps based on respect for the ailing president and his family. When they realized that death would be the final outcome, few believed that the crowds would ever return. When the Pan-American Exposition closed its gates for the last time in November, paid admissions totaled 5,306,859. Chicago's 1893 Columbian Exposition had attracted 21,477,712 paid visitors, in a year that was otherwise financially disastrous for the nation.[11]

One macabre attraction drew thousands before the Exposition closed. The executive committee had planned to return the Temple of Music's Grand Hall to its prior configuration and resume the scheduled concerts. It soon became clear, however, that after Czolgosz's attack, a majority of visitors were demanding to view the site where the president had fallen and where a nation's sadness had begun. Photo postcards of McKinley and of the Temple of Music were selling as fast as they could be printed. Not knowing how much longer any of the other exhibits would capture public attention, management decided to displace scheduled events, maintain the aisles fashioned for the president's reception, and preserve Grand Marshal Babcock's makeshift backdrop. During the Exposition's closing weeks, many thousands walked the path the assassin had taken, pausing a moment at the fateful site. Some even convinced themselves that they could see bloody outlines of the president's body on the floor. Few understood that the only presidential blood spilled in the Temple of Music had been on McKinley's fingertips and clothing. Whether or not they were observing bloodstains that resulted from George Foster's punishing blow to the assassin's nose is not recorded.

Director-General William Buchanan, desperate for any respectable scheme to bring more visitors to the Exposition grounds during its final days, realized that there had never been

a "Buffalo Day," certainly a fitting theme for the officially designated closing day, November 1st. With cooperation from city officials, the event might possibly draw another record-breaking crowd,
Buchanan thought. Unfortunately, he encountered nothing but
resistance, even from Mayor Diehl, whose enthusiastic support of
the Exposition's early development had helped make the undertaking possible. The mayor refused to release city employees from their
jobs so they might attend the planned closing events. Local busi-
nessmen also were cool to the idea of releasing their employees,
even for a half-day "Pan" holiday. Buffalo Day thus began as a pre-
destined failure. It would end in chaos.

As soon as the gates were opened on the first day of
November, those admitted seemed to promptly go mad. Visitors
were barely through the turnstiles before they began attacking
the buildings' surfaces, ripping long strings of electric lights from
their attachments to the still-pliable exterior plaster. Throughout
the Exposition, light bulbs smashed to the ground and windows
shattered. The crunching sound made as hundreds of shod feet
walked over broken glass reverberated through every concourse.
Many of the cafes and restaurants had already been shut down;
these abandoned enterprises were destroyed by the unruly
crowd; the few establishments still open, trying to eke out some
final profit, generally were spared. Severely outnumbered, the
police proved ineffective. Chaos reigned, and by the end of the
day, Buffalo's once-beautiful "Rainbow City" lay in ruins.[12]

Several days later, John Milburn issued public notice that the
Pan-American Exposition had sustained a financial loss exceed-
ing $6 million. This, he added, would mean default on payment
of nearly $3.5 million in outstanding bonds. Nevertheless,
Milburn laced his announcement with superlatives, describing
the event as a "masterpiece," the city of Buffalo's "chosen show-
case!" "The Pan" had in fact displayed its marvels and magnifi-
cence to many thousands of delighted viewers. Yet, from hesitant
beginning to chaotic finale, no one could have anticipated what
people would forever recall of Buffalo's grand spectacle. In time,
historians would argue that the Pan-American Exposition and
the assassination of President McKinley stood as a metaphor for
both the rise and the fall of Buffalo, New York.

Exposition president Milburn and other members of the executive committee later traveled to Washington in an effort to persuade Congress, hopefully with President Roosevelt's support, to appropriate funds for debt relief to the city. They succeeded in part and managed to avoid bankruptcy. Nevertheless, thousands of local investors were never reimbursed for their losses. As for John Milburn, he set to putting both Buffalo and its Exposition behind him. He and his family moved to New York City, where he had accepted a partnership in a law firm. Milburn continued to live there for the rest of his life. The family's home on Delaware Avenue was later sold to the Catholic Diocese of Buffalo and eventually was torn down to make way for a parking lot.

* * * * *

Compensation for the late president's medical care was brought to the public's attention again on February 13, 1902, when the *Medina Tribune* revealed that physicians' claims were in excess of $40,000. Subsequent rumors placed charges in the vicinity of $100,000. On March 19th, the *Buffalo Courier* announced that McKinley's medical bills, mortician fees, telegraphy, and other miscellaneous charges, amounted to $50,000. Congress reached its decision on June 26, 1902. Any remaining conviction that the family should assume this financial obligation had evaporated. The government accepted full responsibility for all charges. The breakdown of payments varied according to the newspapers reporting them. All cited a payment of $10,000 to Mann. Park's fee was variously reported as $2,500 or $5,000, Mynter's as $5,000 or $6,000. Wasdin, as a government employee, received no fee for administering the anesthetic. The physicians brought in as consultants after the surgery—McBurney, Stockton, Janeway, and Johnson—received $2,500 each. Parmenter, although a participant at surgery, also received $2,500. Gaylord, the pathologist, was paid $1,000 for his autopsy examination. Each of the nurses in attendance was paid $100.

Although McKinley's doctors never experienced the ignominy that Garfield's physicians had suffered, the lines remained drawn, especially within the medical community, regarding presumed errors and whether or not Roswell Park could have saved the president's life. Evidence of strong convictions can be found to this day among descendents of the Mann

Treasury Department,

Office of the Secretary,

Washington, D. C., July 31, 1902.

Miss M. Elizabeth Dorchester,

    138 Mariner Street,

        Buffalo, New York.

Madam:

    Congress has provided for expenses of the last illness and death of President McKinley in the deficiency act approved July 1, 1902, as follows:

        To enable the Secretary of the Treasury to pay the unpaid expenses incurred on account of the last illness and death of President McKinley, including compensation of physicians, forty-five thousand dollars, or so much thereof as may be necessary: Provided, That the Secretary shall pay only such expenses and services as he shall determine are just and reasonable and were necessary. All accounts shall be presented to him within two months from the date of the approval of this Act, and no payment shall be made to any officer or employee of the Government for personal or professional services.

    As all accounts, under the law, shall be presented to the Secretary of the Treasury within two months from July 1, 1902, you are respectfully requested to present your account without delay in the form of letter herewith enclosed for not exceeding $100.00 , which sum, as this Department has been advised, covers the amount of your bill.

        Respectfully,

                Secretary.

Letter accompanying payment to each nurse.

and Park families, knowledgeable surgeons in Buffalo, and historians of the McKinley era. When all positions are taken collectively, the prevailing opinion remains that the surgery was botched. Modern historical evaluations of the events contain as much or more criticism than the opinions offered in 1901.

Dr. Park withheld for a dozen years all criticism of the surgical decisions made by his colleagues on McKinley's behalf. He and Dr. Mann maintained a mutual respect and worked together closely to assure a high standard of surgical teaching at the medical school and at Buffalo General Hospital.[13] Each month, they conducted (along with other surgeons in the community) an evening meeting to discuss controversies and new ideas, among them adoption of both antiseptic and aseptic techniques[14] to prevent post-operative infection. The recorded minutes of these meetings do not reveal any public discussion of McKinley's care.[15]

Roswell Park's surgical publications following the death of McKinley document the evolution of his own thinking about the proper treatment of abdominal gunshot wounds. In one paper, he described the case of a woman who had attempted suicide by shooting herself in the abdomen. Immediate surgical exploration revealed stomach perforations and damage to her pancreas. Following suture repair of the stomach, a drain was placed prior to closing the incision. The patient recovered without complication or delay. Even without mentioning McKinley, Park's implication was clear: success following pancreatic injuries requires the placement of drains in the abdomen. Meanwhile, national recognition of Roswell Park's contributions to surgery, particularly in the field of cancer, continued to gather momentum.[16]

In 1908, Dr. Mann joined Dr. Charles Stockton and prominent Buffalo architect George Cary in conducting a dinner to celebrate Roswell Park's twenty-five years as the University of Buffalo's Professor of Surgery. Joining members of the local surgical community at the Iroquois Hotel were a number of renowned surgeons from other cities, including Dr. Frank Billings from Chicago, Dr. George Crile from Cleveland, and Dr. Frederick Dennis from New York City. Dr. William Mayo, in sending his regrets, added these words of praise: "I consider that the profession owes a debt as great to Dr. Park as to any living American Surgeon."

Many other tributes were expressed throughout the evening but none more engaging than those offered by Matthew Mann. He spoke first about Park's prolific writings and then closed with a story that amused everyone present: "Dr. Park has spread the fame of Buffalo all over the world. Out on the lake shore I am the happy (or unhappy, as the case may be viewed) possessor of a farm, where I raise eggs which are worth their weight in gold, and milk which costs about as much as champagne...it is good milk I can assure you. (Laughter.) Not very far from this farm there is a little stream that runs into Lake Erie; it is called Eighteen-Mile Creek. It is a famous point for geologists. They go there because they can find many rare specimens of rocks; in fact, it is known to geologists everywhere. There was once a famous German geologist, and somebody mentioned the fact that he was going to America and would probably stop in Buffalo. He asked the geologist if he knew anything about Buffalo. Oh yes came the reply. It is near Eighteen-Mile Creek. (Laughter.) Well, I think there are a good many surgeons throughout the world who do not know Buffalo as a beautiful city, as a city of handsome residences and beautiful streets lined by noble trees, as a city which is almost the equal of London and Liverpool and Chicago, as a city which has fifteen lines of railroad entering it. They do not know anything about all that, but they do know it as the city which is the home of the distinguished surgeon, Dr. Roswell Park." (Applause.)

Dr. Mann continued his service as dean until 1910, at which time he also retired as chair of the Department of Obstetrics and Gynecology. He continued his busy private practice for several more years. He and Mrs. Mann celebrated their golden wedding anniversary in 1919. Matthew Mann died of heart disease in 1921.

Roswell Park dictated his recollection of the events surrounding McKinley's tragic visit to Buffalo, then put the transcription away for several years. Just prior to his death in 1914, he edited the draft, deleting most references to his colleagues. *Reminiscences of McKinley Week* was published in 1914, according to his specification, in a commemorative volume of his writings. It represented the first public record of his personal thoughts about the days of uncertainty that ended in tragedy. It was a polite document, one whose tone was filled with respect and gratitude for the efforts made by his colleagues. He did not over-play his personal role. Park explained his preparations for assuring adequate treatment of accidents at the Exposition. He was clearly proud of his staff and the care they had rendered to the more than 5,000 visitors who had come to the Pan-American Hospital with a variety of problems during that busy summer. He related the predicament of finding ready transportation back to Buffalo after the message regarding McKinley reached him, explaining that this was what had kept him from attending the president immediately following the assault. He outlined in con-siderable detail the preparations he had made for transferring the president to the Milburn residence, and for his patient's aftercare at that location. He closed with a tribute to McKinley, lauding the president's fortitude and forbearance throughout the difficult week that ended with his death.[17]

Park wrote very little about the operation itself, or so it appeared to readers in 1914. But in 1945, his son, historian Julian Park, made the original draft available to the Buffalo Historical Society. A careful reading of that document reveals an angry and perhaps resentful writer. Park was unsparing in his rebuke of Dr. Edgar Lee who, as the writer explained, "...happened to be on the grounds as a visitor; he had been medical director of one of the western expositions, and was on his way to New York where he proposed to, and did, relocate. He manifested a tremendous amount of nerve in almost forcing his way into the operating room, talking with the president, and virtually offering to do the operation himself. In spite of our injunction to reticence and secrecy, he did a lot of talking the following day in New York." Park added that it had been a difficult matter to remove Lee from the scene, making him more hindrance than help.

References to Dr. Mann were measured carefully, as he did when he commented on the behavior of other surgical colleagues. Nevertheless, he expressed serious concerns about the decision to operate so quickly, about Mann's relative inexperience with gun-shot wounds of any kind, and about the choice of the Pan-American Hospital for surgery instead of the excellent facilities at Buffalo General Hospital. Finally, he disagreed with Mann's decision not to use abdominal drains, omitting any mention that his own opinion on this issue had been sought at the time.

Before examining each of these points, it is necessary to consider what none of McKinley's surgeons knew in 1901, and what surgeons everywhere would not understand for several more decades. Although physicians in that day realized that the circulating blood volume was finite, they did not yet understand that maintenance of other body fluids was equally critical for life. They knew that any significant decrease in the amount of blood in circulation would result in shock and eventually death, if left untreated. They did not comprehend that another kind of shock could develop, even in the absence of blood loss, when other body fluid losses went without replacement.

The body's composition is predominately water. The average male is 60 percent water, an obese man like McKinley somewhat less. Body water is a solvent for vital minerals and salts, and is distributed throughout the body in two well-defined fluid compartments. The intracellular fluid resides in spaces inside each of the body's billions of living cells. The extracellular fluid resides in the blood plasma and in the multitude of tiny spaces that exist between all living cells (interstitial fluid). The contents of the body's fluid compartments are in a constant state of motion. The movement of plasma is rapid because of the pumping action of the heart. The interstitial fluid moves very slowly, in a continuous ebb and flow. Serious injury can radically disrupt the balance of bodily fluids by prompting the development of an abnormal fluid into which extracellular water is drawn. If such a space swells as a result of severe inflammation, ever larger volumes of fluid space may be diverted from their normal locations. The steadily accelerating imbalance in bodily fluids results in shock and if untreated, proves fatal.

In 1901, strict maintenance of the normal life-sustaining body fluid compartments was not the therapeutic obligation it is today. Physicians at that time did know that significant blood loss must be replaced and that nutrition must be sustained. However, the seriousness of the fluid deficit incurred by a patient who could not take fluids by mouth for several days was not yet recognized. Likewise, there was little awareness that a blast injury produced by a speeding bullet could result in swelling of the organs inside the abdomen, with accumulation of fluid drawn from other fluid spaces, especially away from the circulating blood. It was this gradual but deadly process of fluid diversion that the president's body was undergoing during the week that he seemed to be recovering.[18]

McKinley had sustained a serious blast injury when a decelerating bullet discharged its force in the vicinity of his pancreas and surrounding organs. This led to severe internal inflammation and the accumulation of several liters of body fluid within the resulting abdominal cavity. That fluid was drawn from the interstitial space and from the circulating blood plasma. Because all of the body's fluid spaces are in dynamic balance with each other, the circulating blood volume contracted as the abnormal fluid space expanded. Thus, without any visible loss of blood, and entirely independent of the circumstances of his operation, McKinley's condition steadily worsened. The president's heart worked harder and faster to compensate for a diminishing blood volume. Very gradually, he entered a state of shock even though he still appeared well to most observers.

Two important measures of body function were not in use at that time: blood pressure and the concentration of red cells in the blood (hematocrit). Had these indicators been available, McKinley's surgeons would have noted a steady decline in the blood pressure and a reciprocal rise in the hematocrit as plasma was lost from the blood. Instead, they had only urine output and pulse rate to use as gauges. Throughout the days of McKinley's apparent recovery, his urine output was by today's standards abnormally low, a clear indication to modern observers that the kidneys were not receiving enough blood flow. The president's pulse became more rapid as the week passed because his heart was pumping more vigorously to compensate for lost plasma. In summary, McKinley's gradual development of circulatory shock was of a nature not understood in 1901.

To condemn McKinley's physicians for these oversights unjustly imposes current knowledge and standards on bygone therapeutic practices. To avoid the fallacy of anachronism, we must examine the doctors' decisions in the context of what was understood in 1901.

When Roswell Park assessed the McKinley case (in his

unedited draft), he questioned the haste of the surgeons involved. But, unlike Mann and his assistants, Park had the advantage of hindsight: He already knew what his colleagues had yet to discover—that no active bleeding was found when the injury was investigated surgically. Furthermore, as all surgeons present at the Pan-American Hospital that afternoon were aware, the accepted standard of the day, based on the experience of Sims in the 1880's, called for prompt exploration of the injury site. Finally, Mann's decision was also influenced by the actions of the last surgical team to operate on a president with gunshot wounds. Most Americans still blamed Garfield's death on the indecisiveness of his surgeons. Given these parameters, it is clearly unfair to brand Mann and his colleagues as guilty of an error in judgment when they pressed forward with immediate surgery. Park was correct (retrospectively) when he wrote that time was on the surgeons' side. But would waiting have made any difference in the outcome? Unlikely, except, of course, for the fact that Roswell Park might then have been available to serve as McKinley's principal surgeon.

Next, again in the unedited version of his manuscript, Park called attention to Mann's inexperience: "I do not believe that Dr. Mann had ever done a gunshot case before," he wrote. Although he acknowledged that Mynter did have that experience, as did Parmenter, Park added that "...neither of them insisted upon a clean excision of the bullet track and the tissues immediately surrounding." Here too, though, he had the advantage of knowing that McKinley later developed a localized wound infection. That infection contributed very little to McKinley's downhill course following surgery, however.

Critics have pointed to an apparent disparity between Mann and Park regarding their attitudes about the prevention of infection. Mann is cast as an adherent of the "antiseptic (disinfectant) school," Park as a champion of the "aseptic (sterile) method." Actually, all surgeons of that era had passed through the antiseptic period, including both Mann and Park. Park was surely an advocate of asepsis, but there is no indication that Mann wasn't in sympathy with this new doctrine. By 1901, in fact, there was a coalescence of both doctrines that would progress in future decades to extraordinary control of the environment in operating rooms. It must also be remembered that unlike Garfield, who died of overwhelming septic complications, McKinley's demise was not the result of bacteria. The infection of his wound was superficial and constituted a secondary problem.

Park also noted in his reminiscence that as he entered the operating room, "...Dr. Mann was rapping on his assistant's knuckles with an instrument," presumably because Mynter was in his way. What this scene tells us is that Dr. Mynter was actively involved in the surgery, so Mann was certainly not floundering on his own. Even today, when circumstances lead two senior surgeons into helping one another, it is sometimes difficult for each to remember who is the surgeon and who is the assistant. Should Mann have deferred to Mynter instead of agreeing to serve as the president's surgeon? Park implied as much, based on comments later brought to his attention: "... not a few have not hesitated [sic] to express their unreserved opinions to the effect that it was simply a matter of jealousy rather than of urgent haste because of the President's symptoms. It was known that I was hurrying to the scene as rapidly as possible and would soon be there, but perhaps with these few words enough has been said on this score." Park eventually crossed out these passages more boldly than the rest before sending his manuscript to the publisher.

Park's dismissal of the Pan-American Hospital as wholly inadequate for major intra-abdominal surgery is hardly surprising. After all, he had designed the facility himself and knew that it was intended to meet the needs of Exposition visitors with common ailments. Transferring McKinley to the nearby Buffalo General Hospital would have provided the president access to state-of-the-art operating facilities. Certainly, Park's opinion in this regard is unassailable. However, as before, the issue must be considered in historical context. When Mann later recalled the operation he had performed, he was very clear about the problems he and his team faced, specifically, poor lighting, an incomplete set of instruments, and difficulty achieving sufficient retraction to see what they were doing. Yet, the surgeons did achieve their goals. By today's standards, the decision to undertake abdominal surgery in a facility designed to handle only minor emergencies seems foolhardy. However, in 1901, the advantages of conducting surgery in bone fide medical facilities were less widely agreed upon. Hospitals were places where serious infection was the rule, not the exception. The kind of abdominal operations that Dr. Mann performed on the uterus and the ovaries were most often done in private residences because patients resisted having operations in hospitals. Surgeons therefore carried their surgical instruments with them, boiled them prior to use, washed them afterward, and then carried them to the next operation. Patients were also expected to recover from surgery in the home; there was nothing unusual about President McKinley being taken to the Milburn residence for this purpose.

Whether or not an abdominal drain should have been used was a pivotal issue at the time, a technical omission that is still highlighted whenever Mann's surgical judgment is questioned. However, even Park apparently did not consider a drain of paramount importance in the McKinley case; he offered no opinion on its use when Mann asked him at the close of the operation. Contemporary surgeons reading about this issue might imagine the sort of drain in use today—plastic tubing attached to continuous suction device. In 1901, drains usually were long narrow rolls of gauze, one end left inside the wound, the other leading to an absorbent dressing; rubber drains were only slightly more effective. Neither type included a suction apparatus. In any event, the drain issue is probably moot because drains alone would not likely have been sufficient to prevent the shock and heart failure that precipitated McKinley's death.

The autopsy showed enough damage to the pancreas to warrant surgical removal of the injured pancreatic tissue, a recognized option nowadays, but not one that had even been attempted in that day. The use of a drain might have permitted escape of some toxic enzymes produced by the pancreas, but recovery still would have been uncertain because of the serious fluid imbalance that worsened even as New York consultant Charles McBurney was issuing his optimistic reports.

Dr. Park makes no criticism of the post-operative care. He was present; he participated in the decisions made each day. His standards were the standards of his colleagues. Unfortunately, those widely accepted routines included enemas of seemingly endless variety matched to every downturn in the patient's condition, and all based on a deep-seated concern that in the absence of these periodic purges, toxins would accumulate in the intestinal tract. Exaggerated concern for the perils of constipation and misplaced belief in the therapeutic advantage of enemas persisted well into the twentieth century. During McKinley's era, nearly every adverse outcome of abdominal surgery was mistakenly attributed to intestinal toxemia. Thus, all surgeons relied on a flushing of the lower intestines as an essential preventive measure. Regrettably, this practice was self-defeating. Enema fluid is not absorbed by the intestines. Instead, vigorous enemas further drain the body of critical fluids and minerals.

The general public added one more criticism to the list of errors attributed to the president's physicians. Aided by reporters who were quick to invoke judgment before examining the facts, many laymen believed that the missing bullet was the culprit, a foreign body that, left unattended, had stealthily eroded life itself. At the time, reporters questioned the doctors' decision not to use Mr. Edison's miraculous x-ray machine. Historians have since argued-erroneously-that McKinley's surgeons were reluctant to accept new methods that the public willingly embraced as modern. The real answer is that from the start, McKinley's surgeons did not believe much would be gained by retrieving the missing bullet. They were entirely correct in this assessment, and trauma surgeons today agree.[19]

Clearly, errors of both commission and omission characterize the medical treatment President McKinley received. But were the president's doctors to blame for his death? If McKinley's surgeons are judged according to the knowledge available to them at the time, I believe the answer is no. Dr. Mann assumed responsibility at a time of crisis because it was his nature to do so. He was known in his community as a decisive and extraordinarily deft surgeon. He called upon experienced assistants to help him. He chose the operating room that was immediately available to him rather than risk the patient's transfer to another facility. In these decisions, he enjoyed the unanimous agreement of all his colleagues at the scene. Illumination of the operative field did become a serious problem but ingenuity brought them through the operation with their goals met. The routine use of drains was not the accepted standard for surgeons, not yet even the established habit of Roswell Park. Recovery in a private home wasn't an unusual choice in 1901. Finally, all measures commonly used to assure survival following abdominal surgery, some of them now known to be ineffectual and even harmful, were applied by a group of consultants as talented as any available at the time. All who were involved conducted themselves with as much good judgment and skill as could be summoned in Buffalo or anywhere else at the time. President McKinley died when his heart failed, while in a state of shock caused by severe fluid imbalance that went unrecognized and therefore untreated. The notion that Roswell Park could have saved the president's life is fanciful, at best. All glory owed to Matthew Mann and his assistants was stolen by a fatal bullet. William McKinley's wound, in 1901, was a mortal one from the outset. Thus, no justification exists for sinister clouds to hang over Matthew Mann's or Roswell Park's surgical legacy. Any reconsideration of the McKinley tragedy should represent a celebration of medical and surgical progress during the past century, one that witnessed significant contributions from Buffalo's surgical community.

*****

No further speculation about Czolgosz's weapon or its unused cartridges was recorded until a symposium sponsored by the Roswell Park Cancer Institute was held on January 20, 2,000, at the Buffalo and Erie County Historical Society. Viewing the revolver and unspent ammunition (both displayed in a translucent case) prompted an audience member to ask why the gun was only fired twice. The assassin should have been able to empty his revolver within two seconds. Although it is impossible to know for certain why Czolgosz stopped after his second shot, one possibility is that the exposed hammer became entangled in the handkerchief he had used to conceal the weapon.

Another question concerned the bullet that bounced off the president's breastbone. Why had it not entered the chest cavity? A .32 caliber bullet fired from a 1901 Iver Johnson revolver could develop a velocity of 700 ft./sec and a muzzle force of 100 foot-pounds.[20] In order to determine whether any of the ammunition held short gunpowder loads, the three unexploded cartridges were taken to a University at Buffalo School of Medicine laboratory in May, 2000, and weighed on a highly sensitive scale.[21] One of the cartridges was found to be lighter than the other two, by a weight corresponding to the expected gunpowder charge (i.e., approximately nine grains of gunpowder), thus confirming that Czolgosz had purchased defective ammunition. These findings also support the theory that one of the two cartridges fired was short its load, as first proposed in 1901 by a Buffalo police officer.[22]

Any of a number of hypothetical alterations, ranging from changes in the president's itinerary to a different trajectory for the fatal bullet, might have changed the course of history. Perhaps the more interesting counterfactual exercise, however, is to consider how different our nation's history would have been if McKinley had survived his assailant's attack. As the 1904 election approached, the president's sustained popularity and a continuing economic recovery might have led to intense pressure from Republican Party leaders for an unprecedented but Constitutionally permissible third term of office.[8] Taking it one step further, how would Mark Hanna's disregard for "that damned cowboy" and the president's ambivalence regarding his vice president have influenced Roosevelt's fate? Had he been eliminated from the next election ticket, Roosevelt's political career might have come to an abrupt halt. More likely, it would have forced him to seek another path to national leadership.

Instead, the nation experienced a dynamic new leader and one of the most remarkable periods of our history. The progressive era, led by a Republican administration, witnessed the enactment of legislation regulating the behavior of giant trusts and corporations, halted a long string of railroad mergers, passed laws guaranteeing rights for all workers and mandating compensation for workers injured on the job, established meat inspection and pure food statutes, and inaugurated the conservation of natural resources throughout the nation.

Roosevelt would not be immune to criticism, however, nor to attempted violence. Disappointed by the performance of his successor, William Howard Taft, Roosevelt decided to run for president once again. As he entered the open car that was to take him to a political rally in Milwaukee in 1912, he encountered William Shrank. This man, as he later explained, felt compelled to carry out the wishes of the ghost of William McKinley, who urged that his former vice president be shot. Thus, Shrank approached Roosevelt, drew a revolver, and fired one shot. The lone missile bore into the former president's breast pocket and fought its way through the copy of his speech and his metal spectacles case, both of which he had stuffed into that pocket for safekeeping. The bullet came to rest just beneath the surface of his skin. The remaining force of its impact fractured one rib. Since it was the fifty-page manuscript that first interrupted the bullet's progress, Roosevelt's longwinded style was credited with saving his life. Had the bullet penetrated his chest cavity, it would have likely produced a mortal injury.

Roosevelt's aides urged him to leave the scene at once, but to no avail. He refused to cancel his appearance. Now in pain, he entered the hall, bounded onto the stage, discarded the speech that had saved his life, grasped the podium, and shouted to his waiting audience, "I don't know whether you fully understand that I have just been shot! It takes more than that to kill a Bull Moose. The bullet is in me now...I cannot make a very long speech." He proceeded to ad-lib one of the longest and most dramatic addresses of his career. Later, he explained to an aide, "As I did not cough blood, I was pretty sure the wound was not a fatal one." When he felt that he had fully discharged his speaker's obligations, he allowed himself to be taken to a hospital. He remained for a week. Managing to have the final word, he told reporters, "I do not care a rap for being shot. It's a trade risk, which every prominent public man ought to accept as a matter of course."

Emma Goldman drifted from one location to another for nearly a decade after McKinley's death, eventually changing her name to E. G. Smith in order to secure housing and find employment. Temporarily abandoning her political crusade, she relied on prior training and worked as a nurse/midwife. In 1912, just as Roosevelt was beginning to campaign for his Bull Moose Party, Goldman took to the road, once again instigating civil unrest under her own banner. She was arrested in San Diego that year during a free speech demonstration, one of a series of events organized to force the police to pack municipal jails with activist citizens who were willing to stand on street corners and proclaim their political beliefs. Free speech, they insisted, was guaranteed by the Constitution. They were right.

Goldman's political ideology underwent considerable change following the Bolshevik revolution in 1917. She was quoted as observing that the recent events in Russia "...had brought the first ray of hope upon an otherwise hopeless world."[24] Public statements of this kind eventually brought her to the attention of U.S. Attorney General Mitchell Palmer. As our military forces were returning from World War I, widespread concern for the revolutionary events in Russia spawned the "Great Red Scare" in America. Mitchell Palmer was the nation's most ardent Communist hunter.[25] Mass arrests of radicals, referred to as the "Palmer raids," clearly trampled on civil liberties, but they also earned widespread public approval. A highly successful government career would be assured for a young lawyer named John Edgar Hoover who helped with Attorney General Palmer's campaign.[26]

In December, 1920, Emma Goldman and several of her fellow radicals were rounded up by federal agents, transported overnight to Boston, and ushered onto a ship bound for Russia. Among those suddenly finding themselves deported from the United States, she encountered her former mentor, Alexander Berkman.

The incident that prompted these arrests occurred late one night on a quiet residential street in Washington's Georgetown district. Palmer and his wife were awakened by a violent explosion that shattered windows on both sides of the street. Spread all over Palmer's lawn and the front yard of his neighbor, Franklin Delano Roosevelt, were bloody chunks of human flesh. It was immediately clear to everyone who witnessed the ghastly scene what had happened. Palmer's intended assassin had mishandled the fuse and detonated the bomb while he still held it in his hands!

The hapless bomber was most assuredly dead, but politically inspired violence remained alive as it still is today.

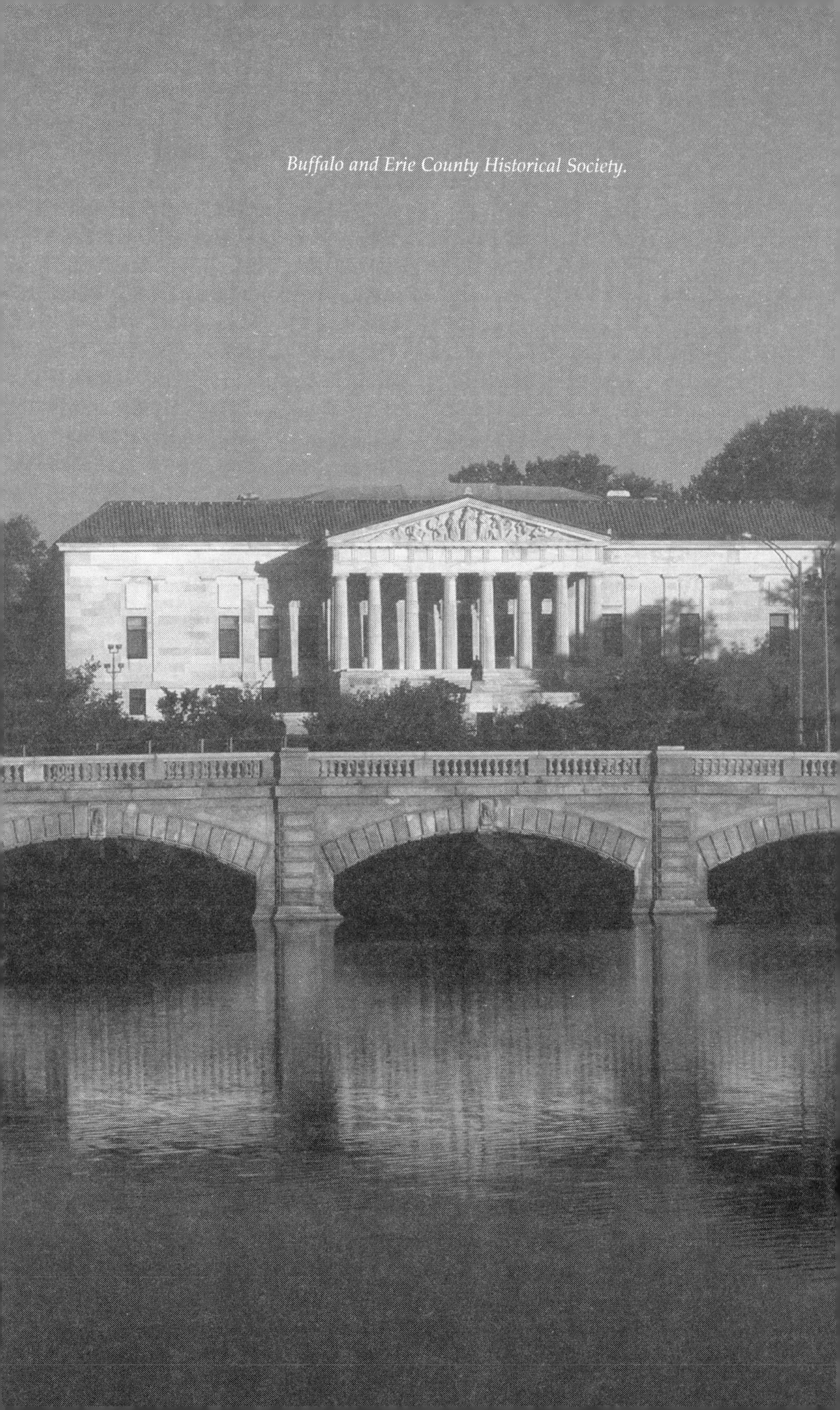

Buffalo and Erie County Historical Society.

EPILOGUE

The Same Injury Treated Today

On Wednesday, January 20, 2000, President William Clinton and Vice President Albert Gore arrived in Buffalo for a political rally.[1] Using the preparations made for that visit as a starting point, it is possible to envision how security would be handled today for an event in Buffalo similar to the one attended by William McKinley in 1901.[2] Similarly, by applying what we know as a result of a century of surgical progress, we can speculate about how contemporary doctors would treat a president who was the victim of a wound identical to the one that killed President McKinley.

Consider this scenario: a modern-day (but wholly imaginary) United States president with physical features and political experiences similar to those of McKinley (58 years old, significantly overweight at 200 lb. but otherwise seemingly healthy, and enjoying widespread popularity at a time of relative world peace) comes to Buffalo to attend a series of events. Among the scheduled engagements is an award ceremony and reception at the Buffalo and Erie County Historical Society, located in the former New York State Building originally built for Buffalo's historic Pan-American Exposition in 1901. The president is expected to arrive at 3:45 P.M. for a scheduled 4:00 P.M. event. In this hypothetical model, the nation's commitment to individual freedom remains intact, and the right to bear arms continues to be fiercely defended. Thus, the potential for an angry dissident taking hostile action against the president is present, but so too is the Secret Service. This agency's responsibilities in the imagined scenario are the same as it assumes in real-life today, namely to protect the president, vice president, president-elect, living past presidents, presidential candidates, their families, selected officials of the U.S. government, and leaders of foreign nations visiting the United States.

The Secret Service's work force of over 2,000 highly trained men and women is distributed across more than sixty field offices (including one in Buffalo) and a central headquarters in

Washington, D.C., three blocks from the White House. In the imagined scenario, the agency was informed of the president's planned visit well in advance (the accepted range of prior notice is two to eight weeks). A senior agent has been designated head of the lead advance team for the visit, and the Buffalo field office has been notified. Once told of the president's intentions, the agency's Protective Intelligence Section began its review of individuals in the western New York State region with a record of making threats to a president or to any other government official. The Secret Service maintains a computer database of more than 40,000 individuals or groups (including several currently active anarchist organizations[3]) with a record of writing or voicing aggressive intent toward any government official.

Routinely, individuals who are judged potentially capable of physical aggression are interrogated, and pertinent information about this subset of people is stored in the agency's database. Approximately 300 individuals in the nation are considered serious threats at all times; any such high-risk person who lives in the vicinity of the designated locale for a presidential visit is contacted in advance by a Secret Service agent or representative of the local police. But, a potential assassin like Leon Czolgosz, an individual who had never written a threatening letter or delivered an incendiary speech, would remain unknown to the Secret Service.

Within a few days of the scheduled visit, the Secret Service advance team visits Buffalo. A transportation officer at the Washington headquarters has already defined many of the travel parameters. For example, Buffalo Niagara International Airport has already been designated as the arrival point for Air Force One (the plane that carries the president is always designated as Air Force One, regardless of the type of aircraft used). The advance team, along with representatives of the local field office and in coordination with the Buffalo police department, establishes the president's actual route. The Erie County highway department is contacted to determine if there are any construction projects underway that might impede the president's travel.

Also contacted and notified of the upcoming visit is Buffalo's regional trauma center located at the Erie County Medical Center (ECMC). All designated drivers, who may be drawn from

Washington headquarters or from the Buffalo field office, will know their primary route, one or more alternate routes, and an emergency route to both the ECMC and the airport. [4]

The advance team visits the Historical Society, where the agents survey all doorways, including emergency exits, for approved entry and exit. Entrances not designated for use during the president's visit are secured. Specially trained dogs are brought in to search the entire building for explosives. When, as is the case in our hypothetical scenario, the designated site is a public building, inspections are scheduled a few days in advance, then repeated immediately prior to the event. After the final inspection, the building is sealed from further use; only individuals specifically cleared to be present for the event are allowed in. All duly authorized persons are asked to submit their social security numbers in advance to facilitate security checks.

The advance team also inquires about demonstrations involving national or local issues that might occur during the president's visit. As was true for the preservationists in 1901, all who champion a cause want the president to be aware of their point of view. The Secret Service may not restrict any citizen's Constitutional rights, including freedom of speech, so demonstrators are assigned space within view of the motorcade, yet not close enough to disturb the principal event or other bystanders. The primary goal is protection, not obstruction, of free expression. By tradition and policy, the Secret Service seeks to maintain itself as an apolitical agency of government.

One day prior to the event, local police erect traffic barriers and cordon off specific areas surrounding the Historical Society. The parking lot in front of the building is configured to allow the motorcade to enter in a wide circular sweep, pull up to the door, and park the vehicles aimed outward to ensure a prompt exit. A zone for television cameramen has been defined approximately fifty feet to the right of the front door. Behind the cameras and near the entrance to a Japanese garden overlooking Delaware Park Lake, another zone is roped off for approximately two hundred bystanders. On the morning of the event, the Secret Service team returns to the site and revises any of these pre-arrangements as they choose. All guests who are scheduled to be present in the building for the president's visit are asked to be in place one hour before his expected arrival. They will pass through metal detectors positioned at a side entrance. The Secret Service is present and observes each guest, politely asking a few with bulges in their suit jacket pockets to extract their small cameras and present them for inspection before entering.

The president and vice president do not often travel to the same events. When they do, they very rarely ride in the same airplane or even in the same automobile. Each has his own security detail. The same advance team, however, is likely to serve both the president and the vice president whenever they appear at the same location. For this hypothetical event in Buffalo, only the president is expected. The vice president is traveling in Vermont, just as Theodore Roosevelt was in 1901.

After the president's airplane touches down, it is isolated from other aircraft on the airport parking apron. Designated ground transportation is brought close to the aircraft. The president's White House protective detail accompanies him wherever he goes, and these individuals remain closest to him as he deplanes. Local agents will form a secondary protective ring. Once the motorcade is underway, the Secret Service activates an encrypted communications link that is independent of normal police radio channels—one that cannot be easily located or interrupted. Although the motorcade will likely take the Kensington and Scajaquada Expressways to the Elmwood Avenue exit before turning right into the entrance for the Historical Society, the lead driver may decide to vary that route, perhaps exiting at Delaware Avenue and approaching the building on Nottingham Terrace, a tree-lined avenue that passes the site where the 1901 Exposition's Triumphal Bridge once stood. Unlike in McKinley's day, when newspapers printed the president's precise route the day before his arrival,[5] today the chosen route is never made public. As the motorcade pulls into the Society's parking lot, the television cameras begin recording the event and reporters start their narratives. This is what is known in the media trade as the "body watch," meaning that the president's public movements are always covered, perhaps in anticipation that something might happen.

A twenty-eight year old man stands among the group of

bystanders who are located behind the bank of television cameras. He is considered a loner by family members and friends and is angry most of the time, though he cannot explain why. He is an avid reader of books about political history, especially revolution; recently, he has been reading about presidential assassinations. Today, he has a revolver hidden in his pants pocket. It is an Iver Johnson, .32 caliber, five-shot double-action revolver, a collector's item he found after searching numerous gun catalogs. Based on his historical reading, he had wanted this revolver to be nickel-plated, but he couldn't find one with that feature. The catalog price was $90.[6]

The president and his party are greeted at the door by William Siener, executive director of the Historical Society, by the mayor of Buffalo, and by several other local political leaders. All individuals near the president are known to the Secret Service, except for those in the small crowd standing behind the television cameras. This is the only place where a would-be assassin can get close enough to make a try.[7] Accordingly, Secret Service agents keep their eyes on this area at all times. Today, the unthinkable will happen.

The president has now fulfilled his responsibilities and leaves the auditorium. As he passes through the foyer, he greets more representatives of the local political leadership. He talks with local volunteers for his own political party, then glances out the window at a terrace overlooking Delaware Park Lake. Someone tells him the story of President William McKinley who, after hosting the first grand social event in this building back in 1901, sat on that terrace to enjoy a cigar from Cuba, recently liberated by the United States. Laughter greets the president's response that he wishes he could liberate the island again so that he too might enjoy a Cuban cigar. Then he turns to leave.

His protective detail takes him into the Society's boardroom where a final communications alert is dispatched to waiting police. Traffic is halted on Elmwood Avenue and on Nottingham Terrace. A motorcycle police escort is already in position; the Secret Service prefers that there be no stops until the motorcade reaches the next location on the itinerary. The president is escorted to the door; there, he bids his hosts farewell. Stepping outside, he descends the stairs and walks toward his waiting car. To the chagrin of his security detail, he suddenly pauses, turns to his left, and extends a wave to the television cameras. As he does so, he feels a sting on his breastbone, followed a fraction of a second later by the loud report of a gun, then the sound of another shot that he does not feel.

Instantly, Secret Service agents close ranks on either side of the president, fully prepared to take the next bullets when they come, but no more shots are heard. Another agent behind the president pushes him toward the waiting car. Meanwhile, an agent standing close to the television cameras spots a man who is crouched, with one arm extended, holding a revolver. The agent leaps upon the man and the two crash to the ground. Less than five seconds have passed since the first shot was heard.[8]

The president and two of his security detail are now inside the car, the door is closed, and a signal to move out is given. At the first hint of an attack, the Secret Service's priorities are to form a protective shield around the president and then remove him from the scene as quickly as possible. The motorcycle police escort turns right onto Nottingham Terrace, as specified in the original plan. But the president's driver makes his own decision and turns left onto Elmwood Avenue and right onto the Scajaqueda Expressway, heading east in the direction of both the Erie County Medical Center and the airport.[9] Inside the car, the fully conscious president feels inside his shirt and discovers blood on his fingertips. Seeing this evidence of injury, one of the agents informs the driver that they must proceed at once to ECMC. The limousine enters the passing lane and accelerates. The driving distance is 4.5 miles. Departing the expressway at Grider Street, the driver turns right and approaches the hospital's emergency entrance six minutes after departing from the Historical Society.

While in transit, special agents in the limousine inform the ECMC trauma center of their approach. Because they do not know the extent of injury, they indicate only that gunshots were heard. At the medical center, the internal paging system is used to send an alpha-numeric message to all members of the trauma team on duty. The message, "Pres arr 5 min GSW," indicates that the president will arrive soon and has likely sustained a gunshot wound. All on-duty trauma team members (7-10 people) reading that message immediately proceed to the receiving area.

Upon arrival, the president is transferred to a gurney and taken into a nearby room specially equipped for trauma resuscitation. Following an established protocol, nurse specialists insert an intravenous line in each of the president's arms and begin to infuse fluids rapidly. Two or three liters will be given in 5-10 minutes if the patient's blood pressure is declining, or over the next 20-30 minutes if it is not. This is more fluid volume in one half-hour than the recorded intake for President McKinley over a span of eight days.[10]

Simultaneously, trauma surgeons are evaluating the president's airway and breathing function, noting whether his respiration is adequate for maintaining normal oxygen levels. In this case, breathing is not a problem, but 100 percent oxygen will be administered anyway through a small plastic tube attached to each nostril. An automatic blood pressure cuff is placed on one of the president's arms for periodic measurement throughout his hospital stay. Electrocardiogram leads are attached to his chest for continuous monitoring of the heart's rhythm.

Surgeons are talking to the president, just as they did with McKinley, to determine his mental status and recollection of events, as well as the location and severity of the pain he is experiencing. Once all of the president's clothing has been removed, the physical examination begins, starting with careful scrutiny of the site(s) of injury. A bruise is noted on the skin overlying the breastbone. Internal injuries are assumed to exist once the surgeons locate the second bullet's entry wound in their patient's left upper abdominal quadrant. The president is turned on each side, and all body surfaces are checked for any additional injuries. Because he has eaten within the past four hours, the president's stomach must be emptied. A nasogastric tube is passed through his nose and into his stomach and suction is applied. All fluid removed from the stomach is observed for visible blood and then sent to the laboratory for analysis. Any evidence of recent bleeding necessarily quickens the decision for surgical intervention. A catheter is inserted into the bladder for continuous measurement of urine output. The presence of blood in the urine would indicate the likelihood of injury to the kidney and would also accelerate a decision for immediate surgery. X-ray technicians stand by, prepared to take x-rays of the president's chest and abdomen.

Approximately twenty minutes has passed since the president's arrival. If his vital signs (breathing, blood pressure, and pulse) are not stable, he will be transferred immediately to a nearby operating room and prepared for surgery. The operating room staff was notified to expect a surgical exploration as soon as the hospital was informed of a patient arriving with a gunshot wound. In this case, the president's vital signs are stable: his pulse, like President McKinley's first recorded pulse, is slightly elevated at 84, not unusual given all the recent excitement. His blood pressure is normal at 120/80 (blood pressure recordings were not available in 1901). No blood is visible in the aspirated stomach contents, or in the urine. The president's oxygen saturation is satisfactory at 100 percent.

While waiting for the x-rays to be developed, the surgical team steps aside to discuss their probable course of action. The president's personal physician, who has accompanied him on this trip and who followed him to ECMC in a separate Secret Service driven limousine, is present and participates in this discussion. Although the Secret Service has retrieved the weapon and is using a computerized national database to trace its serial number,[11] the surgeons do not yet know any details about the assailant's revolver. Their assumption must be that it was a contemporary weapon shooting a bullet of higher velocity and muzzle force than can be produced by a one-hundred-year-old revolver and cartridge. Because of the likelihood of major bleeding, especially in the upper abdomen, they decide on immediate surgery, meaning within 30 minutes of admission to the trauma center.

Meanwhile, the president's assailant has been physically separated from those who subdued him. The agent who first brought the man down protects him from any further attacks from angry citizens in the nearby crowd. The first priority now is to preserve the life and health of the assailant so he can be fully interrogated regarding possible accomplices or potential conspiracies against other government leaders. Like operative Gallagher in the Temple of Music, the apprehending Secret Service agent wants to get his prisoner away from the scene as quickly as possible. Local police oblige, assisting immediately with transportation to the nearest police station. The agent will remain with the assailant until relieved by the FBI.[12] Federal custody of the prisoner is mandatory; 1965 legislation made it a federal offense to assault a president with the intent to kill.

Within a few moments of the president's attack, the Secret Service notified the vice president.[13] In this hypothetical case, the vice president returns promptly to Washington. Any traveling members of the president's cabinet will likewise return to the Capital. No officials will come to Buffalo, as they did in 1901. Today, Washington is considered the place where the Secret Service can most easily assure the security of government officials.

Word of the shooting reaches the trading floor of the New York Stock Exchange shortly before its standard closing time. The Exchange is closed at once.[14] Throughout the ensuing night, the Secretary of the Treasury and the Chairman of the Federal Reserve will confer, making plans to announce support of the dollar in time for the opening of Asian markets. They are responding to the same concerns regarding financial panic that led J. Pierpont Morgan to reassure newspaper reporters of stability in the financial markets after he learned by telegram of the assault on McKinley.

Back at ECMC, the trauma team is studying the x-rays. The chest film is normal, and the abdominal view indicates a bullet lying deep within the abdominal region, behind the stomach, behind the pancreas, and close to the left kidney. Although it was never found, this is likely where President McKinley's fatal bullet lay, imbedded in the spinal muscles behind the pancreas and kidney. The x-ray findings do not change the plans for immediate surgery. This decision is explained to the president, in the presence of his personal physician. His reply, similar to McKinley's, is simply, "I am in your hands."

The anesthesiologist has completed her evaluation of the president, noting his excess body weight and his short neck. Anticipating difficulty inserting the breathing tube into her patient's trachea, she selects her equipment accordingly. Of greatest concern to the anesthesiologist is the fact that, like McKinley in 1901, the imaginary presidential victim finished eating lunch two-three hours earlier. This factor increases the risk of aspiration pneumonitis, a deadly complication that can follow the vomiting of gastric acids into the bronchial passages, sometimes leading to chemical destruction of lung tissue. Aspiration can occur during induction of anesthesia when the stomach is not completely empty; the gastric tube only partially removes this risk. Therefore, pressure is applied to the larynx to constrict the esophagus while the breathing tube is inserted via the mouth into the trachea.

The anesthetic agent will not be chloroform or ether; both were abandoned earlier in the twentieth century. Instead, one from the many available anesthetic agents, recently synthesized and introduced for their more rapid action (within a few seconds) and short-term residual effects, will be selected. Anticipating an incision and the possible discovery of internal bleeding, the anesthesiologist's assistant increases the rate of intravenous fluid infusion. Ten units of O-negative or type-specific blood are available, should they be needed.

With the president now anesthetized, a surgical technician preps the skin surface of both the chest and the abdomen. If major bleeding is encountered during any part of the abdominal exploration, the chest cavity may need to be opened to gain control of bleeding closer to the heart. A midline incision is made from the tip of the breastbone to well below the navel. This is more than double the length of McKinley's incision in 1901. The surgeon and his assistants are prepared to deal immediately with any bleeding, including gross hemorrhage revealed suddenly by release of pressure inside the abdomen during the incision. In this case, as with McKinley, no active bleeding is encountered. The bullet wound on the upper surface of the stomach is found immediately. Ragged edges are trimmed, and the hole is repaired with a double layer of sutures. The gastrocolic ligament, attaching the lower margin of the stomach to the large intestine, is divided horizontally for a distance of ten inches to give the surgeons a clear view of the rear wall of the stomach, the pancreas, and the kidney. A second bullet injury to the stomach, the anticipated exit wound, is encountered, and similarly repaired with sutures.

Careful observation of the pancreas reveals obvious destruction of approximately one-half of that organ. The pancreas can be likened to a fish fillet, both in dimension and texture. Its "tail" has been shattered by the shock of the bullet's penetration. The surgical team decides to remove the damaged portion of the pancreas, a common procedure today, but one not yet practiced in 1901. This step will add about forty-five minutes to the operation. A suction drain is placed within the wound, its tip near the bed of the removed pancreas. The drain is brought out through the skin of the president's left flank. A second and final exploration is made to be certain no other injuries have been overlooked. The bullet has not yet been found, but the operation is not prolonged in order to find it. Following irrigation of the abdominal cavity with several liters of salt solution, the incision is closed with heavy-duty sutures.[15]

The operation now completed, the president is taken to an intensive care unit where his recovery will be closely monitored. His vital signs, oxygen saturation, and blood chemistry levels will be measured at frequent intervals. Any fluid suctioned from the abdominal drain will be monitored for enzymes produced by the pancreas. Assuming that the enzyme levels are not excessive, the nasogastric tube will be removed in three to five days. The president will be out of bed and walking within twenty-four hours; he will continue to walk and move about periodically each day thereafter. He will receive his first nourishment by mouth in five to seven days. He is likely to be discharged from the hospital ten days after the surgery, with a probable return to his desk in six weeks, just as consulting surgeon Charles McBurney had (inaccurately) predicted for President McKinley.

How likely is it that our imaginary president would survive an abdominal gunshot injury like McKinley's in 2001? Very likely, and mainly because the omissions of 1901 would be avoided. Any modern reconsideration of the McKinley assassination represents a celebration of one hundred remarkable years of surgical progress.

APPENDIX I

Letters Threatening Safety of
President William McKinley

Letters received in Washington, D.C. indicating aggressive intent against the president, taken from the Papers of George Courtelyou, Library of Congress, Manuscript Division. Below are summaries of and direct quotes from these letters, along with my own comments.

1898: Approximately 200 letters received. Some threaten death if the sinking of the Maine is not avenged; others threaten the president for unjustified attacks on Spanish-held Cuba.

August 4, 1900: An undated letter written to W. McKinley in Italian, received at the executive mansion and translated by the Secret Service, indicates that an anarchist society meeting in Paterson, New Jersey has recently chosen by lot five of its members for the following assassinations:

> Gaetano Bresci: *King Humbert I of Italy*
> Giuseppe Pucci: *William, Emperor of Germany*
> Allesandro Pasquallini: *Emperor of Austria (unnamed)*
> Alfredo Pasquallini: *President Loubet of France*
> Arturo Giovanetti: *President of the United States*

The letter, unsigned, states that the writer is about to "take flight to South America to escape the vengeance of his companions for having quitted the society." He continues, "Arturo Giovanetti is awaiting his opportunity in Washington." In closing, the anonymous author warns the president to be on his guard.

Comment: On July 29, 1900, five days before this letter was received and translated, one of the five men, Gaetano Bresci, completed his assignment. It was the assassination of Humbert I that captured the interest of Leon Czolgosz.

August 8, 1900: Telegram from Courtelyou who is with the president in Canton, Ohio asking Secret Service Director, John

Wilkie to obtain translation of a message received in cipher from Benjamin Montgomery at the American Embassy in Paris. Translation reveals an intercepted message to the Italian Embassy in Washington from a Count Venosta. The message reads in part, "The man Natale Maresca, born at Piano di Sorrento, formerly a convict, sailed for the United States according to anonymous information, for the purpose of attempting President McKinley's life."

Comment: In a subsequent telegram to Cortelyou, Acting Secretary of State Alvey Adee indicated that Natale Maresca had been arrested upon arrival in New York.

August 14, 1900: Letter addressed to the Honorable John Hay, Secretary of State, Washington, D.C. from William S. Devery, Chief of Police, City of New York, Mulberry Street Station: "Dear Sir - I beg to forward to you herewith a copy of a report made to me by Captain George W. McKlusky of the Detective Bureau...It concerns chiefly the operations of certain anarchists without the jurisdiction of this Department...I leave it to your judgement whether to acquaint the representatives of the Italian Government."

Comment: The report documented in considerable detail the origins of an anarchist movement, beginning with the arrival of Italian lawyer/anarchist Pietro Gori in 1894. Paterson, New Jersey was selected as the site for headquarters, not only because of its working class population but also for the purpose of being less conspicuous outside of New York City. However, with the arrival of many more anarchist Italian immigrants together with additional recruitment in America, the size of the organization eventually drew close attention from local police and, as the report indicated, from New York City authorities as well. The Paterson anarchists were especially pleased to attract from Italy as their leader Enrico Malatesta, who had recently escaped from a prison in Tunisia (see Chapter 1). They would be even more proud of the achievement of their delegated assassin, Gaetano Bresci.

August 20, 1900: Translation of letter written in French received from G. Hartmann from Pruferning, Bavaria. The writer proposed the following method to avoid assassination: "History shows that most of the assassinations of rulers take place in carriages, that there is an instant of time during which a shot or blow or at worst a second one could be averted by means of a mechanism within the carriage composed of a zinc fan which would instantaneously cover the person upon a spring being touched, a mechanism which any carriage maker could contrive and which would not mar the elegance of the vehicle. Please take this into consideration, remembering that an ounce of prevention is worth a pound of cure!"

October 10, 1900: Letter to Director Wilkie from Vincenzo Padula of Gloversville, New York: "I should like to have a 5 minutes private conversation with your Excellency to communicate a new plot of anarchists who are coming from Italy to assassinate you, and two of whom I know. I have no money to travel. If you will furnish me with some immediately I will come and inform your Excellency what ought to be done. The matter must be secret. I enclose my photograph."

November 19, 1900: An apparent blackmail attempt by G. G. Schmidt of Philadelphia who claimed to possess intercepted private letters written at the Executive Mansion that reveal scandal: "...I ask the favor of you to make the Adams Express Company settle their old matter [with me]. They have robbed me of a fortune in four years time. If this is not settled [then I] will expose the scandal. If you decide to favor me [I] will return or destroy all mail."

Comment: Subsequently, Courtelyou forwarded the letter to Wilkie saying he had no information regarding Schmidt. Schmidt was not heard from again.

May 22, 1901: Unsigned letter sent to President McKinley from San Francisco:
"Dear Sir, I will murder you this week."

June 1,1901: Letter received from A. Munson in Madison, Ohio:

"I feel so strongly impressed that President McKinley or his wife or both will meet with bad luck or be the victim of an accident...I cannot get rid of it."

Comment: Following a Secret Service inquiry, Courtelyou was informed that "...the writer is not a spiritualist or astrologer or any sort of seer. Says he cannot explain the presentiment but out of pure friendship feels impelled to warn the President."

APPENDIX II

Secret Service Operatives' Reports

Each of the three Secret Service operatives filed a report to their boss, Secret Service Director John Wilkie. The reports, written on hotel stationery, were executed the evening of the shooting. Verbatim excerpts from these reports appear below.

Albert Gallagher: "I have the honor to submit the following, my report as Special Operative of the Chicago District, for Friday, September 6, 1901, written at Buffalo, N.Y. and completed at 6 o'clock p.m. on the 9th day of September, 1901. "At 8:30 a.m. the Presidential party left the residence of Mr. Milburn, 1168 Delaware Ave., Buffalo, N.Y. Custodian Foster, Specl. Oper. Ireland and myself accompanying them; arrived at the Terminal Station of the Pan-American grounds at 9 a.m. where party took train for Lewiston, N.Y. via N.Y.C.R.R."

George Foster: "The whole party took the gorge electric cars, for Niagara, N.Y. arriving there about 11-30 oclock, after a short drive around Niagara, and out to the middle of the Suspension Bridge, to view the Falls, the President, told me "to have them drive to the Hotel," which we did. Mrs. McKinley retired to her room. The President then reentered his carriage and drove around to all the main points of interest...At every stop I took full charge, making a hollow square, of the four outriders, who were regular army officers, from what I could see of their shoulder straps...I told the commanding officer, that I wanted him to instruct his men that they were to ride down any person who would make an effort to come near the President which order they carried out...As I saw the President's carriage slacking up to stop, I would jump off my carriage, and duck around the army officers horses, and get to the President's side in time to open the door of his carriage for him, being so prompt that he smiled several times...I never took no chances and would be so close up that I could lay my hand on him at any second."

Gallagher: "Whenever the President left his carriage, we were near him; the party returned to the International Hotel, Niagra [sic] N.Y. about 12:15 p.m. and after the President called on Mrs. McKinley he came out on the varanda[sic] of hotel, sit down and talked to friends...In a few minutes luncheon was served. Mrs. McKinley's lunch was served in her room."

Foster: "The President came out on the porch and lit a cigar. I went in and out of all the rooms that was any where close to the place where he was sitting to satisfy myself that no person could possibly get to him."

Gallagher: "Special Operative Ireland and myself joined the party and drove to the Electric Power house where the President made a tour of inspection, Custodian Foster, Special Operative and myself remaining at the door watching that no one but those with the President entered...At 2:45 left for Buffalo, N.Y. arrived at the Terminal Station, Pan-American grounds at 3:30 where the President and party, except Mrs. McKinley who was taken to the Milburn residence, were taken in carriages, to a building where wall paper, shoes and Mexican art was exhibited."

Foster: "At 4 oclock P.M. we arrived at the Temple of Music. We came through a packed crowd of people, enthusiastic, cheering, the President bowing to the right and left. I never saw him in such a pleasant mood, and looking so well."

Samuel Ireland: "The receiving line was formed at the center of the building just under the dome, at the angle of the aisle about eight or nine feet wide...Agents Foster, Gallagher, and I were stationed by Mr. Courtelyou with instructions to keep the line moving as fast as possible as it was a large crowd and the President was tired."

Foster: "The President nodded to the newspaper men, remarking, "Cool and nice in here, isn't it" and turning to me with, "Let them come" the fatal reception was on...I had got back in my place again, and had half turned to take a look at the President to see how he was standing it, when to my horror, I saw and at the same time heard two reports fired directly at the stomach of the President."

Gallagher "The reception had been on about 8 or 10 minutes when I heard two shots fired in rapid succession and standing in front of the President and close to him was a young fellow with a handkerchief in his hand concealing the revolver from which he had shot the President. The President stood erect and seemingly did not realize he had been shot; at almost the same instant Custodian Foster and Special Operative Ireland grabbed the assassin and they with some of the 73 Coast Artillery Corps went down on the floor. I sprang into the crowd, grabbed the assassin by the throat with my right hand and took from his right hand, by my left, the revolver and handkerchief, it being on as the shots had been fired through it; as the handkerchief was blazing my hand was slightly burned. Someone, I don't know who it was, got me by the throat and choked me and while they were choking me the revolver was taken from me but I held to the handkerchief and still have it in my possession properly marked for identification."

Foster: "I gave the order to let him [Czolgosz] stand up so we could search him. He had hardly got on his feet before he took a quick look back at the President. I saw how much that look meant to see if he had done his work well. This so enraged me that I struck him a blow between the eyes, several of the guards caught me but upon assuring them that I was myself again, they took their hands off me."

Ireland: "A Marine tried to put a sabre-bayonet into Czolgosz's body and a negro named James B. Parker tried to get at him to hit him; I got these men to desist as the President was looking at the melee; Gallagher was mistaken for an outsider by some Marines, and they were choking and pushing backward and Agent Foster and I tried to convince them who he was."

Foster: "I immediately went to the aid of the President. We unbuttoned his white vest, on which was a large black spot from the burnt powder, and on his shirt was a round small hole, the blood had started to oze through from the wound."

Gallagher: "I went to the ante room where I found the assassin on a bench with a number of people around him; his nose was bleeding and he seemed to be in a dazed condition. I raised his head and took a look at him – and felt I ought to kill him – I learned he gave the name of Fred Neiman. There was a terrible crowd gathering on outside of building threatening to lynch the villain. I told them before they took him out of the building they had better wash the blood off his face; finally a carriage arrived and the assassin was hurriedly put in it, with some city detective, but the crowd, or mob, made a rush for the carriage and as I was assisting in getting the assassin away, not wanting him mobbed, I was compelled to draw my gun to check the mob from the side of the carriage which I was protecting. The driver whipped his horses to a run and soon distanced the crowd..."

Foster: "The ambulance from the hospital on the Exposition grounds having arrived by this time, we placed the President on their stretcher and carried him with aid of the attendants from the hospital and placed him in the wagon. As they were about to drive away the President gave me one of the saddest looks, as much as to say, "Why don't you come with me." I jumped in over the tail gate of the wagon, went to his head and asked him "if I could do anything for him," and he told me he thought he would feel easier if he sat up so I took him under the arms and with a little assistance from him, I got him in a reclining position, and he told me he "felt a great deal better." I held him that way until we reached the hospital. I forgot to state that in the wagon on our way to the hospital, I noticed him feeling his shirt front, and he said "Foster what is this it feels like a bullet" I felt it very carefully and told him "it was a bullet." He said "that only leaves one." I have that bullet in my possession. It is one of them bull-headed 32 caliber."

Gallagher: "As I did not know what hospital the President had been taken to, I at once came to the Lenox Hotel, where I am stopping, and learned by phone, that he was at the Emergency Hospital in the Pan American Grounds. I immediately returned to the PanAmerican, paid 50 cent admission, not wanting to disclose my identity, went to the Emergency Hospital..."

Foster: "I took charge of his clothes and his jewelry, placed them in the head nurse's little office. When the President was removed I went with the ambulance until it was out of the Exposition grounds, then returned to the hospital and in company and in the presence of the head Doctor and the head nurse, I made an itemized list giving the doctor a duplicate..."

Ireland: "Secretary Courtelyou told me voluntarily that no blame could be attached to the Secret Service men, taking into consideration a number of other men in line had handkerchiefs with which they wiped perspiration; etc., etc., etc."

Gallagher: "The following are my charges for services rendered and expenses incurred this day:

Incidentals, admission to Pan American	.50
Car fare	.10
Services	5.00

Respectfully submitted,
Albert L. Gallagher, *Specl Operative*"

On September 17, 1901, Samuel Ireland wrote another letter to Director Wilkie, apologizing for an article that appeared in a Buffalo newspaper under the heading, Secret Service Guard Ireland Tells Story of Anarchist's Deed. Ireland's apology reads, in part:

"I have deferred writing this until it should reach you after today, not wishing to intrude it upon your mind at such a time.

Custodian Foster read me portions of two telegrams from you to him in which you censured me for being interviewed on the subject of the President's assassination..."

"I have no knowledge of what went out of Buffalo in the press about me, except what appeared in Rochester papers...hence I am in the dark as to exactly what accounts you refer to as being interviews with me...I submitted to no formal interview...When at the Hospital I was asked questions by Representative Alexander or Colonel Mills of West Point...and may have been overheard by reporters or these gentlemen may have quoted me to newspaper men. I made no comment on the shooting to anyone, however, except touching matters that were of common knowledge to all present..."

"Feeling as I do about the death of the president, and the horror under which I rest from my closeness to the assault upon him, I am not capable of feeling the anger I should feel at having been misinterpreted or misrepresented by unthinking friends...I can only lodge this explanation with you and ask your kindly credence."

Respectfully,
Samuel R. Ireland, *Special Operative*

APPENDIX III

Remarks on the Operation[1]

Matthew D. Mann M.D.

The difficulties of the operation were very great, owing partly to the want of retractors and to the failing light. The setting sun shone directly into the room, but not into the wound. The windows were low and covered with awnings. After Dr. Rixey aided us with a hand mirror, the light was better. Toward the end of the time a movable electric light[2] with reflector was put in use. The great difficulty was the great size of President McKinley's abdomen and the amount of fat present. This necessitated working at the bottom of a deep hole, especially when suturing the posterior wall of the stomach.

The operation was rendered possible and greatly facilitated by a good operating table and the other appliances of a hospital, and by the presence of many trained nurses and assistants. Still, the hospital was only equipped for minor emergency work, and had but a moderate supply of instruments. Unfortunately, when called I was not told what I was wanted for, and went to the exposition grounds entirely unprepared. Dr. Mynter had his large pocket case, the contents of which were of great use.

As has already been noted, further search for the bullet was rendered inadvisable by the President's condition. The autopsy shows that it could not have been found, and that the injuries inflicted by the bullet after it passed through the stomach, were of such a nature as to render impossible and unnecessary any further surgical procedure. A bullet after it ceases to move does little harm. We were often asked why, after the operation, we did not use the x-ray to find the bullet. There were several reasons for this. In the first place, there were, at no time, any signs that the bullet was doing harm. To have used the x-ray simply to have satisfied our curiosity would not have been warrantable, as it would have greatly disturbed and annoyed the patient, and would have subjected him also to a certain risk. Had there been signs of abscess-formation, then the rays could and would have been used.

My reason for not draining was that there was nothing to drain. There had been no bleeding nor oozing; there was nothing to make any discharge or secretion;[3] the parts were presumably free from infection, and were carefully washed with salt solution. As there was no peritonitis and the abdomen was found post mortem to be sterile,[4] we may safely conclude that no drainage could have been provided which would have accomplished anything. My experience teaches me never to drain unless there is a very decided indication for it, as a drain may do harm as well as good.[5]

In conclusion, I wish to thank all the gentlemen who so kindly and skillfully assisted me. They were all surgeons of large experience in abdominal surgery, and their aid and advice were most valuable. Especially I wish to acknowledge my great obligation to my associate, Dr. Mynter. Not only was he an assistant, but he was much more, and helped me greatly by his skill as a consultant, with his good judgment and extensive knowledge of abdominal work. Although called first, he waived his claim, and generously placed the case in my hands, willingly assuming his share of the responsibility.[6]

The anesthetic was most carefully administered by Dr. Wasdin, and the knowledge that he had charge of this very important duty relieved me of any anxiety on that score.

In the eventful week that followed the operation, Dr. Park and Dr. McBurney were towers of strength in helping to decide the many difficult questions which came up.

Dr. Rixey was in constant charge of the sick-room, aided later by Dr. Wasdin, who was detailed to this special duty.[7] Both were unremitting in their care, and faithful to the end.

Dr. Stockton helped us in the last three days with the highest skill and best judgment.

Never, I am sure, under like circumstances, was there a more harmonious or better-agreed band of consultants. That our best endeavors failed was, I believe, no fault of ours; but it must be an ever-living and keen regret to each one of us, that we were not allowed the privilege of saving so noble a man, so attractive a patient, and so useful a life.

APPENDIX IV

In 1901, Roswell Park dictated his recollections of the events following the attack on President McKinley; he then put the transcribed draft away for several years. Eventually, he revised the manuscript for publication in 1914. His text deletions appear in italics.

Reminiscenses of McKinley Week[1]

When the directors of the Pan American Exposition made me its medical director, I began my work with the conviction that it was quite necessary to have upon the grounds a sufficiently equipped hospital in which care could be given to any emergency cases that might occur within the Exposition limits, for I could not forget that in all previous affairs of the kind serious as well as minor accidents and illnesses had happened which called for immediate attention. The fire which occurred in Chicago during the World's Fair, and various happenings in St. Louis and elsewhere, had profoundly impressed me with this need. I had difficulty at first in impressing this conviction upon the officials, but succeeded first in equipping a temporary assignment of a few rooms in the main office building, and as the need became more apparent in obtaining an appropriation for the erection of a small but convenient structure near the Elmwood Avenue entrance. The lower floor of this building was given up to the usual hospital purposes, while the upper floor contained rooms for the superintendent (Miss Walters) and for half a dozen nurses. The latter were changed every month, thus during the six months of the Fair an opportunity for at least thirty trained nurses from various parts of the country, who were thus given an opportunity to act in their professional capacity as well as to see the Exposition. These assignments to a month's tour of duty for each were eagerly sought, and many more applications were received than could be granted. Thus it happened that both during the construction period, as well as during the progress of the fair, first aid was offered to a large number of individuals.

That the erection and the conduct of the Pan-American Exposition Hospital was amply justified was proven not only by the principal tragic event, which for the time being made Buffalo the centre of the world's interest, but by the fact that at the close of the Exposition some 5400 individuals received aid or comfort of some character as recorded by our books. A complete duplicate card system was put into effect, the cards giving a brief history of each case, while all accident cases were carefully observed and recorded, in order that should controversy arise and suits be instituted we should have a first hand account for our own protection. One set of cards was kept in the hospital, while the duplicates were transmitted daily to the

legal bureau for reference there, should occasion require.
During the construction period minor accidents were frequent,
and one or two fatalities occurred. During the progress of the
Exposition one of the government officials suffered very serious
injury from a fall from the cupola of the Government Building on
to the roof beneath. One or two apoplectic strokes also occurred
during the fair, while faintings, convulsions or epileptic seizures
and cases of heart failure were not infrequent.

It was the rule of the hospital that no patient should be kept
there over night; this rule was practically observed in all but
one or two cases which were too serious to be moved, or in a
few instances of illness occurring among the concessionary
inhabitants on the grounds; thus, late one night I had to operate upon a case of appendicitis on one of the latter who, being
a foreigner and not speaking English, was allowed to remain
throughout his convalescence where his people could have
easy access to him so that his wants would be made known.

It was to us a curious feature that the esquimos[2] wore their furs
even during our hot weather, while during the spring they
seemed to suffer from the cold more than did our own people
during the previous winter. They were unexpectedly susceptible;
at one time it was necessary to quarantine their village because
of measles; two or three cases being sent to the General Hospital,
while one young woman developed a rabid tubercular condition
of which she subsequently died. In fact among the various villages there was considerable sickness and a notable carelessness
obtained regarding all sanitary precautions. Dr. Nelson Wilson ,
who acted as medical inspector during the Fair, had much trouble, especially in the "Streets of Cairo," in forcing ordinary and
necessary precautions, and more than once it became necessary
for us to call in the highest official aid in compelling these people to observe our simple rules.

Dr. Kenerson was the deputy medical director, while three
recent University of Buffalo graduates constituted the house
staff, of whom two usually, and always one, were constantly on

duty. At first, I had great trouble with the reporters and news-paper men who sought details regarding our patients, thus endeavoring to give a publicity to their private affairs which savored too much of yellow journalism. From the outset it was made a positive rule that patients who sought relief should be afforded the same privacy that their own homes would furnish, and absolutely nothing was given out from the hospital regarding any individual or case.

But the event which surpassed all others in interest and importance was the murderous attempt on the life of President McKinley which occurred September 6th, 1901. The principal features of this tragedy are still fresh in the minds of the people, and have become matters of common history. It is regarding my own personal experiences and observations during the trying week which followed the assault in the Temple of Music that I wish to recall in these notes.

The President spent the forenoon and noontide of that eventful day in Niagara Falls, reaching Buffalo in the afternoon in time to make his promised appearance and address in the Temple of Music. Early that afternoon I had myself gone to Niagara Falls in order to operate upon a Mr. Ransom, of Ransomville, at the Memorial Hospital in that city. His was a case of malignant lymphoma of the neck, requiring careful dissection, and constituting a difficult and serious operation. Drs. Campbell and Chapin were assisting me. Just as I had completed the most serious part of the operation someone entered the operating room bearing a special message to me that the President had been shot, and that I was wanted upon the Pan-American grounds at once. As soon as I had recovered my equanimity I turned to Dr. Campbell, who knew all the railroad people at the station, and asked him to go at once and make the necessary arrangements for a special engine or train, saying that Dr. Chapin and I would finish the operation and be at the station by the time things could be ready.

Leaving the dressings to Dr. Chapin, I hurried to the railway station, reaching there shortly after Dr. Campbell's arrival. There I found everything in confusion, everybody upset by the sad news, and the station master, not only confused, but waiting for orders from Buffalo. It has always seemed to me that an engine might have been speedily detached or furnished for the emergency, but I was told that a Michigan Central through train would be along shortly, and that I should be sent up on that, while a special engine would be waiting at the Black Rock junction to take me round on the Belt Line and down upon the special tracks which had been laid into the Exposition grounds. Dr. Campbell requested that he might accompany me. We had to wait fifteen or twenty minutes for this train, but upon its arrival Dr. Campbell and I jumped upon the engine, and the train was hurried toward Buffalo. At the junction, we alighted and then mounted a special engine which was awaiting me, and lost no time in reaching the grounds. I had the engine stop at the Elmwood Avenue crossing, not far from the hospital, and we entered the grounds through the Elmwood Avenue entrance, scarcely a stone's throw from the hospital.[3] A large crowd surrounded the hospital, but were kept at a reasonable distance by the city and the Exposition police. Passing the lines I hurried into the little building, where I found Mr. Milburn, Mr. Buchanan, Mr. Charles Goodyear, and others, with Mr. Cortelyou, to whom I was at once introduced.

I was promptly informed that the operation upon the President was then in progress, with Dr. Matthew D. Mann in charge. Hastily preparing myself for admission to the operating room, I entered and found Dr. Mann at work assisted by Dr. Herman Mynter, John Parmenter and others. Very briefly the principal incidents were told me, and as Dr. Mann was then ready to close the wound my opinion was asked regarding the advisability of drainage. To this I could only reply that he knew the actual situation better than I, as well as what he had already done, and that I thought he was the best judge as to whether to drain the wound or not. After brief consultation it was decided to close the incision without drainage, a decision which subsequent events proved to be probably unfortunate.

Dr. P. M. Rixey, Surgeon General of the Navy,[4] who had been travel-
ling with the President and Mrs. McKinley as their family physician,
had arrived upon the scene but a very few minutes before I entered;
hearing my name mentioned, he at once came up to me and asked me
who it was doing the operation; I explained to him who Dr. Mann
was, and assured him regarding his experience and ability where-
upon Dr. Rixey said to me "well you are the only man here I know
anything about, and I want you to take charge of the case." I explained
to him the impossibility of assuming this charge at least at that
moment, but said the whole matter would be adjusted later.

A very few moments of observation in the operating room and
a little reflection convinced me that everybody's attention and
interest were centered upon the event of the moment and that
no thought nor care had been given by anyone present as to
what was to be done after the operation was concluded, and
that I could be of the greatest service by attending to the immediate future of the case. Accordingly I joined the group of gentlemen above mentioned and at once raised the question,
which I had already practically decided, that our little hospital
was no place for the President to remain in after leaving the
operating table. Mr. Milburn, however, settled the matter by
saying that he had promised the President that he should be
removed to the Milburn house as soon as possible, to which Mr.
Courtelyou added his assertion that his removal was to be
effected in the speediest and best possible manner.

At once I turned to Miss Walters and directed her to detail the
two nurses of the six then on duty who seemed best fitted for
the purpose, and have them prepare to go at once to Mr.
Milburn's house and have everything ready. I also directed her
to select a surgical bed, with ample supply of bedding, and also
everything that could be required, utensils, etc., in the care of
such a case. These were all quickly put in readiness, and were
sent down with the nurses in a police patrol wagon, in which
they reached Mr. Milburn's home and so efficiently made
everything ready in the room selected, a large, rear one con-

necting with an equally large front room, so that when we reached the house with the ambulance conveying the President, everything was ready down to the smallest detail for his reception. To illustrate the rapidity and the perfection of the arrangements, Mr. Huntley, of the General Electric Company had run in a special wire, and installed electric fans, with possibilities for anything else needed in this direction, and the fans were actually in operation by the time we reached the house.

Immediately after the conclusion of the operation I hastily gathered in my little office the men principally interested and closing the door spoke to the following effect – that through Mr. Cortelyou's direction we were practically under a sort of military discipline, if not martial law, and that first of all we were to follow directions laid down by him, first of which was absolute reticence so far as giving out any definite information was concerned; that whatever bulletins or information were given out were to be transmitted through him, and that the President was to be promptly removed to Mr. Milburn's house. To this I added that everything was ready for this transference both at the house and at the hospital, where the ambulance was in waiting. I furthermore added an injunction to the effect that we must by all means preserve a united appearance, and that we must avoid all the discussions and differences of opinion which had so conspicuously marked the conduct of President Garfield's case, and other cases which they might easily recall to mind.

At once, Dr. Mynter voiced a protest against the removal of the patient in which he was joined by, at least, one other (I do not remember which one). Thereupon began a discussion which I quickly checked by saying that it was useless since the order had been given and everything had been prepared for carrying it out. In spite of this Dr. Mynter protested but to no avail.

I then called for definite action as to who should be in charge of the case, and suggested that in as much as Dr. Rixey was there in his official capacity, and as the President's own Medical Advisor he should be allowed to select those whom he wished to serve with him. *This was agreed to but I do not think the agreement was exactly unanimous or hearty, but it seemed to me as the wisest and most politic thing to do. Immediately Dr. Rixey turned to me and said, "well Dr. Park you know I told you in the other room that I wanted you to take charge of this case," to which I replied that that was hardly fair to Dr. Mann, but that I was sure that both Dr. Mann and the others would cheerfully join in rendering all possible services in any desired way.* Dr. Rixey spoke to the effect that he did not know any of the men present and that it would be well for us to make our own selections, which all resulted in the selection of Dr. Mann, Dr. Mynter, Dr. Wasdin, and myself, it being thought that too many would constitute an unwieldy and unnecessarily large number. It was understood furthermore that the others would cheerfully join at any desired moment, and in this way, Dr. Stockton was subsequently added to the staff, and at the last, Dr. Cary as well. Dr. Kendall of the Army would have been invited to join had we known him, but at that time he had only only just arrived at Fort Porter and was not known to any of us. Others present at this conference were Drs. Van Peyma, Nelson, Wilson, John Parmenter and a Dr. Lee of St. Louis. *Regarding this Dr. Lee, he happened onto the grounds as a visitor; he had been medical director of one of the Western Expositions, and was on his way to New York where he proposed to and did locate. He manifested a tremendous amount of nerve in almost forcing his way into the operating room, talking with the President, and virtually offering to do the operation himself, it was appearing as though he tried to bring this about. He left for New York the same evening, and in spite of our injunction to reticense and secrecy, he did a lot of talking the following day in New York. In reality he was more hindrance than help although it was a somewhat difficult matter to eliminate him.*

The conference in my office was brief and at its conclusion those who had been doing the operating retired to dress themselves, while Dr. Wasdin and myself entered the ambulance in which the President had been already placed and we took up our leisurely passage toward the Milburn home. We were surrounded by military escort and city police, while just behind the ambulance rode two of the Government Secret Service officials on bicycles. The little procession passed no faster than men could easily walk, this partly because many of the escorts were on foot, and because, although the streets were smooth, we did not want to jostle the patient any more than was necessary. The passage of that small procession through the crowd and down Delaware Avenue was one of the most dramatic incidents I have ever witnessed. The Fair grounds were crowded that day, and it seemed as though the entire crowd had gathered to witness this event. Every man's hat was in his hands, and there were handkerchiefs at many eyes. I never saw a large crowd so quiet; not even the President's funeral was marked by so much evidence of profound sympathy. On arriving at the house the transfer of the patient from the ambulance to the bed was effected in the easiest possible manner, and before his recovery from the anesthetic. Everything had been placed in the most complete readiness by the nurses detailed from the Pan-American Hospital and within five minutes after the patient's arrival the room presented only the ordinary appearance of a sick room.

I cannot refrain[5] from mentioning a few reflections and incidents connected with the operation. Just as I entered the operating room the first incident that attracted my attention was Dr. Mann rapping Dr. Mynter's fingers with one of the instruments because said fingers were apparently in his way. This was but a sample of Dr. Mann's petulance when excited during an operation, nevertheless it was an unfortunate time at which to make such an exhibition of annoyance. Dr. Mann at once turned to me and complained of the absence of such needle holder and needles as he wished to use; leaving the room for an instant I went to my own portable instrument case and selected a needle holder and needles, returned with them after seeing that they were efficiently though hastily sterilized by use of the alcohol flame. This case of mine, by the way, contained everything which would have been needed for such an operation, but no one knew of its being at hand. It appeared that in their effort to find me Mr. Goodyear[6] had stopped at my house and my maid had given him the case which she knew I always took with me to operations; in this way it happened to be in my office at the hospital, and instantly available.

The operation concerned was a difficult one because there was a layer of, at least, two inches of fat between the skin and the abdominal muscles; The abdomen was large and protuberant, and the deeper portion of the bullet track would not have been easy to expose under the best of auspices, and while the operating room was practically sufficient for all ordinary purposes it must be acknowledged that both light and equipment were not all that could have been desired.

Had I been present at the time the President arrived at the hospital all this would have been changed or else I should have insisted upon his being taken to the General Hospital where the admirable facilities would have permitted easier work. Referring again for the moment to the operation itself, I have been assured by both Drs. Parmenter and Wilson that they saw drops of perspiration fall into the wound from Dr. Mynter's forehead. (Mynter by the way always perspired freely when doing any of this work in a warm room.) I do not recall caps or gauze were worn by anyone in the room. I mention this fact about the drops of perspiration because they might be supposed to have produced septic infection but nothing of this kind was shown at the autopsy, nor by the bacteriologic examinations made by Dr. Matzinger. Regarding the performance of the operation, and voicing some personal considerations I have never yet, except to two or three of my most intimate friends, permitted myself to say anything in the way of criticism either in the way of operative work, or with the haste with which they proceeded toward it. It was generally accepted however that undue haste was one of the features attending it, and that the gentlemen principally involved hurried into it in order to, at least, begin it before I could reach the scene, since had I been there it would certainly have fallen to my lot to be the principal operator. Not a few have not[sic] hesitated to express their unreserved opinions to the effect that it was simply a matter of jealousy rather than of urgent haste because of the President's symptoms. He, in fact, as the moments went by gained in strength, and his pulse steadily improved, and there was no reason to fear immediate collapse, nor to suspect serious, internal hemorrhage. It was known that I was hurrying to the scene as rapidly as possible and would soon be there, but perhaps with these few words enough has been said on this score.

I do not believe that Dr. Mann had ever done a gunshot case before, Dr. Mynter had, however, of course seen them and handled them, but neither of them insisted upon a clean excision of the bullet track and tissues immediately surrounding it through the whole thickness of the abdominal covering, i.e., some three inches, and this contused and minutely ragged tubular wound was closed with the rest of the incision which all seemed to me unfortunate. Regarding the question of drainage upon which I was hurriedly consulted as above mentioned it must be said neither of the principal surgeons had had much experience with such injuries in the upper abdomen, nor did they learn so far as I can recall, during the progress of the operation that the pancreas or even the kidney had been injured in any way. This case was an epoch-making one in more senses than one. At that time no one present had ever practiced posterior or through and through drainage of this area, and while the patient's body was so stout that to have made it in this case would have been difficult still, had it been done the patient's chances would have been improved rather than the reverse while nothing could have made the case any more serious or fatal then it proved to be. While therefore probably no one would, at that time, have drained posteriorly it certainly would have been wiser had an anterior drain been made. Whether this would have saved the patient or not I cannot say, but I have always regretted that it was not put into practice.

Only six or seven weeks later I had a case, at the General Hospital, of a similar kind in every respect as nearly as could be made out, of a woman who attempted suicide by firing a bullet into the upper abdomen. I found perforation of the stomach, and injury to the pancreas; at all events I closed the stomach perforation and made posterior as well as anterior drainage; this case recovered without an untoward symptom.

But to return to the events of that day and period; I still felt myself charged with making most of the arrangements, and in fact the others seemed almost paralyzed for the time being. The first question was of nursing. While the two nurses detailed from the hospital were to remain during the night, they were not there in any permanent capacity and were to be relieved the following morning. After conference with Dr. Mann I secured the services of Miss Mohan and Miss Connolly, who both reached the house the following morning at eight o'clock, thus relieving the Misses Shannon and Dorchester. I also felt that we ought to have male nurses and for obvious reasons, and for this purpose and in order to secure efficient men I appealed, through Mr. Cortelyou, for the assignment at duty of men from the hospital corps which was connected with the Government exhibit, where a detachment of hospital corpsmen formed a part. If I remember correctly, two men were promptly sent from this corps and one from the hospital at Fort Porter; at all events by midnight we had three efficient male nurses and had established for each of them a tour of duty of eight hours out of the twenty-four. A tent was put up for these men on a vacant lot across the street, where were also encamped a detail of soldiers from Fort Porter, who maintained around the house a strict military guard, no one being allowed to pass the lines except those whose duty required their presence within. The most efficient arrangements were everywhere made, and by nine o'clock that same evening the northwest corner of Delaware Avenue and Ferry Street was essentially a military post under martial law. The city police drew their lines a block distant in each direction, and all traffic and passage of vehicles was arrested, thus preventing any possible noise from such a source. Our own teams and those carrying various officials were alone permitted to drive up to the adjoining corner. The vacant lot at the northeast corner of Delaware Avenue and Ferry Street presented the appearance of a small camp, where were encamped not only soldiers compromising the guard, but the press representatives, who had a large tent to themselves. Into this were run special wires, while into the Milburn house passed another set of wires connecting directly both by telephone and telegraph with the White House, and a telegraph operator was on constant duty from early the first morning.

Government officials quickly gathered from various directions. The cabinet officials who were not guests of private citizens (as

Mr. Root, for instance, who was the guest of Mr. Sprague) were given rooms at the Buffalo Club, and here special Cabinet meetings were held; thus, for the time being, the Milburn house became the White House of the country, and this home, with the Buffalo Club, was for a week the capitol of the United States.

Arrangements were made with marvelous rapidity; by the following morning a corps of servants, including the chef, had been transferred from the private car in which the President was traveling, bringing with them White House service for both dining room and kitchen. These were later augmented by more help, and more service from the White House, as well as by other help secured from the city. In this way a complete corps of servants were ready to serve meals or refreshments at any hour of the day or night, and I remember that one day some one hundred and forty dinners were served. I remember also that at no time during the day or night did I fail to secure anything desired, solid or fluid. The Milburn house was on a lot next to the corner lot where was the handsome residence of Mr. William H. Glenny. His family were of course permitted to pass the lines at all times although his residence was partically within the limits of the military guard.

To return to the patient. He bore his illness and such pain as he suffered with beautiful, unflinching and Christian fortitude, and no more tractable or agreeable patient was ever in charge of his physicians. No harsh word of complaint against his assassin was ever heard to pass his lips. As the days went by, the peculiarity of his Christian character became ever more apparent, and was particularly noticeable at the last, up to the very moment of his lapsing into unconsciousness. Up to this time I had hardly ever believed that a man could be a good Christian and a good politician. His many public acts showed him to be the latter, while the evidence of his real Christian spirit were most impressive during his last days. His treatment of Mrs. McKinley during the many trying experiences which he had with her fortified a gentleness in his manly character, while the few remarks or expressions which escaped from him during his

last hours stamped him as essentially a Christian in the highest
and most lovable degree.

Comment: Roswell Park clearly reveals his angst in the italicized
passages (later edited out before publication). Surly, his convictions were strongly held. Readers of the document above can
form their own opinions about the validity of Park's criticisms
of Mann, and whether or not it was the surgery itself that
caused the president's death. Note that there is little mention of
the post-operative management. Why? Because so little was
known at the time about the care of a severely injured patient
following surgery.

✛

BIBLIOGRAPHY

I have relied predominately on primary sources, including the official medical reports, the autopsy and bacteriologic reports, and the personal recollections written at the time or soon after by Drs. Matthew D. Mann, John Parmenter, P. W. Van Peyma, N. W. Wilson, C. W. MacDonald, and, of course, Roswell Park. The published recollections of Emma Goldman, Louis Babcock, James Quackenbush, and Police Superintendent Bull were invaluable.

This historical interpretation of the McKinley assassination also has been assisted by the recent release of documentation held in the archives of the United States Secret Service, particularly the written reports of all three operatives present in the Temple of Music, George Foster, Samuel Ireland, and Albert Gallagher. Selected documents from the papers of William McKinley and of George Courtelyou (held at the Library of Congress) were also helpful.

Primary Sources

Babcock, Louis L. "The Assassination of President McKinley." *Niagara Frontier Miscellany* 34 (1947): 11-30. (Volume available at Buffalo and Erie County Historical Society [BECHS])

Buchanan, William, T. *Final Report, Pan-American Exposition,* 1901. (BECHS)
Bull, W. *Annual Report, Buffalo Police Department,* 1901. (BECHS)

Channing, W. "The Mental Status of Czolgosz, the Assassin of President McKinley." *American Journal of Insanity* 59 (1902): 233-278.

Courtelyou, George et al. "The Official Bulletins." *Buffalo Medical Journal* 57 (1901): 220-225.

Foster, George. Letters and telegrams. Prepared at request of John Wilkie, Secret Service. U.S. Dept. of Treasury, September 1901.

_____. "Report." Prepared at request of John Wilkie, Secret Service. U.S. Dept. of Treasury, September, 1901.

Gage, P. T. "What I Saw at the Shooting of President McKinley." *Metropolitan Magazine* 14 (1901): 594-603.

Gallagher, Albert. "Report." Prepared at request of John Wilkie, Secret Service. U.S. Dept. of Treasury, September, 1901.

Gaylord, H. R. "Report on the Autopsy." *Buffalo Medical Journal* 57 (1901): 284-291.

Goldman, Emma. "The Assassination of McKinley." *The American Mercury* 24 (1931): 53-67.

Ireland, Samuel. "Report." Prepared at request of John Wilkie, Secret Service. U.S. Dept. of Treasury, September, 1901.

Kropotkin, Peter. *Memoirs of a Revolutionist.* New York: Doubleday & Co., 1962 (originally published 1899).

____. *Mutual Aid.* London: Heinemann, 1902.

MacDonald, C. F. "The Trial, Execution, Autopsy, and Mental Status of Leon F. Czolgosz, Alias Fred Nieman, The Assassin of President McKinley." *Philadelphia Medical Journal* 9 (1902): 31-42.

Mann, Matthew. "Remarks on the Operation." *Buffalo Medical Journal* 57 (1901): 275-276.

Matzinger, H. G. "Report on the Bacteriologic Examination." *Philadelphia Medical Journal* 8 (1902): 648-649.

McKluskey, George. "Report on Anarchists in Paterson, New Jersey and Role of Enrico Malatesta." Prepared at request of Chief of Police William S. Devery, New York City, 1900. In George Courtelyou Papers, Library of Congress, Manuscript Division.

Park, Roswell. "Reminiscences of McKinley Week." 1914. Original manuscript on file at BECHS.

____. "Report of the Medical Department of the Pan-American Exposition, Buffalo, N.Y." *Buffalo Medical Journal* 57 (1902): 417-431.

Parmenter, John "The Surgery in President McKinley's Case." *Buffalo Medical Journal* 57 (1901): 205-206.

Quackenbush, James L., "Statement Describing Events

Observed at Temple of Music, Sept. 6, 1901." *Buffalo Express,* 9 September 1901.

Rixey, P. M., M. D. Mann, H. Mynter, R. Park, E. Wasdin, C. McBurney, and C. G. Stockton. "The Official Report of the Case of President McKinley." *Buffalo Medical Journal* 57 (1901): 271-293. Also published in *American Medicine,* 19 October 1901 and *Journal of the American Medical Association,* 19 October 1901.

Spitzka, E. A. "The Post-Mortem Examination of Leon F. Czolgosz: The Assassin of President McKinley." *American Journal of Insanity* 58 (1902): 368-411.

"Trial of Leon F. Czolgosz for the Murder of President McKinley, Buffalo, New York." *American State Trials* 14 (1901): 159-231.

Van Peyma, P. W. "Last Hours of McKinley." (Buffalo) *Daily Bazaar* 28 November 1902.

Wilkie, J. E. "Memorandum Regarding Presidential Protection." Prepared at request of Chas. Norton. U.S. Dept. of Treasury, 1910.

Wilson, N. W. "Details of President McKinley's Case." *Buffalo Medical Journal* 57 (1901): 207-225.

Secondary Sources

I. GENERAL REFERENCES

Barnard, Harry. *Eagle Forgotten: The Life of John Peter Altgeld.* Indianapolis: Bobbs-Merrill, 1938.

Barry, Richard H. *An Historical Memento of the Nation's Loss: The True Story of the Assassination of President McKinley at Buffalo.* Buffalo: Robert Allan Reid, 1901.

Belknap, Michal R. *American Political Trials.* Westport, CT: Praeger, 1994.

Berkman, Alexander. *Prison Memoirs of an Anarchist.* New York: Mother Earth Publishing, 1912.

Brands, H. W. *TR: The Last Romantic.* New York: Basic Books, 1997.

Brooks, Stewart. *Our Murdered Presidents: The Medical History*. New York: Frederick Fell, 1966.

Caroli, Betty Boyd. *First Ladies*. Oxford: Oxford University Press, 1987.

Clarke, James W. *American Assassins: The Darker Side of Politics*. Princeton, NJ: Princeton University Press, 1982.

David, Henry. *History of the Haymarket Affair*. New York: Farrar & Rhinehart, 1936.

Donovan, Robert J. *The Assassins*. New York: Harper & Bros., 1955.

Fisher, Jack C. *Lead Pencil Miner*. La Jolla, CA: Alamar Books, 1998.

Freidel, Frank B. *The Splendid Little War*. Boston: Little Brown, 1958.

Goldman, Emma. *Living My Life*. New York: Alfred A. Knopf, 1931.

Goldman, Mark. *City on the Lake*. Buffalo: Prometheus Books, 1990.

____. *High Hopes, The Rise and Decline of Buffalo, New York*. Albany: State University of New York Press, 1983.

Gould, Lewis L. *The Spanish-American War and President McKinley*. Lawrence: Regents Press of Kansas, 1982.

____. *The Presidency of William McKinley*. Lawrence: Regents Press of Kansas, 1980.

Harvey, George. *Henry Clay Frick*. New York: Scribners, 1928.

Heilbroner, Robert L. *The Worldly Philosophers: The Lives, Times, and Ideas of the Great Economic Thinkers*. New York: Simon & Schuster, 1953.

Hogg, Ian V. *Illustrated Encyclopedia of Firearms*. Secaucus, NJ: Chartwell Books, 1978.

Johns, Wesley A. *The Man Who Shot McKinley*. New York: A. S. Barnes, 1970.

Jones, Rebecca C. *The President Has Been Shot!* New York: Penguin Putnam, 1996.

Kerensky, Alexander. *The Crucifixion of Liberty*. New York: John Day, 1934.

Leary, Thomas, and Elizabeth Sholes. *Buffalo's Pan-American Exposition: Images of America Series*. Charleston: Arcadia, 1998.

Leech, Margaret. *In The Days of McKinley*. New York: Harper Bros., 1959.

Leffler, J. J. "Ida McKinley." In *American First Ladies*, edited by Lewis Gould, 227-293. New York: Garland, 1996.

Martin, F. S., and R. U. Boehlert. *The American Presidents: A Bibliography*. Washington, DC: Congressional Quarterly Inc., 1987.

McCarthy, D. V. N. *Protecting the President*. New York: Wm. Morrow, 1985.

McElroy, Richard L. *William McKinley and Our America: A Pictorial History*. Canton, Ohio: Stark County Historical Society, 1996.

Morgan, H. Wayne. *William McKinley and His America*. Syracuse, NY: Syracuse University Press, 1963.

Morris, Richard B. "Ordeal by Jury: Trial of the Chicago Anarcho-communists." In *Fair Trial: Fourteen Who Stood Accused*. New York: Knopf, 1952.

Olcott, Charles S. *The Life of William McKinley*. Boston: Houghton Mifflin, 1916.

Park, Roswell. *Roswell Park: Selected Papers, Surgical and Scientific*. Buffalo: Published for subscribers, 1914.

_____. *Principles and Practice of Modern Surgery*. Philadelphia: Lea Bros., 1907

_____. *Surgery by American Authors*. New York: Lea Bros., 1901.

Strouse, Jean. *Morgan: American Financier*. New York: Random House, 1999.

Townsend, G. W. *Memorial Life of William McKinley*. Philadelphia: Memorial Publishing Co., 1901.

Tuchman, Barbara. *The Proud Tower*. New York: Macmillan, 1962.

Tyler, John W. *The Life of William McKinley: Soldier, Statesman, President.* Philadelphia: Ziegler & Co., 1901.

Wilkie, Don. *American Secret Service Agent.* New York: Frederick & Stokes, 1934.

II. ARTICLES, PAMPHLETS

Adler, Selig. "The Operation on President McKinley." *Scientific American* 208 (1963): 118-130.

Buckley, J. M. "The Assassination of Kings and Presidents." *The Century Magazine* 63 (1918): 136-142.

Damon, Allan L. "The Great Red Scare." *American Heritage* (February 1968): 22-27.

Edelman, M., and R. J. Simon. "Presidential Assassinations: Their Meaning and Impact on American Society." *Ethics* 79 (April 1969): 199-221.

Ernst, E. "Colonic Irrigation and the Theory of Autointoxication: A Triumph of Ignorance over Science." *Journal of Clinical Gastroenterology* 24 (1997): 196-198.

Fine, S. "Anarchism and the Assassination of McKinley." *American Historical Review* 60 (1955): 777-799.

Gladden, W. "Two Kinds of Anarchists." *Leslie's Weekly* 28 (1901): 278.

Harper, S. B. "Gunshot Wounds of the Presidents of the United States." *Proceedings of the Mayo Clinic* 19 (1944): 11-19.

Hastings, D. W. "The Psychiatry of Presidential Assassins." *Lancet* 85 (1965): 93-100, 157-162, 189-192, 294-301.

Kaiser, Frederick M. "Presidential Assassinations and Assaults: Characteristics and Impact on Protective Procedures." *Presidential Studies Quarterly* 11 (1981): 545-558.

____. "Origins of Secret Service Protection of the President: Personal, Interagency, and Institutional Conflict." *Presidential Studies Quarterly* 18 (1968): 101-127.

Logan, J. A. "A Day of the President's Life." *Leslie's Monthly* 48 (1899): 339-343.

Loria, F. L. "Historical Aspects of Penetrating Wounds of the Abdomen." *International Abstracts of Surgery* 87 (1948): 521-524.

Morton, T. S. K. "Abdominal Section for Traumatism, with Reports of Five Cases." *Journal of the American Medical Association* 8 (1887): 225-232.

Murphy, E. C. "Theodore Roosevelt's Night Ride to the Presidency." Adirondack Historical Association, 1996.

Palmer, M. L. et al. "Dr. Roswell Park and the McKinley Assassination." In *Medical History in Buffalo 1846-1996: Collected Essays*. 179-191. SUNY Buffalo, 1996.

Park, Roswell. "Surgical Treatment of Injuries and Diseases of the Pancreas." In *Roswell Park: Selected Papers, Surgical and Scientific*. 188-200. Buffalo: Published for subscribers, 1914.

____. "After Treatment of Abdominal Operations." *In Principles and Practice of Modern Surgery*. Philadelphia: Lea Bros., 1907.

____. "Gunshot Wounds Made by Modern Missiles and their Treatment." *Buffalo Medical Journal* 38 (1898): 1-11.

Pillitteri, A. "OR Nursing 100 Years Ago: Nursing Care of President McKinley." *Today's OR Nurse* 13 (1991): 19-24.

Sherman, Richard B. "Presidential Protection during the Progressive Era: The Aftermath of the McKinley Assassination." *The Historian* 46 (1983): 1-20.

Sims, J. M. "The Treatment of Gunshot Wounds of the Abdomen in Relation to Modern Peritoneal Surgery." *British Medical Journal* 1 (1882): 184-186.

Stockton, C. G. "Roswell Park: A Memoir." *In Roswell Park: Selected Papers, Surgical and Scientific*. vii-xx. Buffalo: Published for subscribers, 1914.

Sullivan-Fowler, M. "Doubtful Theories, Drastic Therapies: Autointoxication and Faddism in the Late Nineteenth and Early Twentieth Centuries." *Journal of the History of Medicine and*

Allied Sciences 50 (1995): 364-390.

Weisz, A. E., and R. L. Taylor. "American Presidential Assassinations." *Diseases of the Nervous System* 30 (1969): 649-658.

III. SCRAPBOOKS

Several collections of clippings from newspapers* and weekly publications** assembled by the participants at the time provided a wonderfully organized way to evaluate contemporary popular reporting of the events.

Matthew Mann Scrapbook, held at University at Buffalo Archives, Amherst, N.Y.

Roswell Park Scrapbook, held at University at Buffalo Archives, Amherst, N.Y.

Charles G. Stockton Scrapbook, held at University at Buffalo Archives, Amherst, N.Y.

Ansley Wilcox Scrapbook, held at Theodore Roosevelt Inaugural Site, Buffalo, N.Y.

Pan-American Exposition Scrapbooks, Buffalo and Erie County Historical Society, Buffalo, N.Y.

*Additional background information was drawn from the following newspapers: *Buffalo Commercial, Buffalo Courier, Buffalo Express, Buffalo Evening News, Buffalo Times, Chicago Tribune, Cleveland Plain Dealer, Niagara Falls Gazette, New York Herald,* and *New York Times.*

**Weekly publications that covered the events in detail are *Leslie's Weekly, Harper's Weekly, The American Mercury,* and *Metropolitan Magazine.*

❖

Notes
Prologue

1. For attendance and revenue data, see William T. Buchanan, *Final Report, Pan-American Exposition*.

2. Many of these letters can be found in the George Courtelyou Papers, Library of Congress, Manuscript Division. See Appendix I for a sampling.

3. The three Secret Service "operatives" (as they were then termed) filed individually authored reports regarding the events of that day. See Appendix II for extracts from their reports.

4. Theodore Roosevelt was born on October 27, 1858. Thus, although he would not be 43 until a month after he assumed the office of president, historians often list his age as 43 at the time of his inauguration.

5. Buffalo, one of America's fastest growing cities in 1901, was hardly a backwater, medically or in any other way. Still, this comment testifies to the medical elitism to be found in Boston, New York, and Philadelphia at the time. The insult overlooks the presence of Dr. Charles McBurney, a consultant from New York City, throughout the president's aftercare.

6. At the urging of Buffalo attorney Ansley Wilcox, the doctors did sign and make public a formal statement that reiterated their unwavering consensus concerning the president's post-operative care (see Chapter 8). They took no other legal action, however.

7. See Appendix IV for a complete transcription of Roswell Park's original, unedited draft.

8. Graduates of the University of Buffalo School of Medicine may recall this bookstore at the corner of Main and High Street, very close to the Buffalo General Hospital. I cannot remember the store's name, but I can still recall the owner and his wife, and I retain in my library several historical volumes purchased there after I found my copy of Park's *Selected Papers*.

9. Roswell Park, *Selected Papers: Surgical and Scientific*.

10. Economic data show twelve quarters of growth in the economy dating from 1896. For additional detail, see G. M. Walton and H. Rockoff, *History of the American Economy*.

11. Numerous versions of Hanna's emotional statement exist. Some include the words "that damned cowboy," and others do not.

12. Most of the Roosevelt quotes are taken from his speeches or from H. W. Brand's thoroughly engaging biography, *TR: The Last Romantic*, 426.

13. Only in Lincoln's case does there appear to be evidence of a gen-

uine conspiracy. A group of assassins led by John Wilkes Booth and John Suratt hoped to achieve the simultaneous murders of President Lincoln, Vice President Johnson, and Secretary of State Seward. The attempted assassination of Truman might also be called a conspiracy, but of course it failed. Otherwise, presidential assassinations, actual and failed, have been the work of solitary gunmen.

1
Anarchists

1. Prince Peter Kropotkin, *Paroles d'un Revolte*, cited in Barbara Tuchman, *The Proud Tower*.

2. For an overview of the late nineteenth century anarchist movement, see chapter 2 of Tuchman's *The Proud Tower*.

3. For additional background, see Sidney Fine, "Anarchism and the Assassination of McKinley," in *The American Historical Review* 60 (1955): 777-799.

4. For an excellent summary of Marx's life and philosophy, see Robert L. Heilbroner's *The Worldly Philosophers*.

5. Alexander Herzen, cited in Tuchman, *The Proud Tower*, p. 66.

6. Peter Kropotkin, *Memoirs of a Revolutionist*. Originally published in 1899.

7. The arrival of Enrico Malatesta in Paterson, New Jersey is cited in the report of New York City Captain of Detectives, George McKluskey, 1900. See abstract in Appendix I.

8. Anarchists insisted that all creatures of nature had been preserved through mutual assistance. See Peter Kropotkin, *Mutual Aid*.

9. Alexander Kerensky, *The Crucifixion of Liberty*.

10. Cited in Fine, "Anarchism and the Assassination of McKinley."

11. Henry David, *History of the Haymarket Affair*.

12. The Haymarket trial is evaluated for its fairness in Richard B. Morris, "Ordeal by Jury: The Trial of the Chicago Anarcho-communists."

13. Harry Barnard, *Eagle Forgotten: The Life of John Peter Altgeld*.

14. For two views of this affair, consult George Harvey, *Henry Clay Frick* and Alexander Berkman, *Prison Memoirs of an Anarchist*.

15. Emma Goldman, *Living My Life* . She wrote her biography after returning to Canada, more than a decade following her 1919 deportation from the United States.

16. No historical record regarding Czolgosz precedes his premeditated attack on McKinley. Existing knowledge of his family background and the lonesome course of his life is the product of intense police interrogation following the shooting. Police investigators grilled the

assailant, interviewed his family, and conducted conversations with those who recalled their interactions with Czolgosz. Most of this information was not revealed until the trial; it was recorded in the court stenographer's summary. Additional information was revealed during medical evaluations conducted prior to Czolgosz's execution. Newspaper accounts of Czolgosz and his whereabouts prior to the shooting often include inaccuracies such as identifying his weapon as a Derringer. Buffalo police and district attorney interrogation was not available to reporters until they listened to testimony during the trial.

17. The assassin is often mistakenly identified as an immigrant. Although it is known that his father emigrated from Poland, the name Czolgosz is Hungarian. The vagaries of the Austro-Hungarian empire and moving borders between nations suggest that the family's heritage is not Polish but Hungarian.

18. This version is based on Tuchman. See also Appendix I for the indication of planned assassinations of King Humbert and President McKinley.

19. The police found this clipping among Czolgosz's personal effects. The pistol that he likely shot rabbits with at the family farm, and brought with him to Buffalo, also was found in his east side rented room. Apparently, he did not deem it worthy of a presidential assassination.

20. Emma Goldman later wrote (for *The American Mercury*) her recollection of the circumstances surrounding the McKinley assassination, including her first meeting of Czolgosz (Nieman), her knowledge of his interactions with other anarchists, and her thoughts about his eventual fate. Cited under primary sources.

21. Schilling provided these recollections to police and reporters.

2
McKinley

1. This was a common theme in McKinley's speeches, and there were many variations, such as "A government like ours rests upon the intelligence, morality, and patriotism of the people." Delivered in Columbia, S. Carolina on Dec. 20, 1898.

2. The term "White House" was popularized by Theodore Roosevelt during his presidency. Prior to that time, the president's residence was usually referred to as the executive mansion.

3. For a detailed accounting of President and Mrs. Cleveland's security concerns, refer to Frederick Kaiser, "Presidential Assassinations and Assaults: Characteristics and Impact on Protective Procedures."

4. Rebecca Jones, *The President Has Been Shot!*

5. I have drawn from several sources for biographical details of William McKinley's life. Several biographies published soon after his death serve to memorialize him and embellish details of the assassination, based primarily on often inaccurate newspaper accounts. Examples are G. W. Townsend's *Memorial Life of William McKinley* and the Rev. Samuel Fallows' *Life of William McKinley: Our Martyred President*. These sources are rich in McKinley's boyhood and military years. Perhaps the first serious biography was Charles S. Olcott, *The Life of William McKinley* in 2 volumes. I found most useful the engaging narrative of Margaret Leech: *In the Days of McKinley*. Wayne Morgan has more recently provided an analysis of McKinley's political life in *William McKinley and His America*. Another important biographer of McKinley is Lewis Gould, who has written extensively on the Spanish-American War in *The Spanish-American War and President McKinley*, and *The Presidency of William McKinley*.

6. When a judge's daughter presented him with his first taste of ice cream, he thought the custard had frozen accidentally. When corrected, he explained that he was only a simple country boy from faraway Ohio.

7. Betty Boyd Caroli, in *First Ladies*, characterizes Ida McKinley as an especially demanding first lady, perhaps a match for Mary Lincoln, although without prompting as much controversy or criticism as the latter.

8. These were both likely the result of complications during the second pregnancy or subsequent delivery. Historians have termed her problem as petit mal seizures, which is not medically accurate. Petit mal disorders occur in childhood and are often outgrown. Ida McKinley's periodic lapses were not true convulsions (grand mal seizures); they were likely due to a brain lesion. Contemporary neurologists would point to the location of the problem as in one of her temporal lobes. The cause might have been an unperceived and untreated elevation of blood pressure during pregnancy and/or delivery, followed by a limited but clinically significant brain hemorrhage. An unconfirmed observation that Ida McKinley never had another seizure after her husband died is difficult to explain or even believe. Her many lapses of consciousness would have to have been a form of hysterics, which seems highly unlikely, their origin being so closely related to a pregnancy.

9. As this book neared completion, television viewers of the Bush vs. Gore election were reminded of the contested election of 1876 that left Samuel Tilden without the presidency, based on an 8:7 Republican advantage on the electoral commission, five of whose members were

Supreme Court justices. Should we conclude that nothing was new about the 2000 election?

10. Grover Cleveland was elected twice; he was the twenty-second (1885-89) and the twenty-fourth (1893-97) president.

11. When he opened Chicago's ill-timed Columbian Exposition during the summer of 1893, Cleveland chose for his theme, "...the stupendous results of American enterprise." Anarchist critics promptly drew attention to the fact that within a few hundred yards of his stage and extending for several miles, many thousands lived in cardboard shacks, drank contaminated water, and ate very little.

12. Bryan would run for president three times and lose all three elections. Later, he prosecuted the Scopes "Monkey Trial" in Dayton, Tennessee.

13. An unnamed observer took a broader view of the winning ticket and said, "I feel sorry for McKinley; he has a man of destiny behind him."

14. Jack C. Fisher, *Lead Pencil Miner*.

15. The practice of reviewing the parade from a comfortable stand in front of the executive mansion eventually became an inaugural tradition.

16. Andrew Carnegie did not misunderstand the implications of this conflict. Vigorously opposed to the U.S. becoming a colonial power, he offered to write a $20 million check to the government if it would grant independence to the Filipinos, that being the price the U.S. had paid to Spain for transfer of Philippine sovereignty...an extraordinary example of trying to buy influence one might say.

3

Exposition

1. William McKinley's descriptive characterization of fairs like the Pan-American Exposition, spoken near the beginning of his final speech, delivered in Buffalo on Sept. 5, 1901.

2. For a history of world's fairs and national expositions, I have relied on the online versions of the Britannica and Encarta encyclopedias.

3. For greater detail regarding Pan-American Exposition history, refer to Mark Goldman's *High Hopes: The Rise and Decline of Buffalo, New York*. In addition, the pictorial essay by Thomas Leary and Elizabeth Sholes, entitled *Buffalo's Pan-American Exposition: Images of America Series*, provides abundant, interesting historical detail.

4. This appropriation was reduced to $300,000 in 1899, despite the support of then Governor Theodore Roosevelt, who continued to endorse the original sum.

5. For a financial history of "The Pan," from early fundraising until calculation of the ending deficit, see William Buchanan's *Final Report of the Pan-American Exposition, 1901.*

6. Mark Goldman's *High Hopes...* offers a colorful rendition of Buffalo's development prior to the Pan-American Exposition.

7. In 1901, Buffalo consumed approximately 12,000 horsepower daily, which is equivalent to 9,000 kilowatts or 9 megawatts (MW). Today, the daily electricity consumption of a city of 350,000 would equal 350 MW, or about 40 times the amount used a century ago. I am grateful to Stephen Baum, CEO of San Diego Gas and Electric for these comparative figures.

8. Roswell Park discussed his planning for the Exposition's hospital and other health measures in his 1902 summary, published in the *Buffalo Medical Journal.*

9. President McKinley did send a message in time for the grand opening in May. It read in part, "I send you a greeting from the shores of the Pacific, with heart-felt welcome to our guests from sister republics, for whom we wish continued abundant prosperity."

10. The term "Midway" originally referred to a unique feature of Chicago's Columbian Exposition, namely a concentration of amusements in an area called "The Midway Plaisance." The shortened form quickly made its way into popular usage and continues to be synonymous with an amusement area at fairs, circuses, and carnivals.

11. A copy of this speech is filed in the Pan-Am Expo folder of the George Courtelyou Papers, Library of Congress, Manuscript Division.

12. This data and much of the descriptive detail are taken from an undated *New York Herald Tribune* supplement issued near the beginning of the Exposition. Mrs. Harry Metcalf was kind enough to lend me her family's well-preserved copy.

13. George Courtelyou wrote in 1902, "...twice before leaving Canton for Buffalo, the reception in the Temple of Music was stricken from the program, each time to be put back at the request and direction of President McKinley. Upon its going back on the program the second time, the direction was well-nigh imperative." Letter from Courtelyou to Louis Babcock, cited in Babcock, "An Account of the Assassination of President McKinley and the Trial of Czolgosz."

14. Czolgosz likely did pay this debt; a well-used pistol, perhaps the one he liked to shoot rabbits with and not the one he used at the Temple of Music, was found in his room at Novak's.

15. Buffalo police questioned everyone at Novak's Hotel who saw or spoke with Czolgosz.

16. Many of Buffalo's senior journalists, such as Richard Barry of the *Buffalo Enquirer*, described such scenes almost poetically.

4

Gunshots

1. According to McKinley biographer Margaret Leech, these words were uttered by the president in Canton, Ohio when Courtelyou attempted one last time to cancel the visit to the Buffalo exposition.

2. The *Buffalo Enquirer's* Richard Barry recalled this attribute of the sunrise on Sept. 6th. His implication is obvious (never mind that the sun's color at any given moment is a function of atmospheric conditions).

3. Numerous accounts of this fateful day have been written; not surprisingly, no two are the same. The present narrative, unlike any of its predecessors (as far as I know), benefits from access to the written reports of the three Secret Service operatives who shadowed the president on his itinerary that day, stood within ten feet of him in the Temple of Music, and played their own roles in subduing the assailant. I am grateful to Michael Sampson, Historian of the Secret Service, U.S. Department of Treasury, for access to these manuscripts. Variations in these three reports can be observed in Appendix II.

4. Taken from police interrogation and the trial summary.

5. Surprisingly, no sitting president had yet traveled beyond the nation's borders. John Adams and Thomas Jefferson completed their foreign travel before serving as the nation's second and third presidents. Theodore Roosevelt had gone to Cuba, but that was before he became the 26th president. He would also be the first to travel outside the country as president, visiting Panama in 1908.

6. A newspaper reporter caught this exchange and later described it as Mrs. McKinley's final wave to her husband. The American public was well aware of the couple's longstanding habit of waving to one another, adding poignancy to the gesture on that day.

7. In a statement published in the *Buffalo Express* three days after the incident, James Quackenbush described his observations at the scene. He had traveled to Niagara Falls that morning with the president's party, then excused himself before lunch to return to help Babcock prepare the site for the afternoon reception.

8. This information is drawn from the statement Louis Babcock provided to District Attorney Thomas Penney and later published (see references). Because of the detail and apparent accuracy of his observations and those of Quackenbush, Penney asked both men to testify at Czolgosz's trial.

9. There are no photographs of the scene. Newspaper photogra-

phers weren't present for the reception because one man, C. D. Arnold, had been contracted to take all official photographs of the Exposition. He snapped McKinley departing his carriage outside the Temple of Music but he did not follow the president into the building. Artists' renderings of the shooting exist but none is entirely accurate when compared with eyewitness accounts. The most popular of these views mistakenly creates the impression that Czolgosz approached from the president's right instead of his left. Although C. D. Arnold was summoned to the Temple of Music following the shooting, he was not allowed inside to take pictures until after the president had been removed to the hospital.

10. Parker later made himself available to reporters for interviews. They described him as a "tall Negro man," a waiter at a nearby cafe who had taken the afternoon off to see if he could greet the president. Eventually, Parker made a statement in which he described the scene and took some credit for preventing further injury to McKinley. This offended some people, including Secret Service Director John Wilkie, who was not interested in having his men share credit for subduing Czolgosz with anyone. Parker was not asked to testify at the trial.

11. From operative Gallagher's report to Secret Service Director John Wilkie.

12. Several versions of the president's words are provided in the historical record. I have taken the simplest and most commonly reported quotes. There is general agreement, however, that his first three utterances following injury were on behalf of the assailant, then his wife, and finally the Exposition. Considered typical of the man, his words were duly reported to the nation.

13. Picture a hack as a small, not very fancy, horse-drawn carriage.

14. Louis Babcock's eyewitness account of the Temple of Music events describes the action Newcomb Carlton, director of works for the Exposition, took after he noted the police attempting to distract the public while Czolgosz was being transferred out of the Temple of Music. Carlton walked to a nearby telephone and instructed the man at the front gate of the Exposition to close it as soon as the carriage holding the prisoner passed through, further impeding anyone who thought the vehicle could be stopped.

15. In his recollection of the operation, Mann explained the paucity of instruments by saying that he had not been told why he was being summoned to the Pan-American Hospital. However, this incident, as reported in the newspapers, suggests that he had been told enough to warrant the sudden interruption of his haircut.

16. Strychnine sulfate, a potent alkaloid compound, is a lethal poison only at much higher doses than were used medically in 1901.

17. The 56-year-old Mynter had been born in Denmark in 1845. He graduated from medical school in Copenhagen in 1871 and served as an assistant surgeon in the Royal Danish Navy until emigrating to the United States in 1882. He moved to Buffalo and served a four-year apprenticeship (referred to as a surgical residency today) at Buffalo General Hospital. Appointed Professor of Surgery at the Niagara Medical School, he transferred his affiliation to the University of Buffalo in 1898, taking the title Professor of Clinical Surgery.

18. Eugene Wasdin was a 40 year-old government employee stationed at the Marine Hospital in Buffalo at the time McKinley was shot. As the reader will learn, the theory he introduced into the assassination story created a public sensation.

19. Little more is known about Dr. Lee than what appears here. It is not even certain that he had surgical training. Years later, in his "Reminiscence of McKinley Week," Park expressed his extreme annoyance with Lee.

20. In 1939, Buffalo City Hospital on Grider Street was renamed in honor of Edward J. Meyer. Today, it has been rebuilt as the Erie County Medical Center.

21. Matthew Darbyshire Mann was born in Utica, New York in 1845. He was 56 years old when he performed the surgery on McKinley. He graduated from Yale College in 1867, studied law for a few months, then transferred his interest to medicine. He graduated from New York's College of Physicians and Surgeons in 1871. After traveling and studying in Vienna and Paris, he established a practice first in New York and then in Hartford, Connecticut. When James Platt White, Buffalo's eminent Professor of Obstetrics and Gynecology retired, Mann was recruited to replace him. In 1887, Mann was appointed dean of the University's Medical Department.

22. This is taken from Selig Adler's 1963 discussion of the McKinley assassination in *Scientific American*. Adler's account was based largely on evidence compiled by the medical consultant to McKinley, Charles Stockton, who knew much about the reputations of Buffalo's surgeons.

5

Operation

1. In 1898, Park published in the *Buffalo Medical Journal* an original

communication entitled, "Gunshot Wounds Made by Modern Missiles and Their Treatment." In 1902, he published in *American Medicine*, "Surgical Treatment of Injuries and Diseases of the Pancreas."

2. The *Niagara Falls Gazette* of Sept. 7, 1901, identified Roswell Park's patient as Mr. William Powley of Ransomville, New York. The article went on to detail the journey of Dr. Campbell, who accompanied Park back to the Pan-American Hospital.

3. This tale was not recorded at the time. Over the years, it has come to be considered apocryphal. Its source for this writing is Park's son, Julian, who attached a written account of it, with other notations, to the original draft of his father's "Reminiscence" before donating the materials to the Buffalo Historical Society. It is interesting that it is attributed to Campbell and not to Park, who likely would have repeated the story around the family dinner table.

4. Parmenter, who was 40 years old, had trained at Buffalo General Hospital.

5. Later, people would note a host of similarities: both presidents were from Ohio, both died in September, both were hit twice, only one shot inflicting mortal damage to each, and in both cases, the lethal bullets remain undiscovered.

6. A new building had recently opened on High Street, known today as the East Building, the oldest existing structure in the Buffalo General Hospital complex.

7. For additional detail, refer to Frank L. Loria, "Historical Aspects of Penetrating Wounds of the Abdomen."

8. Although the sixteenth century French surgeon Ambrose Pare had advocated probing wounds to locate and retrieve the ball, his technique never gained wide acceptance.

9. See Appendix III for Mann's recollection of the operation.

10. It was commonplace for surgeons in that day to carry their instruments with them because surgery was conducted in private homes as well as in the hospital.

11. There was telephone contact between the hospital facilities in Buffalo and Niagara Falls, but no one has documented what information was exchanged in each of the calls made. Such a record would be revealing.

12. For a very detailed description and evaluation of the activities in the operating room, I am grateful for the research of Adele Pillitteri, reported in her "OR Nursing 100 Years Ago: Nursing Care of President McKinley."

13. By today's standards and probably the standards of that day as well, Miss Walters had loaded the operating room with nursing staff, perhaps assuring that each one on duty would have their place in histo-

ry. Other nurses who played roles at the Milburn residence were Miss Hunt (who looked after Mrs. McKinley) and Misses McKenzie, Mohan, and Connelly (Johns Hopkins Hospital). Of course, there were also more medical students and surgeons present than were required for the task.

14. G. W. Townsend, Memorial *Life of William McKinley*.

15. In 1937, *Buffalo Times* reporter Edward Tighe reported demolition of the old police headquarters building and, the resultant fleeing of "wretched ghosts," among them Leon Czolgosz. *Buffalo Sunday Times* May 23, 1937.

16. Although aspects of the procedure are commented on by Dr. Mann in the *Buffalo Medical Journal*, details of the entire procedure are described in the official medical report: P. M. Rixey et al. "The Case of President McKinley." Also some details are to be found in N. W. Wilson, "Details of President McKinley's Case."

17. Roswell Park was born in Pomfret, Connecticut in 1852, making him nearly 49 years old at the time of the assassination. His family moved to Racine, Wisconsin and Park attended college there, then earned his M.D. at Northwestern University in 1876. He taught anatomy for three years before pursuing additional study in Germany, France, and Austria. Returning to Chicago, he served as lecturer of surgery at the Rush Medical College until he was recruited in 1883 to serve as Chairman of Surgery for the University of Buffalo's Medical Department.

18. In Park's "Reminiscences of McKinley Week" (see Appendix V).

19. For details, refer to H. W. Brands, *TR: The Last Romantic*.

20. Cited in Jean Strouse, *Morgan*.

21. As related by Emma Goldman in her recollection published in *The American Mercury*.

22. See Appendix II for abstracts of these reports, provided to the author by the Secret Service.

6

Recovery

1. These reassuring words were expressed by Charles McBurney, summoned as a consultant from Roosevelt Hospital in New York City by Dr. Rixey. He departed the following Thursday morning still convinced that recovery was assured.

2. Much of the content of this chapter is based on newspaper reporting and on the official bulletins issued by Secretary Courtelyou. For the full text of the latter, see P. M. Rixey et al., "The Case of President McKinley," *Buffalo Medical Journal*; this official report was also published

in several other journals (see references).

3. Margaret Leech, *In the Days of McKinley*.

4. See Micaela Sullivan-Fowler, "Doubtful Theories, Drastic Therapies: Autointoxication and Faddism in the Late Nineteenth and Early Twentieth Centuries" and E. Ernst, " Colonic Irrigation and the Theory of Autointoxication: A Triumph of Ignorance over Science."

5. The official reports do not list further nursing staff changes. Nurses worked eight-hour shifts. One nurse, Miss Hunt, was assigned to care for Mrs. McKinley.

6. And indeed they were. Even before news of the attack elicited bipartisan sympathy, the public response to his last speech was uniformly praiseworthy. One journalist even suggested that McKinley's speech would rank with George Washington's Farewell Address.

7. Meetings of the Clearinghouse Committee served some of the functions fulfilled by the Governors of the Federal Reserve Bank today.

8. The New York Stock Exchange customarily traded six days a week in 1901.

9. Jean Strouse, *Morgan*.

10. Emma Goldman, *The American Mercury*.

11. Henry Deringer (1789-1868), an American gunsmith from Philadelphia, invented single- and double-barrel pistols. They were small, light, and of large caliber, but effective only at close range. The company that manufactured these firearms used the spelling "Derringer." Over time, this kind of weapon has become known as a derringer. John Wilkes Booth assassinated President Abraham Lincoln in 1865, firing one shot from a single-barrel, .41 caliber derringer.

12. H. W. Brands, *TR: The Last Romantic*. 410.

13. The president's cabinet also used the Glenny House at Ferry and Delaware for some meetings because of its proximity to the Milburn home.

14. This is based on newspaper accounts collected by Buffalo reporter Wesley Johns in his engaging book, *The Man Who Shot McKinley*.

15. It is remarkable that Czolgosz said,"... Kill the President"on the day following the surgery, as if he knew the outcome. We don't know whether police were keeping him informed of the president's condition, but that seems highly unlikely. District Attorney Penney of course asked,"Did you intend to kill the president?"

16. All quotations attributed to Czolgosz are taken from reports of interrogations and confessions as reported in *The Trial of Leon F. Czolgosz for the Murder of President McKinley*, Buffalo, New York, 1901.

17. As reported by Dr. Charles Stockton in a 1914 tribute to

Roswell Park. See Park's *Selected Papers: Surgical and Scientific.*

18. According to one version of this story, the 6 inch coil the machine arrived with was eventually replaced with the needed 10 inch coil. Therefore, x-rays could have been taken, but they were never deemed necessary.

19. The remarks of Secretary Hay were recalled by Louis Babcock, in "The Assassination of President McKinley."

7

Death

1. McKinley, in conversation with Courtelyou, Courtelyou diary, December 29, 1899.

2. When everything else failed, physicians in 1901 turned to calomel (mercurous chloride) and oxgall, their most powerful cathartics.

3. The pulse was listed as 128 for that report, certainly not a clinically significant decrease from 130. The two numbers are closer than the range of error for recording pulse rate.

4. The Adirondack Museum in Blue Mountain Lake, New York in 1977 published a booklet by Eloise Cronin Murphy, descendant of Mike Cronin, third driver in the relay team, entitled "Theodore Roosevelt's Night Ride to the Presidency."

5. This of course was unproven therapy at the time, beyond the limits of actual medical knowledge. At best, it was a shot in the dark. Since Thomas Addison's mid-nineteenth century discovery of the suprarenal (adrenal) gland hormones and diseases based on deficiencies of those hormones, there had been only very modest progress in their understanding. The discovery of hydrocortisone would come later in the twentieth century.

6. From his "Reminiscences of McKinley Week." See Roswell Park, *Selected Papers: Surgical and Scientific.*

7. Roosevelt's recollection of his thoughts, and the details of this journey appear in his letters to Henry Lodge and are cited in H. R. Brands, *TR: The Last Romantic.*

8. H. R. Gaylord, "Report of the Autopsy." *Buffalo Medical Journal.*

9. Cited in P.M. Rixey et al., "Official Report," *Buffalo Medical Journal.*

10. Both the arraignment and the trial were recorded by Mr. Horace E. Story. In 1901, court stenographers took notes and a summary was prepared for reference in court the next day. Word for word transcription was not yet a developed technology. When Mr. Story

retired in 1953, after more than a half century of service to Erie County, he recalled the Czolgosz trial for a *Buffalo Evening News* reporter. It was one of the first in which his use of carbon paper allowed for immediate production of a copy which he passed to grateful newspapermen. *Buffalo Evening News*, Nov. 19, 1953.

8

Punishment

1. The many quotes from newspapers and medical journals presented in this chapter are taken from scrapbooks of clippings maintained by Park, Mann, Wilcox, and Stockton.

2. For the full text of the statement, see P. M. Rixey, "Official Report," *Buffalo Medical Journal*.

3. Story related in Goldman's recollection of the McKinley assassination in *The American Mercury*.

4. In keeping with procedures of that day, summaries rather than word-for-word transcriptions were made of the proceedings of each day in court. Summaries of both the arraignment and trial are published in American Trials 14 (1901):159-231.

5. In 1965, Donald Hastings, a professor of psychiatry at the University of Minnesota, declared the Czolgosz trial to be "a conspicuous blot on the record of American justice." He was not the first to believe that the issue of mental insanity had not been taken seriously. Dr. Walter Channing of the Tufts Medical School argued in 1902 that a diagnosis of insanity could have been made easily from behavioral evidence, independent of the assassin's declarations of complete sanity, which were immaterial. See Hastings, "The Psychiatry of Presidential Assassinations" and Channing, "The Mental Status of Czolgosz..."

6. Letter provided from files of the Secret Service, U.S. Treasury Department.

7. In 1901, the criminal brain was believed to be anatomically and functionally different from other brains.

8. The voltage used is known. The amperage, the measure of electrical current, is not because it is a function of the resistance represented by the body, which varies.

9. An electrical current of this power is likely to send the heart's rhythm into ventricular fibrillation. Alternatively, a state of asystole may occur, meaning no beat at all. Both are inconsistent with life. At the autopsy, the pathologist noted that the heart had ceased purposeful motion in systole, meaning during full contraction.

10. Prevailing belief in ethnic variations in brain size and configuration at that time stimulated the recording of data according to racial or national origin.

11. Spitzka was a century ahead of his time in suggesting that mental illness could exist on the basis of chemical imbalances in the brain. Today, we know much about neurohormones and have developed drugs that reestablish proper chemical balances in the brain.

9

Aftermath

1. Taken from Roosevelt's first speech to Congress following the McKinley assassination.

2. Emma Goldman relates her struggle following the McKinley assassination in an article she wrote in 1931 for *The American Mercury* .

3. Origins of this law and its Constitutional challenge are cited in Sidney Fine, "Anarchism and the McKinley Assassination," p. 793.

4. Based on Barbara Tuchman, *The Proud Tower*, and Fine, "Anarchism and the McKinley Assassination."

5. A photograph of the brothers watching the 1865 funeral procession can be found among the memorabilia at the Theodore Roosevelt birthplace in New York City.

6. Roosevelt recounted these thoughts later in a letter he wrote to his friend Henry Cabot Lodge. Cited in H. W. Brands, *TR: The Last Romantic*, 411-413.

7. Legislation detailed in Fine, "Anarchism and the McKinley Assassination."

8. Roosevelt retained Courtelyou as his secretary until appointing him as Secretary of Commerce.

9. Courtelyou, "Report of meeting regarding Presidential security." George Courtelyou Papers, Library of Congress, Manuscript Division.

10. For details concerning the evolution of this legislation, see Frederick Kaiser, "Origins of Secret Service Protection of the President..." and Richard Sherman, "Presidential Protection During the Progressive Era..."

11. Paid admissions data for both the Buffalo and Chicago expositions and financial data taken from William Buchanan, *Final Report, Pan-American Exposition*.

12. Another bizarre scene would unfold two days later in the Exposition's stadium. Animal trainer Frank Bostock decided that his

prized elephant, Jumbo, had gone mad and should be put out of his misery. Electrocution was the chosen mode of death. After all, it wouldn't be the only famous electrocution that season! Exposition officials were at first appalled but later relented when they realized the stadium would be packed with paying customers one more time. At the appointed hour, Jumbo stood before the crowd wrapped, in wires attached to a power source. When the switch was closed, 11,000 volts of energy pulsed through the wires—and had no visible effect on the elephant. The crowd urged that Jumbo be set free and he was. Apparently an elephant's skin is an excellent insulator. Story related by Mark Goldman in *High Hopes*.

13. An isolated report of disagreement between Mann and Park appeared in the *Buffalo Enquirer* on November 6, 1902. Under the title, "The Fractured Contract of Doctors," the writer asserted that neither surgeon was referring patients to the other. The choice of words (e.g., "butchery" instead of surgery) suggests the style of a gossip columnist working on the basis of unconfirmed rumor.

14. Some use the terms interchangeably today, but in 1901, these concepts were distinct. Antisepsis, involving the use of disinfectants such as carbolic sprays to limit the propagation of bacterial growth, came first, typified by the innovations of Joseph Lister in London. Asepsis, involving the use of techniques to prevent bacterial contamination in the first place, was a newer concept.

15. The minutes are held at the research library of the Buffalo and Erie County Historical Society. Other than the official reports and the Park reminiscence, there are no records of formal discussions of the care rendered to McKinley; such discussions apparently were held only in private.

16. Roswell Park would later be honored by the establishment of a research laboratory for the study of cancer, and ultimately by the Roswell Park Memorial Cancer Institute.

17. Park's draft is reproduced in entirety in Appendix IV.

18. Modern surgeons refer to the abnormal fluid space as the "third space" or "pathological third space" and recognize it as a serious but reversible condition. The development of a third space can be anticipated and accommodated through the administration of extra fluids (this approach is discussed in the Epilogue). This principle came from experimental studies conducted during the 1930's by two surgical giants, Owen Wangensteen and Alfred Blalock. Wangensteen's experimental model used dogs as subjects and involved tying off the principal artery to the intestinal track, thus producing ischemia

(severely diminished blood supply). The resulting injury induced swelling that inevitably led to shock. Blalock's model was simpler. It called for applying a tourniquet to the hind leg of a dog, then releasing the tourniquet and measuring the fluid accumulation in that ischemic limb as circulating blood volume diminished and shock occurred. Both models produced what has been called distributive (as opposed to hemorrhagic) shock, that is, shock resulting from an abnormal redistribution of body fluids. If this form of shock is left untreated, death follows, as McKinley's case demonstrates.

19. Metallic fragments are rarely the source of problems once they have come to rest, and attempts to remove all of them often produce more tissue damage than opting to leave them be.

20. This is a force sufficient to penetrate three 7/8 inch pine boards at fifteen feet.

21. My thanks to Dr. Bruce Holm for the use of his laboratory and gram scale, and for the cooperation of William Siener and William Mayer of the Buffalo and Erie County Historical Society (the repository for Czolgosz's weapon). In total, three unspent cartridges, two fired casings, and the bullet that bounced off McKinley's breastbone were weighed.

22. The possibilty of defective ammunition was first proposed by an unnamed police officer during a *Buffalo Courier* reporter's interview, Sept. 7, 1901.

23. McKinley had already stated that he would not serve another term. Throughout history, political declarations of this nature have proven subject to revision, however.

24. Cited in Michal R. Belknap *American Political Trials.*

25. During the early 1950's, Senator Joseph McCarthy made numerous public accusations but never succeeded in finding many Communists in high government posts. Palmer, on the other hand, believed that his periodic round-ups of radicals succeeded in ridding the nation of a dangerous segment of the population.

26. Hoover came to the Department of Justice directly after he graduated from George Washington University Law School. His first position was as an aide to Palmer, in charge of the Office of Enemy Alien Registration. Cited in Allan L. Damon, "The Great Red Scare."

Epilogue

1. See the *Buffalo News*, January 19, 20, and 21, 2000 for coverage of that visit.

2. For additional background regarding contemporary presidential security procedures, see former Secret Service Agent Dennis V. N. McCarthy's book *Protecting the President*. The incident I have imagined is based on John Hinkley's attack on President Reagan and McCarthy's role in that incident.

3. Anarchist groups met (peacefully) at the time of nominating conventions for both the Republican and Democratic parties during the summer of 2000. (As reported in the *New York Times)*, Aug. 5, 2000.

4. Policies such as these were already in place when President Kennedy visited Dallas in 1963, although they have been refined since. During the week prior to President Clinton's January, 2000 visit to Buffalo, 55 inches of snow had fallen on the city. The streets were cleared in time for the president's arrival, but, in order to be certain of visual references that might be obliterated by the high snowdrifts, the drivers assigned to the Buffalo field office had driven and re-driven all of the designated routes of the president's motorcade.

5. Czolgosz would not have experienced any difficulty figuring out where President McKinley would be at each moment of his visit and with whom. Local newspapers published this information, as it had been given to them by Exposition officials. The president's schedule never varied from the published account (until the shooting).

6. Czolgosz paid $4.50 for his revolver, which would be the equivalent of $90 today, correcting for inflation. In fact, a weapon of this type was listed for $110 in a gun collectors' catalog at the time of this writing.

7. Random bystanders are now kept at greater distances than was John Hinkley when he awaited the exit of President Reagan from the Washington Hilton Hotel in 1981.

8. As described by Agent McCarthy in *Protecting the President* (see pp. 15-18 and 50-64).

9. Following Reagan's injury, the police escort became separated from the president's limousine when the president's driver made a sudden decision to head for the hospital instead of the White House. In our hypothetical case, the driver would likely prefer the expressway to city streets since that route would allow the quickest access to either the airport or the medical center, as circumstances dictated.

10. Dr. Roger Seibel, Director of ECMC's Regional Trauma Center provided me with a detailed account of how a president arriving with President McKinley's wound would be managed.

11. Within fifteen minutes of President Reagan's shooting, the serial number of the weapon had been traced to its owner, John W. Hinkley, who was at that moment in custody and giving his full name to interrogators.

12. Special Agent McCarthy stood by John Hinkley at District of Columbia Police Headquarters, despite personal injury, until relieved by the FBI.

13. George Bush was airborne when President Reagan was shot. His plane landed only to refuel before returning to Washington.

14. When John Hinkley shot President Reagan, the NYSE closed within six minutes of the attack.

15. Dr. David Hoyt, head of the Trauma Division at the University of California, San Diego and chairman of the American College of Surgeons Committee on Trauma kindly offered his analysis of the McKinley surgery and how a similar wound would be handled today.

Appendix III

1. Ref. In *Buffalo Medical Journal*.

2. The incandescent bulbs used at the Exposition were 8 watts.

3. Dr. Mann is mistaken, of course. Today we are aware that a damaged pancreas may produce abundant and caustic discharge.

4. Dr. Mann overlooks the fact that bacteriologic cultures did reveal the presence of bacterial organisms. These could have been contaminants introduced at the time of autopsy, however, since no gross manifestations of infection were observed.

5. Dr. Mann refers here to the possible introduction of microorganisms along a drainage tract.

6. Dr. Mann passes up this opportunity to explain the circumstances that led him to accept the assignment rather than suggest to Milburn and McKinley that Mynter was the more experienced choice. We are left only with the evidence that Milburn knew of Mann and indicated that he was the best option.

7. Of all those involved in the president's care, only Rixey and Wasdin were employees of the federal government. Following the shooting, Wasdin received official military orders to attend to the president's aftercare.

Appendix IV

1. Original document held in the library of the Buffalo and Erie County Historical Society.

2. This draft is reproduced with the original spelling and punctuation used by the secretary who transcribed Dr. Park's dictation.

3. Park does not recall hailing a car, but several reporters

described his arrival at the hospital in a car.

4. Not his actual title, but one that Park mistakenly recalled.

5. Years later, of course, he did refrain from including his remarks critical of the operation itself.

6. Never explained was why no one present at the hospital during the operation called attention to the availability of Dr. Park's instrument set.

Acknowledgments

I wish the Buffalo bookseller who long ago sold me a copy of Roswell Park's Selected Readings: Surgical and Scientific were still in business. I would like her to know that my purchase stimulated a career-long fascination with the McKinley assassination and its medical circumstances. I am also grateful to the unknown exhibit designer at the Buffalo Historical Society whose decision to display Park's unedited manuscript reawakened my interest years later.

During my research for this book, I benefited greatly from access to the collections located at three institutions: the Buffalo and Erie County Historical Society (BECHS), the Theodore Roosevelt Inaugural National Memorial Site in Buffalo, and the U.S. Secret Service. At each, the assistance I received was invaluable. BECHS Executive Director William Siener offered intellectual stimulation, continued interest and wise counsel. To Curator of Collections William Mayer, I offer special thanks; his cooperation was critical for a re-examination of Czolgosz's weapon and its unused ammunition. The help provided by BECHS librarians Linda Kennedy and Pat Virgil deserves separate mention, as well. Roosevelt Inaugural Site Director Molly Quackenbush, Curator Lenora Hensen, and Interpreter Mark Comito each offered enthusiastic support and patient assistance. And, at the United States Department of Treasury, Historian of the Secret Service Michael Sampson generously provided me with access to files from his agency not previously available to the public, thus opening a new and rich primary source for my perusal. His cooperation and critical review of my phrasing of events is fully appreciated.

For their reliable and capable assistance, I would also like to thank the many librarians and archivists at the following institutions: Geisel Library, University of California at San Diego (UCSD); University Research Library, University of California at Los Angeles; Widener Library, Harvard University; and New York Public Library. I am particularly grateful to John Haynes of the Manuscript Division of the Library of Congress; Christopher Densmore of the University at Buffalo Archives; Linda Lohr of the Robert Brown History of Medicine Library, University at Buffalo; Cynthia Van Ness and William Loos of the Buffalo and Erie County Public Library; David Valenzuelas and Joan Jadusckewicz of the Buffalo News Library; and Richard McElroy and Bud Weber of the Ramseyer Research Library, William McKinley Memorial and Museum (Canton, Ohio).

Valuable on-site research assistance in Buffalo was provided by Frances Wilson, Linda Fisher, and Philip Morey. Also, the city's Recorder of Vital Statistics, Charles Michaux, helped me close important gaps in some of the data.

At draft stage, the manuscript benefited from the help of readers from many walks of life, including a tool and die maker (from whom I learned that it is a die, not a dye) and a retired helicopter pilot (who taught me that an airplane parks on the runway's apron, not on the runway). These readers of preliminary chapters include Jack Anthony, Bradley Aust, Chester Buck, Mark Comito, Linda Fisher, Pat Fisher, William Greiner, David Hoyt, William Loos, Bradley Nemeth, Sydney Pool, Roger Seibel, William Siener, Bruce Stabile, Ronald Stein, and Paul Wolf. Ronald Batt, my Buffalo counterpart (a retired surgeon pursuing graduate study in U.S. history), offered many important insights and technical corrections.

I am also extremely grateful for the careful attention the manuscript received from several professional historians. I could not have achieved my goal without the critical commentary offered by the following UCSD professors: Michael Bernstein (U.S. political and economic history), Michal Belknap (legal history), and Robert Edelman (Russian history). University at Buffalo professor of history Michael Frisch provided continuing encouragement and sensible advice.

Katherine Mooney was essential to the editing process; and Burt Brockett once again applied his marvelous creativity to the task of book design.

Finally, it is to "Uncle Jack" Anthony that I extend my most sincere appreciation, both for his advisory on historic firearms and ballistics technology and for the Saturday afternoons we shared in the 1950s prowling the exhibit halls of the Buffalo Historical Society, the ramparts of Fort Erie, and many other historic sites. From those experiences came my lifelong interest in history.

❖

Photo Credits

McBurney, Charles Stockton Scrapbook; Secretary of State John
Hay, Library of Congress.

101   Theodore Roosevelt Inaugural Site (former Ansley
       Wilcox Mansion) contemporary photograph (courtesy TR Site);
       Roosevelt and Hanna: Charles Stockton Scrapbook.

113   Certificate of Death courtesy of the Bureau of Vital Statistics,
       City of Buffalo.

117   President Roosevelt, Wilcox Mansion draped in
       mourning: Library of Congress.

123   Funeral scenes: Library of Congress.

124   The assassin: Buffalo Police photo.

138   McKinley political cartoon: Library of Congress.

141   President Roosevelt addressing Congress: Library of Congress.

148   Letter accompanying payment for nursing services courtesy of
       Leland Dorchester, nephew of nurse Mabel Dorchester.

162   Buffalo and Erie County Historical Society.

Author's note: Most of the photographs were originally taken by various newspaper photographers. I have listed above the source where I found them best duplicated.

❖

Index

About the Author

Dr. Fisher graduated from the University of Buffalo School of Medicine in 1962. He is Emeritus Professor of Surgery at the University of California, San Diego. Currently, he is pursuing a Masters degree in U.S. History at UCSD. He lives with his wife in LaJolla, California.